Student Notes from Latin Europe (1400–1750)
A Research Companion

Student Notes from Latin Europe (1400–1750)

A Research Companion

Edited by
Xander Feys
Maxime Maleux
Andy Peetermans
Raf Van Rooy

LEUVEN UNIVERSITY PRESS

Published with the support of the KU Leuven Fund for Fair Open Access and the KU Leuven C1-project "'Ad fontes!' in the Classroom: Teaching Latin, Greek, and Hebrew Texts in the Early Modern Southern Low Countries" (C14/18/030; 2018–22)

Published in 2025 by Leuven University Press / Presses Universitaires de Louvain / Universitaire Pers Leuven. Minderbroedersstraat 4, B-3000 Leuven (Belgium).

All TDM (Text and Data Mining) rights are reserved.

Selection and editorial matter © 2025, Xander Feys, Maxime Maleux, Andy Peetermans, and Raf Van Rooy
Individual chapters © 2025, The respective authors

This book is published under a Creative Commons Attribution Non-Commercial Non-Derivative 4.0 License. For more information, please visit https://creativecommons.org/share-your-work/cclicenses/

Attribution should include the following information:
Xander Feys, Maxime Maleux, Andy Peetermans, and Raf Van Rooy (eds), *Student Notes from Latin Europe (1400–1750): A Research Companion*. Leuven: Leuven University Press, 2025. (CC BY-NC-ND 4.0)

Unless otherwise indicated all images are reproduced with the permission of the rightsholders acknowledged in captions. All images are expressly excluded from the CC BY-NC-ND 4.0 license covering the rest of this publication. Permission for reuse should be sought from the rightsholders.

ISBN 978 94 6270 456 5 (Paperback)
ISBN 978 94 6166 640 6 (ePDF)
ISBN 978 94 6166 641 3 (ePUB)
https://doi.org/10.11116/9789461666406
D/2025/1869/12
NUR: 680

Typesetting: Crius Group
Cover design: Daniel Benneworth-Gray
Cover illustration: Michael Hayé, *Systema Ptolemaei* and *Systema Copernici*, colored engravings in Leo Josephus Daco, *Physica. Metaphysica*, 1678. KBR, MS II 106, fol. 244^r & 250^r, and *Pen drawing in anonymous lecture notes*, ca. 1676-1696. BN, MS 12349 II, fol. 186^v

Contents

Introduction   11
Raf Van Rooy and Maxime Maleux, on behalf of the editors
     1. Education in early modern Latin Europe: A scene from Leuven   12
     2. Structure of the research companion   17
     3. Why Leuven?   19
     Acknowledgments   20
     Notes   21
     References   22

Part I—The Basics of Student Notes Research   25

Chapter 1—The Making of Student Notes   27
Ann M. Blair
     1. The survival of student notes   27
     2. The forms of student notes   31
     3. Methods of note-taking in the classroom   34
     4. What can and cannot be learned from student notes   37
     Notes   42
     Suggestions for further reading   44
     References   45

Chapter 2—Getting a First Grasp of Student Notes   49
Raf Van Rooy and Xander Feys
     1. Introduction   49
     2. Referentiality, fragmentariness, and provenance   50
     3. Paleography   54
     4. Drawing up a typology for student notes   60
         4.1. *Form*   60
         4.2. *Structure*   63
         4.3. *Contents*   65
     5. Conclusion   67

6. Exercise	67
Notes	69
References	69
Transcription and model solution	71

Chapter 3—The Materiality of the Student Notebook — 73
Jarrik Van Der Biest

1. Introduction	73
2. From paper mill to preservation	76
3. Analysis	79
3.1. Quire structure	80
3.2. Distribution of watermarks	83
3.3. Dates	85
3.4. Textual divisions, codicological blocks	86
Notes	91
Thematic bibliography	91

Chapter 4—Book History: The Basics with Two Case Studies — 95
Natasha Constantinidou, Dieter Cammaerts, and Violet Soen

1. Introduction	95
2. An increasingly interdisciplinary field	96
3. Production and distribution of printed books	98
4. From production to consumption: An inquiry into material objects	104
5. Analyzing printed text editions: Aspects of book history in practice	110
6. Conclusions	118
Notes	119
Thematic bibliography	120

Chapter 5—How to Make Student Notes Accessible — 125
Raf Van Rooy

1. Introduction	125
2. Choose wisely from the start	126
2.1. Diplomatic and semi-diplomatic transcription	126
2.2. XML	126
2.3. The act of transcribing: Benefits and tools	127
2.4. Good practices	128

3. Conclusion	130
Notes	131
References	131

Student Notes Toolkit   133

Part II—The Potential of Student Notes Research   135

Chapter 6—History of Education   137
Daniel Gehrt and Michael Stolberg
1. Introduction   137
2. The diversity and flexibility of basic academic education   138
3. Training for professional practice: Medical students' notebooks   143
4. Conclusion   148
Notes   149
References   152

Chapter 7—Intellectual History   157
Lorenz Demey, Marc Laureys, Maxime Maleux, and Andy Peetermans
1. Introduction   157
2. Revolutionary rhetoric versus didactic continuity: Juvenal in Bologna   160
3. Official policies versus didactic non-conformism: The university of Leuven and the *Wegestreit*   162
4. Textbook canonicity versus didactic creativity   164
    4.1. Aristotelian diagrams beyond the square of opposition   164
    4.2. Hebrew in Leuven and Paris   168
5. Conclusion   170
Notes   171
References   172

Chapter 8—Book History   175
Xander Feys and Raf Van Rooy
1. Introduction   175
2. Book circulation   175
3. Interleaving for intermezzi   179

4. Student practices in handling books and their flaws ... 182
  5. Pedagogic pragmatism ... 184
  6. Conclusion ... 186
  Notes ... 187
  References ... 188

Chapter 9—Visual History ... 189
Alicja Bielak and Gwendoline de Mûelenaere
  1. Introduction ... 189
  2. Visual elements in notebooks ... 191
     2.1. Heterogeneous visual languages ... 192
     2.2. Diagrams ... 197
     2.3. The materiality of the image ... 201
  3. Classification of images in student notebooks ... 204
     3.1. Traditional university iconography ... 204
     3.2. Scientific drawings and engravings ... 205
     3.3. Symbolic language ... 205
  4. Emblems as didactic and mnemonic devices ... 205
     4.1. *Scientific* emblemata ... 205
     4.2. Recuperation of emblematic devices ... 207
     4.3. Emblems as memory aids ... 212
  5. Conclusion ... 215
  Notes ... 217
  References ... 219

Chapter 10—History of Orality ... 223
Tomás Antonio Valle and Raf Van Rooy
  1. Introduction ... 223
  2. Conversational culture at Wittenberg university c. 1550 ... 224
  3. The oral/aural challenges of teaching and learning ... 228
  4. Conclusion ... 231
  Notes ... 232
  References ... 233
  Further reading ... 235

Chapter 11—Socio-Cultural History 237
Maximilian Schuh, Xander Feys, and Raf Van Rooy
   1. Introduction 237
   2. Case study 1: The arts faculties at Uppsala and Ingolstadt 238
      2.1. Uppsala 239
      2.2. Ingolstadt 241
   3. Case study 2: Triangular teaching in Milan in about 1465 245
   4. Case study 3: *Aeneid* 12 and the Turkish threat 248
   5. Conclusion 251
   Notes 253
   References 253

Multilingual Glossary 257

Introduction*

Raf Van Rooy and Maxime Maleux, on behalf of the editors

Early modern student notes are a particularly challenging object of research but can bring fresh perspectives on our understanding of human history and cognition. Student notes can elucidate the history of teaching institutions, of knowledge and books, of art and images, of conversation and everyday life. It is our firm belief that a research companion like the present can help scholars interested in the potential of student notes overcome hurdles more easily than by struggling on their own. This brief companion, in fact, reflects for a large part the experience that academics from various parts of Europe and North America have had when struggling with student notes—failing forward one may say. The contributions in this companion, on the one hand, provide information on the phenomenon of early modern student notes and the background you ideally have to approach these kinds of documents—ideally, because no one scholar can come to master all required competences fully. This is the main goal of Part I, with its five chapters and toolkit. On the other hand, the companion aims to kaleidoscopically showcase the research opportunities offered by student notes. Our account is certainly not exhaustive but rather reflects the experiences of the editors and scholars featured in this book, which we have consciously not tried to make overly uniform.

This research companion is ultimately the product of a workshop on May 20–21 and 27–28, 2021, which took place online due to the COVID pandemic. The workshop was entitled, "How to Investigate Student Notes from the Renaissance (*ca.* 1300–1600)?" and was one of the first to focus exclusively on the phenomenon of early modern student notes. Rather than producing traditional proceedings of this conference, we deemed it to be more stimulating—especially for junior researchers in this field—to present some of the key insights of this Leuven-based conference in the form of a brief research companion for student notes from Latin Europe. Therefore, this companion pursues first and foremost a practical aim rather than delving too deeply into theoretical details. As such, it is addressed primarily to students in the fields of early modern (intellectual) history and classical reception studies who for their research want to work with student notes. We conceive student notes here broadly as writings created by people engaged in learning and studying, typically in a traditional classroom context or in private tutoring. As a consequence, we leave self-study largely out of consideration, where teacher and student coincide and a different dynamic of knowledge transfer is at work, even though we acknowledge the interest of these sources for various questions.[1] In this introduction, we briefly sketch the nature of early modern education, taking sixteenth-century Leuven as our illustrative example, before elaborating on the structure of this handbook. We adopt this micro-historical approach since it would be a Herculean task to survey the scholarship on early modern education here, and we want to avoid overwhelming the uninitiated reader with too much information. The well-documented individual chapters will offer the necessary references to standard works, in addition to the ones mentioned in the next sections.

1. Education in early modern Latin Europe: A scene from Leuven

October 23, 1543. The Fish Market in Leuven. The students Gerardus Aemilius of Rotterdam and Johannes Aegidius were happy to sit on a bench this breezy autumn afternoon. Their middle-aged professor, Rutgerus Rescius (c. 1495–1545), was giving his opening lecture on Homer's *Odyssey* at the local Trilingual College (Collegium Trilingue). Outside the college, the Brabant city of Leuven was bristling with student and commercial life: fishmongers and booksellers cohabited on the Fish Market ever since the Trilingue had been established in 1517, serving the flocks of students who lived in the local college or came to study there. This Trilingual College enriched the curriculum of the only university in the Low Countries at that time, which had been founded in 1425, with advanced language and literature courses on Latin, Greek, and Hebrew that took place daily, except for Sundays. In 1568, Latin was taught in the morning (9–10am), Hebrew and Greek in the afternoon (2–3pm and 3–4pm, respectively).[2]

For Gerardus and his fellow students, the comfortable benches at the Trilingual College must have been a welcome change from the cold and hard floors in the college halls at the *vicus artium*, "the arts quarter," where the courses of the faculty of arts took place during regular hours. These courses were obligatory for any student starting at the university, before they could move to one of the higher faculties: medicine, law, and theology. They could take them either in Leuven or at another university, as Johannes had done. For Trilingue student Johannes Aegidius had already finished law studies in Orléans, graduating in 1541, before returning to Leuven and attending the Trilingue classes there. In other words, not only regular students of the university attended the Trilingue but also those who had already graduated and simply had an interest in what was taught there. Indeed, the courses at the Trilingue were extracurricular, scheduled to take place before and after the regular lectures at the *artes* faculty, which other students of the college probably attended as well.

Studying Greek language and literature must have reminded Gerardus and Johannes of their first steps in writing Latin when they attended their local Latin schools before going to university, where they may have had a taste of Greek as well.[3] Gerardus probably frequented a Latin school in the vicinity of his native city of Rotterdam, incidentally—or not?—the city Erasmus hailed from, the intellectual founder of the Trilingual College in Leuven.[4] Erasmus had also appointed in 1518 the college's first Greek professor, the young Rescius, a somewhat fickle man but a talented Hellenist who would educate entire generations of students in Greek language and literature. By 1543, Rescius had about thirty years of experience of teaching, which he did in Latin, as was customary at European universities in the early modern period. During his opening lecture, his experience and advancing age must have given him an aura of *auctoritas*, "authority," as he made his case for why Christians should engage with pagan Greek literature like Homer's epic poems:

> Divus Basilius Magnus dicit totum opus Homeri nihil aliud esse quam laudem virtutis. Vnde etiam a Christianis legendum.[5]

> The holy Basil the Great says that the entire oeuvre of Homer is nothing else but a praise of virtue. Therefore it should also be read by Christians.

Student Johannes used his quill and ink to dutifully record this piece of information in the margin of the textbook he had just bought, issued in 1535 by the printing press run by his professor. He took notes while knowing that the extracurricular courses of the Trilingual College did not involve any evaluation like exams or disputations. His fellow student Gerardus apparently found it irrelevant to write down this information in his copy of the same textbook. Perhaps the students scribbled further notes down on blank sheets of paper, whether loose or bound in some way, in the typical manner of taking notes at the old university of Leuven, quite often under dictation.[6] What is sure is that they helped each other out. Johannes' copy of the textbook contained a passage where the ink had not come through well. No doubt looking at a fellow student's copy, he mimicked the printed Greek when adding the missing text. Such student interaction was probably also needed when one of them had not understood the professor's uttering, seeing that teaching took place almost wholly orally, with no or limited visual support.

Gerardus and Johannes would have bought their textbooks shortly before the course at one of the local bookshops at the Fish Market, probably Hieronymus Cloet's, whose well-filled shelves gave students what they needed for their courses and other books that may have elicited their interest. Cloet's bookshop would still have been a mess after the investigation it was subject to in the spring of 1543, when authorities had become suspicious of the owner's religious orthodoxy and had accused him of reformed sympathies. Cloet testified that people asked him for "suspect books" on a daily basis.[7] Seeing that the summer of 1543 had been particularly bloody in Leuven, with five heretics being publicly executed, Gerardus and Johannes must have been somewhat cautious about their interests in Greek, a language increasingly associated with Protestantism and hence growing ever more suspect.[8] The fact that their own professor, Rescius, published the textbooks for the Trilingue probably took away some of the suspicion at least, since he apparently never was accused of being a heretic—even though he was involved in other criminal investigations and lawsuits.[9] Rescius ran his printing business alongside his job as a professor in order to be able to sustain his wife and children, who may have assisted in his publishing house.[10]

As one of the official booksellers of the university, acknowledged by the rector, Cloet had strategically moved from another part of town to the Fish Market and specialized in books for the Trilingue. Yet, this smart bookseller was involved in the local knowledge economy in other ways, too, since he acted as a scribe, copying texts, and offered training in basic literacy to the son of the innkeeper of De Gulden Librije, which was next to the first location of his bookshop, and where he would meet fellow booksellers to discuss business and the day's news. Besides selling books to one of the most advanced institutes for higher learning, then, Cloet was also active at the lowest end of teaching and literacy training.

* * *

The case of the Trilingue at the old university of Leuven presents many idiosyncrasies, of course, but also shares a lot with other knowledge economies around schools and universities in early modern Latin Europe.[11] Throughout Europe, there was a standard trajectory from basic literacy training through secondary education to higher studies at university level, starting with the propaedeutic curriculum at the faculty of arts. One had to study the *artes* of the so-called trivium (grammar, rhetoric, and dialectic) and quadrivium (arithmetic, music, astronomy, and geometry), before moving on to one of the higher faculties: typically, medicine, civil law, canon law, or theology, the queen of all faculties. A doctorate in theology was the highest academic degree one could aspire to.[12] At the same time, depending on one's time and resources, students could tailor their personal trajectory by taking extracurricular courses publicly or privately, by self-study, by moving around to various universities, or by a combination of these and other strategies. From a young age, Latin was a crucial competence, especially at the many secondary schools and colleges, notably those of religious orders like the Jesuits. Not unsurprisingly, this level of education is sometimes called the Latin school, where students received extensive training in all aspects of that classical language and literature as well as ancient history.

The knowledge economy at early modern European universities was in essence a male business of (young) adults, although the contributions and agency of other marginalized groups are attracting more and more attention in contemporary scholarship.[13] Interest in girls' schools, where training in the vernacular was the focus and could be provided by both men and women, has been rising as well.[14] Not much is known thus far about student notes from these institutions, and most research has focused on the male-dominated Latin schools and especially universities, a focus inevitably reflected in this research companion, too.[15] Some scholars have recently also made a case for studying basic literacy training using student notes, even though the source basis is much thinner for that level of training because the ratio of survival for these documents is far lower.[16] Others have emphasized the importance of looking beyond Europe.[17] We are enthusiastic about all these approaches and hope that many of the insights shared and the skills mentioned in this book will be of use to researchers working on student notes in other contexts, too.

Although it would be worthwhile to investigate and compare student notes from different time periods and regions, this handbook has opted to focus on the early modern period (roughly from 1400 until 1750) and on those parts of Europe in which Latin was the scholarly lingua franca. Yet this primary focus on Latin does not inhibit the treatment of other relevant languages with which the early modern student interacted. Greek and Hebrew, two learned languages that profoundly shaped humanism, also emerge in several of the contributions, as do certain vernacular languages. As such, the various contributions constitute a representative mosaic of student notes in the Latin-molded European universities of the early modern era.

Latin may lend unity to the historical-educational context that is the subject of this research companion, but it also may form a considerable obstacle for the student notes researcher who has a background in early modern history. Yet, a sound knowledge of Latin and its postclassical peculiarities is therefore in many cases a *condicio sine qua non* for this kind of study, although this competence is presently waning. The vast corpus of Latin texts from the medieval and early modern periods is at risk of becoming forgotten due to this evolution.[18] Indeed, by looking only at notes in the vernacular languages of Europe, a significant body of sources are overlooked, as is the case with studies like Petrella's (2022), which focuses exclusively on Italian marginalia—even though such studies obviously have their merits, too. Another seemingly daunting skill related to language is its handwritten manifestation, especially in the case of notes recorded with haste or in tiny letters. Paleographical skills are typically a smaller obstacle than language knowledge. The present companion contains a section with some convenient tips and tricks for often recurring abbreviations and ligatures but does not attempt to offer a Latin language course, for which many alternatives exist (for example, taking a course or self-study). While classicists are well equipped to tackle student notes linguistically and paleographically, they may need an extra effort to study the historical context. The general conclusion may be that an early modern historian with a thorough knowledge of Latin or a classicist who has familiarized themself with early modern history probably best approaches the ideal profile of a student notes researcher. It is these profiles, in any case, that we find mostly among the contributors to this research companion.

2. Structure of the research companion

The present research companion is divided into two parts. The first part focuses on the phenomenon of early modern student notes, aiming to guide the reader through the technical and practical aspects of the reading, interpreting, and editing of student notes. Chapter 1 surveys the making of student notes in all of their diversity. The second chapter aims to acquaint the reader with some of the practical aspects that will come in useful when studying student notes for the first time, like paleography and provenance marks. The following two chapters delve deeper into the material aspects of student notes. Whereas Chapter 3 focuses on skills related to codicology and the manuscript book, Chapter 4 discusses book-historical aspects of the handpress technology that are relevant for understanding the nature of student notes in relation to print. Finally, Chapter 5 briefly addresses various methods of editing student notes, which should be tailored to the nature of the source corpus.

In the second part, we move from the background knowledge that student notes researchers ideally possess to the question of what student notes can contribute to scholarship. The individual chapters in this part highlight specific fields to which student notes have something to offer by means of concrete case studies, without aspiring to be complete, as student notes can be relevant for other fields not represented in this research companion, too. These chapters reflect the diversity we find both in student notes corpora and in present-day scholarly approaches. The authors argue in a plethora of ways that student notes can shed new light on established disciplines, especially history and its various subfields, as well as classical reception studies. Following the humanist motto *varietas delectat* ("variety pleases"), we have given contributors the liberty to shape their chapters as they saw fit, as long as they wrote it accessibly and coherently, both internally and in the broader context of the research companion. As almost every early modern book could theoretically be used as a school textbook and be adorned with notes (Grafton 2008), the range of possible fields and topics to which student notes are relevant is much wider than a brief research companion like this one could possibly cover. The most obvious field to which student notes research can contribute is the history of education, tackled in Chapter 6. In this chapter, the authors argue that student notes help nuance prescriptive documents and university curricula and shed light on educational methods, which could be very hands-on in the case of medicine. The field of intellectual history, the subject of Chapter 7, is another obvious beneficiary of the bottom-up perspective granted by student notes, since the ideas of many a scholar have come down to us partly through their students' writings: think only of Aristotle, Philip Melanchthon, and Ferdinand de Saussure, to name but a few great names of different eras. This chapter features three subdisciplines of intellectual history: the history of classical scholarship, the history of logic, and the history of linguistics, with case studies focusing on Bologna and Leuven. Chapter 8 argues that student notes constitute a key source for book-historical information, as this source type enables one to study book use and circulation, as the authors illustrate by means of notes from Leuven. Chapter 9 subsequently highlights that, while we associate student notes primarily with textual materials, they may also contain many images. This fact makes student notes relevant sources for visual history, too, while the images themselves contribute to our understanding of early modern teaching and learning practices. The authors make their case by means of student notes from Leuven and the Polish–Lithuanian Commonwealth. Shifting from the visual to the oral, Chapter 10 investigates what student notes can bring to the table for the cultural history of orality, by relying on student notes from Wittenberg and Leuven. As such, student notes provide a glimpse of the fleeting everyday interactions between students and their professors. Chapter 11, finally, continues in this line by addressing the sociocultural lessons to be learned from the study of student notes. The authors present three case studies from the Holy Roman Empire, Italy, and the Low Countries to make this point.

Finally, as an appendix to this research companion, we provide a multilingual glossary of key terms used and discussed in the contributions. This glossary at the same time serves as a basic index to the companion, which may be useful to those working with a physical copy of the book.

3. Why Leuven?

The old university of Leuven, founded six centuries ago in 1425, ranks among the universities that have received the most historiographical attention. Over the years, local scholars have devoted various research projects to the history of education at this institution, a tendency that has become even more pronounced as the university's sixth centenary approached in 2025 with projects like STUDIUM.AI. In particular, academic interest in Leuven student notes started to boom in the wake of a project that ran in the early 2010s within LECTIO (the KU Leuven Institute for the Study of the Transmission of Texts, Ideas and Images in Antiquity, the Middle Ages and the Renaissance): Magister Dixit. It was—and still is—the aim of this project to inventory all student notebooks reflecting lessons at the old university.[19] The notebooks on logic and physics have been studied most intensively up to this point.[20] Over the past decade, LECTIO has continued to foster further research into these student sources. The open access Magister Dixit platform is moreover open-ended, meaning that new finds keep being added, and that new partnerships with GLAM (galleries, libraries, archives, and museums) institutions are being made in addition to the original three partnerships with the libraries of KU Leuven, UCLouvain, and the KBR in Brussels.[21] Ad hoc collaborations with minor institutions are in place, too. After the initial focus on logic and physics, a second wave of research projects followed, turning from arts to the faculties of law and theology in the context of the *@aulam* project (2019–24), and to the extracurricular Trilingual College, which was the setting for Section 1 above. The next step would be to tackle the faculty of medicine and certain *artes* disciplines that have not yet received closer scrutiny (for example, grammar).

The Trilingue was studied in the context of the *Ad fontes* project and two PhD fellowships included in it (2018–24). The student notes that bear witness to the Trilingue lessons on Latin, Greek, and Hebrew language and literature, inspired by the innovative pedagogical ideas of Erasmus of Rotterdam (Papy 2018), have been integrated into DaLeT (Database of the Leuven Trilingue). The database illustrates how these languages were taught in the first decades of the sixteenth century, when the Trilingue was at the height of its popularity and was widely acclaimed as a pioneering institute. It was members of this project who hosted the workshop in 2021, mentioned above, and subsequently oversaw the creation of this research companion. This background explains the strong presence of Leuven, in general, and the Trilingue, in particular, which is clear to anyone who browses through this volume. The Leuven case offers a relevant example that in some respects may be representative of early modern student life more broadly. We are well aware, however, that not every particular source type or insight will be transferable to other contexts, which is also why we have made sure to include case studies from other parts of Europe. Far from a systematic survey, we envision this research companion to serve as a steppingstone toward that goal.

The Trilingue project and the digital resource developed within it, DaLeT, have provided the principal incentive to produce this research companion. During the project and especially the workshop the team hosted, we realized that the trial-and-error process we experienced while working with our student sources has yielded many valuable lessons. Together with the participants of the workshop, we thought it more useful to share these lessons with aspiring student notes researchers than to offer a traditional volume of proceedings. Indeed, we hope that this open access research companion may contribute, however slightly, to creating a common body of knowledge and experience. May this companion inspire further research and also spare future generations of student notes researchers not only some time but also various frustrations.

Acknowledgments

The workshop and resulting research companion have been made possible by generous funding from the KU Leuven C1-project "'Ad fontes!' in the Classroom: Teaching Latin, Greek, and Hebrew Texts in the Early Modern Southern Low Countries" (C14/18/030; 2018–22) and from the KU Leuven Fund for Fair Open Access. Additional support came from two PhD fellowships sponsored by the Research Foundation—Flanders (FWO): Xander Feys' project "Language and Literature Teaching in the Sixteenth Century: Vergil and Homer at the Leuven Collegium Trilingue" (11H8220N | 11H8222N; 2019–24) and Maxime Maleux's project "The Teaching of the Old Testament Revolutionized? The Sixteenth-Century Low Countries and the First Institutionalized Hebrew Curriculum" (1145321N | 1145323N; 2020–24). Raf Van Rooy's ZAP Starting Grant (STG/22/004; 2022–24) made it possible to finalize the manuscript in a busy period of starting up new projects, among other things by prolonging the appointment of co-editor Andy Peetermans.

As editors, we are also enormously thankful to the contributors, who have shown punctuality and patience with this project. Ann Blair provided welcome advice on the multilingual glossary and was always available to discuss ideas for certain chapters, including Chapter 2 and the Toolkit at the end of Part I. We have moreover appreciated the encouragements we received from several participants in the workshop, who ended up not contributing to the research companion but showed themselves warm supporters of this endeavor or helped materialize this research companion in some way. This group includes but is not limited to: Asaph Ben-Tov, Elia Borza, Martine Furno, Anne-Hélène Klinger-Dollé, Ray Schrire, Luigi Silvano, and An Smets.

This research companion would moreover never have materialized without the support of the senior members of the *Ad fontes* project: first and foremost, Jan Papy, who supervised the project until 2022 and rekindled the interest in student notes at KU Leuven by means of various projects. This book stands as a testimony to his scholarly legacy in student notes research and his pioneering role in it. We are indebted to Toon Van Hal and Pierre Van Hecke for having supported the *Ad fontes* project from the very start and helped us turn the project into what it has become. Pierre paved the way for the particularly thorny Hebrew side of the story, whereas Toon gave us precious advice on various things, including technical aspects related to the development of DaLeT. Finally, we owe a lot to the two generous reviewers, whose remarks we have gratefully incorporated, and to the team of Leuven University Press, especially Veerle De Laet and Nienke Roelants.

This research companion concludes a productive yet turbulent chapter in our academic careers, in which we have come to realize that productive turbulence may be the only way to survive the present state of Western academia.

Notes

* We thank Ann Blair for polishing both our ideas and English expression.
1 In other words, we adopt a less liberal approach than, for example, Durand-Guédy and Paul (2023), which focuses on personal manuscripts across cultures, which may include student notes, but we

do not limit ourselves to dictates and annotated prints either. A comprehensive history of self-study remains to be written, as far as we know, but see, for example, Ben-Zaken (2011).

[2] See Vander Linden (1908). Nannius, too, taught at 9am: see Feys (2024: Chapter 1.2.10). In 1550, Greek was taught before Hebrew, it seems, at 1–2pm, judging by a testimony of Roger Ascham: see Feys (2024: Chapter 2.4.2). On Hebrew teaching, see Maleux (2023).

[3] Bot (1955); Vanhoutte and Van der Eycken (2007).

[4] For details on these students, see Feys (2024). On the Collegium Trilingue, see most recently Papy (2018) and the extensive bibliography there as well as the database DaLeT.

[5] Standardized text and translation of DaLeT Annotation ID 21.

[6] But see Van Der Biest (2024) for nuance.

[7] Delsaerdt (2001: 123). Biographical data on Cloet offered in the following paragraphs are drawn from Delsaerdt (2001: 121–4).

[8] See Delsaerdt (2001: 119sqq.).

[9] On Rescius, professor, publisher, and *enfant terrible*, see Van Rooy (2022) and especially Feys (2024), with the references there.

[10] There is no direct evidence that Rescius' wife Anna Moons was involved, but there is plenty of evidence for the involvement of wives in other publishing houses in Leuven: see Wyffels (2021).

[11] Cf., for example, the impressive recent study of Lines (2023).

[12] See, for example, de Ridder-Symoens (1996) and Goeing et al. (2020).

[13] For example, by Wyffels (2021), mentioned in note 10.

[14] See, for example, van de Haar (2019: Chapter 4).

[15] See the seminal collection of studies in Campi et al. (2008) as well as, for example, Bénévent and Bisaro (2019) and Bénévent et al. (2020). The research companion will offer many other references throughout.

[16] For example, Smith (2019).

[17] For example, Casalini et al. (2021).

[18] Leonhardt (2013). It can only be hoped, for the sake of student notes research but also for other disciplines, that medievalists and early modern specialists support the study of this language, as there is still so much to be gained from it for the study of history.

[19] The Magister Dixit platform can be accessed through https://www.kuleuven.be/lectio/magisterdixit/solr-search.

[20] For logic, see Coesemans (2019); Geudens (2020). For physics, also known as natural philosophy, see Mantovani and Cellamare (2022: especially Chapters 15–17 for Leuven).

[21] GLAM stands for Galleries, Libraries, Archives, Museums.

References

Bénévent, Christine, and Xavier Bisaro, eds. 2019. *Cahiers d'écoliers de la Renaissance*. With the collaboration of Laurent Naas. Tours: Presses universitaires François-Rabelais.

Bénévent, Christine, Emmanuelle Chapron, Cécile Boulaire, and Xavier Bisaro, eds. 2020. *Paroles d'élèves dans l'Europe moderne*. Turnhout: Brepols.

Ben-Zaken, Avner. 2011. *Reading Ḥayy Ibn-Yaqẓān: A Cross-Cultural History of Autodidacticism*. Baltimore, MA: The Johns Hopkins University Press.

Bot, Petrus Nicolaas Maria. 1955. *Humanisme en Onderwijs in Nederland*. Utrecht: Het Spectrum.

Campi, Emidio, Simone De Angelis, Anja-Silvia Goeing, and Anthony Grafton, eds. 2008. *Scholarly Knowledge: Textbooks in Early Modern Europe*. Genève: Droz.

Casalini, Cristiano, Edward Choi, and Ayenachew A. Woldegiyorgis, eds. 2021. *Education beyond Europe: Models and Traditions before Modernities*. Leiden–Boston: Brill.

Coesemans, Steven. 2019. "Faculties of the Mind. The Rise of Facultative Logic at the University of Louvain." Unpublished PhD dissertation, Leuven: KU Leuven.

DaLeT: Database of the Leuven Trilingue. www.dalet.be. Last accessed April 4, 2024.

Delsaerdt, Pierre. 2001. *Suam quisque bibliothecam: Boekhandel en particulier boekenbezit aan de oude Leuvense universiteit, 16de–18de eeuw*. Leuven: Leuven University Press.

De Ridder-Symoens, Hilde, ed. 1996. *A History of the University in Europe 2: Universities in Early Modern Europe 1500–1800*. Cambridge: Cambridge University Press.

Durand-Guédy, David, and Jürgen Paul, eds. 2023. *Personal Manuscripts: Copying, Drafting, Taking Notes*. Berlin–Boston: De Gruyter.

Feys, Xander. 2024. "Language and Literature Teaching in the Sixteenth Century: Vergil and Homer at the Leuven Collegium Trilingue." Unpublished PhD dissertation, Leuven: KU Leuven.

Geudens, Christophe. 2020. "Louvain Theories of Topical Logic (c. 1450–1533): A Reassessment of the Traditionalist Thesis." Unpublished PhD dissertation, Leuven: KU Leuven.

Goeing, Anja-Silvia, Glyn Parry, and Mordechai Feingold, eds. 2020. *Early Modern Universities: Networks of Higher Learning. Early Modern Universities*. Leiden–Boston: Brill.

Grafton, Anthony. 2008. "Textbooks and the Disciplines." In *Scholarly Knowledge: Textbooks in Early Modern Europe*, edited by Emidio Campi, Simone De Angelis, Anja-Silvia Goeing, and Anthony Grafton, 11–36. Genève: Droz.

Leonhardt, Jürgen. 2013. *Latin: Story of a World Language*. Translated by Kenneth Kronenberg. Cambridge, MA–London: The Belknap Press of Harvard University Press.

Lines, David A. 2023. *The Dynamics of Learning in Early Modern Italy: Arts and Medicine at the University of Bologna*. Cambridge, MA–London: Harvard University Press.

Magister Dixit. https://www.kuleuven.be/lectio/magisterdixit/solr-search. Last accessed April 4, 2024.

Maleux, Maxime. 2023. "The Teaching of the Old Testament Revolutionized? The Sixteenth-Century Low Countries and the First Institutionalized Hebrew Curriculum." Unpublished PhD dissertation, Leuven: KU Leuven.

Mantovani, Mattia, and Davide Cellamare, eds. 2022. *Descartes in the Classroom: Teaching Cartesian Philosophy in the Early Modern Age*. Leiden–Boston: Brill.

Papy, Jan, ed. 2018. *The Leuven Collegium Trilingue 1517–1797: Erasmus, Humanist Educational Practice and the New Language Institute Latin – Greek – Hebrew*. Leuven–Paris–Bristol, CT: Peeters.

Petrella, Giancarlo. 2022. *Scrivere sui libri. Breve guida al libro a stampa postillato*. Rome: Salerno Editrice.

Smith, Marc. 2019. "L'apprentissage de l'écriture au début du XVIIe siècle d'après des fragments d'exercices nouvellement découverts." In *Cahiers d'écoliers de la Renaissance*, edited by Christine Bénévent and Xavier Bisaro, with the collaboration of Laurent Naas, 187–209. Tours: Presses universitaires François-Rabelais.

van de Haar, Alisa. 2019. *The Golden Mean of Languages: Forging Dutch and French in the Early Modern Low Countries (1540–1620)*. Leiden–Boston: Brill.

Van Der Biest, Jarrik. 2024. "An Augustinian Revolution in the Lecture Hall? Michael Baius (1513–1589) as Regius Professor of Theology in Leuven." Unpublished PhD dissertation, Leuven: KU Leuven.

Van Rooy, Raf. 2022. "In Rutger Rescius' Classroom at the Leuven Collegium Trilingue (1543–1544): His Study Program and Didactic Method." In *Trilingual Learning: The Study of Greek and Hebrew in *a Latin World (1000–1700)*, edited by Raf Van Rooy, Pierre Van Hecke, and Toon Van Hal, 179–205. Turnhout: Brepols.

Vander Linden, Herman. 1908. "L'université de Louvain en 1568." *Bulletin de la Commission royale d'histoire* 77: 9–36.

Vanhoutte, Jürgen, and Johan Van der Eycken. 2007. *Latijnse scholen in de Zuidelijke Nederlanden (16de–18de eeuw): Repertorium en archiefgids, Vlaanderen en Brussel.* Edited by Eddy Put and Mark D'Hoker. Algemeen rijksarchief en rijksarchief in de provinciën: Studia 116. Brussel: Algemeen Rijksarchief.

Wyffels, Heleen. 2021. "Women and Work in Early Modern Printing Houses: Family Firms in Antwerp, Douai, and Leuven, 1500–1700." Unpublished PhD dissertation, Leuven: KU Leuven.

PART I
The Basics of Student Notes Research

CHAPTER 1

The Making of Student Notes

Ann M. Blair*

1. The survival of student notes

Note-taking has been a feature of the student experience across countless cultures, time periods, and kinds of study. What makes the context of Renaissance and early modern Europe especially valuable to study is the remarkable survival of student notes of multiple kinds. From earlier periods in the European tradition we can surmise that various transmitted texts originated in student notes. This is likely the case for some works of Aristotle and of medieval scholasticism, for example which originated in oral teaching, whether lectures or discussions. Evidence to support this conclusion for ancient and medieval periods comes predominantly from clues in the transmitted texts, including formal features (for example, a succession of answers to a question in the case of Aristotle's *Problemata*) or an explicit statement. For example, an early fourteenth-century scribe noted that Heinrich von Friemar's *quaestiones* on Lombard's *Sentences* were recorded "by the method of notes" (*per modum notabiliorum*) and further explained (as if that expression were uncommon) that the note-taker (*reportans*) could not keep up with the speaker because he was not dictating (*non legebat ad pennam*); therefore if something was wrongly omitted, the fault lay not with the speaker but with the note-taker.[1] As the final clause suggests, this note was likely inserted to protect the reputation of the lecturer from any omission that might be noticed, but it also offers the historian fascinating detail about how oral events were put into writing. Similarly, sermons delivered orally were generally recorded in writing by the note-taking of listeners. Already in the early Christian period Augustine employed *notarii* skilled in tachygraphy (or fast writing) to take down his sermons that he then edited and put into circulation (for example, Boodts and Dupont 2018: 178). Medieval preachers, like Bernard de Clairvaux among many others, proceeded in the same way. In addition, especially from the thirteenth century on, we have notes taken during sermons by listeners acting on their own. Many medieval texts likely survive as recorded *per modum notabiliorum* but unless they include explicit mention of such an origin we might not be aware of it. The surviving notes themselves, called *reportationes*, may be numerous, but are often not readily identifiable as such.[2] By contrast starting in the fifteenth century we have more abundant collections of surviving notes. Crucial factors that fostered the composition and survival of notes in the Renaissance include the availability of paper as a relatively inexpensive yet durable medium for writing, the explicit advice of humanist pedagogues to take notes while studying or reading, new habits of saving those notes as potentially useful to one's later self or to others (who might come to own them through inheritance or purchase), and long-lived institutions that preserved these manuscripts even through periods of disinterest in them. Notes survive in impressive quantities from all across early modern Europe. The majority of them are probably not "student notes" in the narrow sense but rather "reading notes" formed through a lifetime of copying excerpts from books, following the advice of teachers and manuals outside an instructional context, but we are not yet in a position to quantify either kind of corpus.

Identifying student notes among the many kinds of surviving notes is a challenge. This is easiest to do when the notes state explicitly that they were written in a pedagogical setting. An ex-libris mark indicating ownership of a manuscript or book offers an initial clue. More detailed statements might be found on the opening title page or a closing colophon that provide the names of the student and/or the teacher, the date, institution, and course topic and grade level involved (see Figures 1.1 and 1.2 for examples). Surviving student notes also differ from other kinds of notes in that they usually take the form of a bound volume. In part this correlation is likely due to survival bias. Students may well also have taken notes on loose sheets or slips but anything left unbound was at higher risk of loss in the intervening centuries. Furthermore, notes taken in a pedagogical setting were likely considered of little use unless they were nicely kept and bound. In other words, while the personal archives of famous figures like Robert Boyle (1627–1691) or G.W. Leibniz (1646–1716) or even rather obscure ones like Joachim Jungius (1587–1657) include loose sheets and slips, these were notes relevant to their work as adults and considered worth saving even if they proved difficult to consult; by contrast student notes could be assumed to contain nothing original that would warrant saving if left in a messy state.[3]

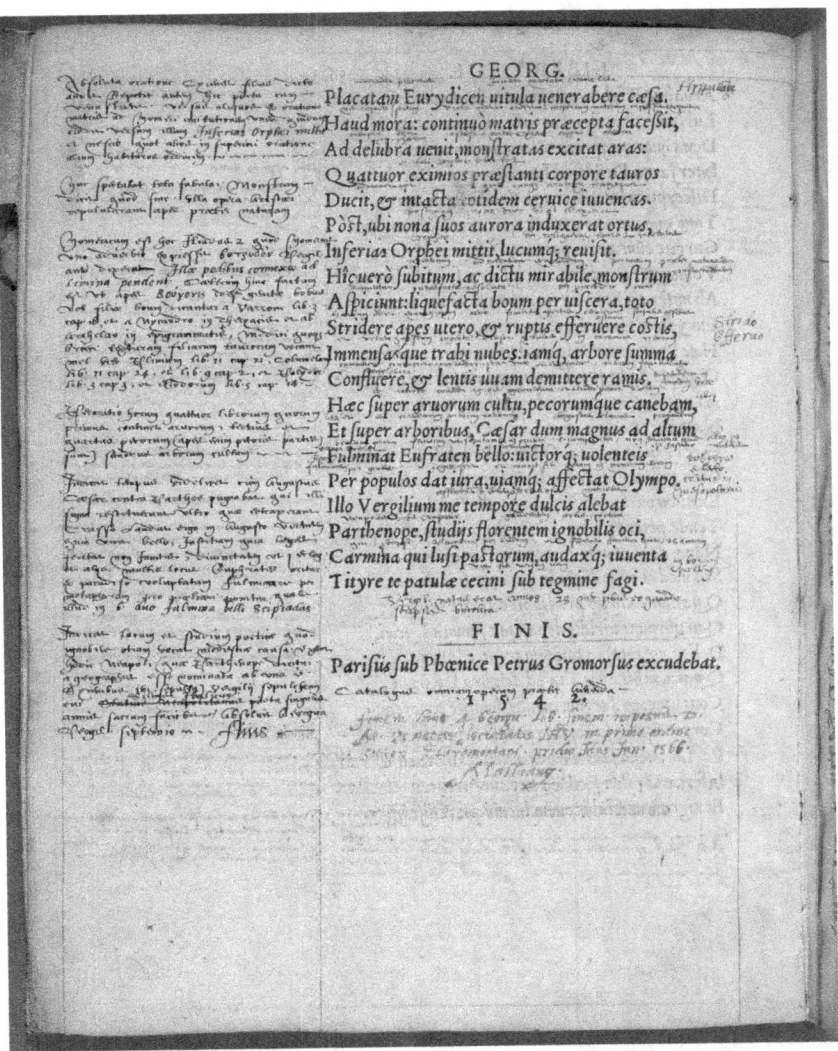

Figure 1.1. From a *Sammelband* containing twenty-six school editions. Here from the second text: Virgil, *Georgicon liber quartus* (Paris: Petrus Gromorsus, 1542), last printed page featuring, after the printer's colophon, a manuscript colophon in red ink: Mallianus, January 1566, in the class of M. Venegas S.J. in the first (highest) class (*primo ordine*) at the Collège de Clermont (Paris). The interlinear paraphrase and marginal comments are probably first-order notes, but the student has failed to enter the lemmata drawn from the text for comment, which earlier in the book he added in a larger script, in black ink, presumably as second-order notes in the space left blank for the purpose. Houghton Library, Harvard University: *FC5.A100.B565v, seq. 52.

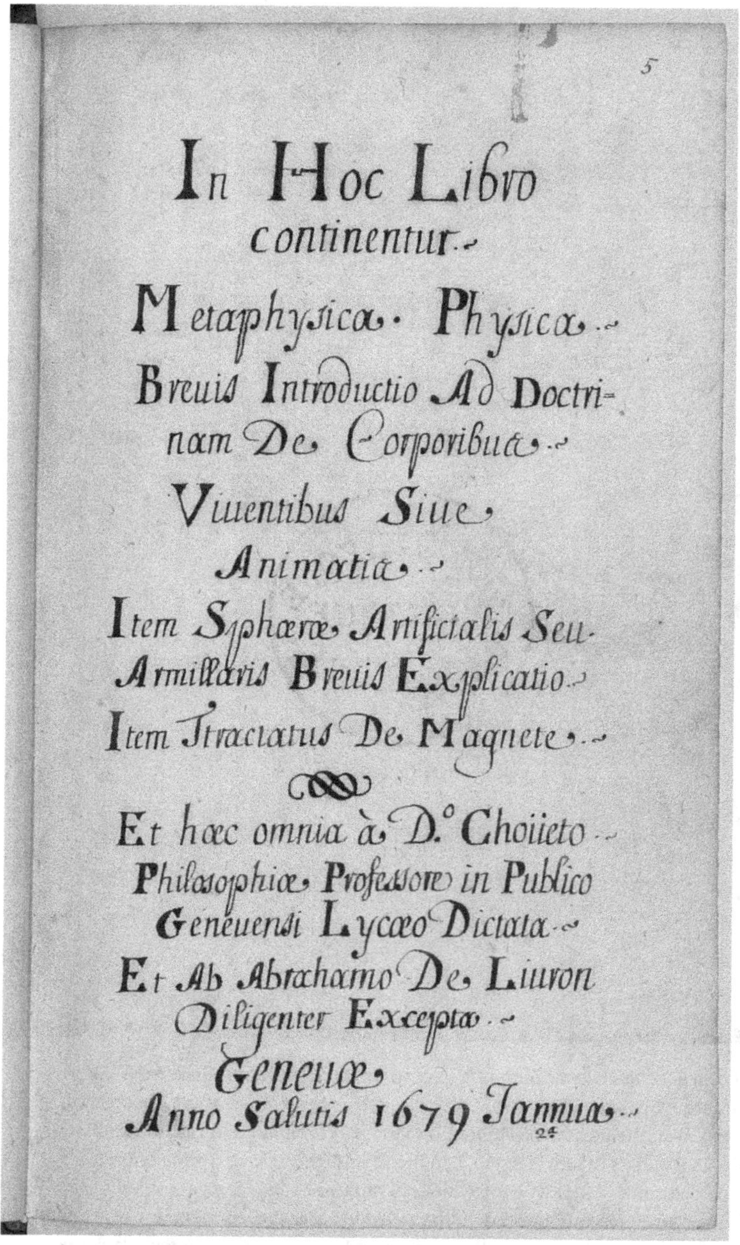

> In Hoc Libro
> continentur
> Metaphysica. Physica.
> Breuis Introductio Ad Doctri-
> nam De Corporibus
> Viuentibus Siue
> Animatis
> Item Sphæræ Artificialis Seu
> Armillaris Breuis Explicatio
> Item Tractatus De Magnete
>
> Et hæc omnia à D.° Choüeto
> Philosophiæ Professore in Publico
> Geneuensi Lycæo Dictata
> Et Ab Abrahamo De Liuron
> Diligenter Excepta
> Geneuæ
> Anno Salutis 1679 Januar.

Figure 1.2. "In hoc libro continentur Metaphysica, Physica [...]": the title page announces the many topics dictated by Chouet and *excepta* (captured from orality, as distinct from *excerpta*) by Abraham de Livron, in Geneva, 1679. Bibliothèque de Genève, MS lat 323. For a full description, see Jeger (2016: 1,399–406).

Another reason why student notes survive in bound form is that they were likely produced under a teacher's guidance or supervision to meet certain standards of legibility and neatness, even beauty. We have few details about how exactly teachers might have reviewed their students' notes. Occasionally, student notes contain corrections, but we cannot say whether these were made by a teacher or by the same student on re-reading the notes or by a third party, for example, possibly in view of a plan to publish the notes. Since student notes contain uncorrected errors, of spelling or aural misunderstanding, it seems unlikely that close teacher review was the norm. Students probably exercised considerable independence in keeping their notes. The sizes of the surviving bound volumes range from octavo to folio and the bindings (when they are original, which is not always easy to determine) vary from cheap parchment to expensive stamped leather. The handwriting and presentation range from hasty to so regular as to suggest professional scribing. Some illustrations were integral to the subject matter and likely mandated by the teacher, for example, depictions of the three cosmological systems (Ptolemaic, Copernican, or Tychonic). These can be found tucked into a portion of a page (or the space for them occasionally left blank when the student failed to return to fill them in) or spread out over a whole page; many are simple ink drawings made with minimal tools like ruler and compass, while others were also elaborately colored and adorned with decorative elements. Some surviving manuscripts are stunningly illustrated, which suggests that the student was also seeking to display their skills of draughtsmanship, whether in ink alone or with pigments, whether for their own personal enjoyment or to please a teacher or family member.[4]

2. The forms of student notes

Bound student notes typically survive in one of two forms. Either the volume comprises one or multiple printed texts in which the student has added notes on the printed pages and interleaved blank ones, or it consists of an entirely manuscript text organized into chapters and sections to look like a printed textbook. The first of these formats, the annotated school edition of a classical text—called the *feuille classique*—could of course only develop after printing was well established; it is documented from at least the early 1500s (Compère 2004). But instruction of the same kind predated printing. Prior to being able to purchase low-cost printed editions of the assigned text, a student would have had to first write out the source text before annotating it, as Guillaume Gisenheim or Beatus Rhenanus did as boys in Sélestat (Schlettstadt) in the 1490s for example. The fourteen-year-old Rhenanus wrote out, presumably under dictation, verses from Virgil's *Bucolics* in a large hand with wide interlinear spacing, then the teacher's comments in a smaller hand in the margins of and between the lines of Virgil's text.[5] By the early sixteenth century the initial task of writing out the classical text was abandoned in favor of each student purchasing an inexpensive school edition, printed locally and probably specifically for their coursework, which comprised only the assigned classical text with no paratext nor printed commentary.[6] Clusters of annotated school texts in the *feuille classique* genre have been studied for a variety of contexts, including Leipzig in the 1510s, Leuven's Collegium Trilingue starting in 1517, or the *collèges* of Paris from the 1560s and following decades.[7] Examples from these clusters are abundant enough that some have ended up on the modern rare book market and dispersed from there, for example, into the rare book collections of American universities among other locations.

While the *feuille classique* represents the schoolwork of younger adolescents acquiring a humanist mastery of classical languages and cultures, typically in colleges associated with universities, the freestanding manuscript coursebook is the result of the study of philosophy or other fields that students entered once they had acquired sufficient training in Latin and humanist methods. Students would write down, typically under dictation during many class sessions, a complete course on topic so as to come away with their own personal textbook, divided into sections and chapters. Manuscript coursebooks addressed one of the four parts of philosophy as mandated by the university curriculum—logic, physics, metaphysics, ethics—or any number of other topics taught on an extracurricular basis. Courses on the parts of Aristotelian philosophy were often framed around questions that would be answered with definitions and distinctions, responses and objections, in commenting on Aristotelian passages, following patterns characteristic of medieval teaching. But the form of a dictated course was supremely versatile and could easily stray from assigned authors, formats, and topics. François Dainville emphasized the role of Jesuit colleges in bypassing received opinion and introducing new topics (like geography) that spread to universities too, as instructors responded to the request of their students in extracurricular teaching. He called the greater latitude that dictated courses allowed "the pedagogical expression of a serious revolution, that which gave birth to Descartes."[8] The dictated course remained the main vehicle for classroom instruction in philosophy in the seventeenth and eighteenth centuries across the full range of philosophical opinion—from Cartesians to *novantiqui* who sought to combine Aristotelian and Cartesian philosophies, to traditional commentaries on the eight books of Aristotle's *Physics*, which were still offered at the university of Cervera near Barcelona in the mid-eighteenth century.[9] The form was supremely adaptable and could equally well ignore or embrace a philosophical authority.

While these two forms of student notes are the focus of the rest of this chapter and of this volume more generally, we should keep in mind that early modern students also took **notes in other forms**. For example, a student recorded in a freestanding manuscript the commentary by Angelo Poliziano on Suetonius' *Lives of the Caesars* in 1490–1 (Fera 1983). In another case a student transcribed into his copy of the text under study the marginal annotations that the teacher had made in his own copy; the teacher (Heinrich Glarean, 1488–1563) evidently expected students to have access to his books and to use them in this way.[10] In another instance where we can compare the notes of two students in the same class (taught by the Swiss humanist Vadian at the University of Vienna in 1517), they took each their own notes from oral teaching without dictation and independently from each other; only on technical matters did the student transcripts match, likely from copying something that the teacher circulated or wrote on a blackboard (Grafton and Leu 2013: 263). The multiple stages of note-taking in the private tutoring of a young nobleman have also exceptionally been preserved through the long-lived library founded by Duke August the Younger of Brunswick-Lüneburg (1579–1666).[11] The Herzog August Bibliothek owns notes that young August took as a child, probably at an earlier stage of education from the *feuilles classiques* and freestanding coursebooks. These include a copy of Cicero's *De officiis* with underlining by the child at the age of about eight to eleven and two notebooks that gathered selections excerpted from this and other classical texts. In the first of these notebooks, the *Sentenzensammlung* ("collection of sentences"), the boy copied (quite neatly) excerpts arranged by author and work, for example, Cicero, *De officiis*, *sententiae* numbered 1, 2, etc. In the second, entitled *loci communes* ("commonplaces"), he copied over some of the excerpts from the *Sentenzensammlung* along with others, sorting them under topical headings arranged alphabetically.[12] The presentation was messier, which suggests that the contents of these pages were not planned but added whenever August encountered an appropriate passage for a heading. We can reasonably call these reading notes, since they resulted from the same practices by which adults formed large collections of excerpta, but given August's age these reading notes were presumably taken in a pedagogical context though not in a classroom setting. Many other notes taken by students in a variety of forms also existed that did not benefit from belonging to a founder of a major library and some may survive without our being aware of their pedagogical origins. For example, an otherwise unknown student at Wittenberg kept notebooks that mixed printed texts and manuscript ones (Lepri 2022: 79). Note-taking was an individual practice that could be quite idiosyncratic, as even early modern pedagogues advocating a particular method acknowledged.[13]

3. Methods of note-taking in the classroom

For student notes taken in a classroom setting, whether in the form of the *feuille classique* or a freestanding coursebook, students frequently wrote under dictation by the teacher. Evidence for dictation includes explicit indications in opening or closing statements in the manuscript notes ("dictata a ...," that is, "dictated by ..."), contemporary remarks in other kinds of sources (for example, letters or memoirs), and instances where two or more sets of notes taken in the same class have been studied and found to be very closely matched except for some aural misunderstandings or misspellings (see, for example, Leonhardt 2008). Repeated rules against dictation also suggest that the practice was common even when it was forbidden, notably at the University of Paris in the fourteenth century (Hajnal 1959: 117–23). The bans on dictation may have been designed to distinguish university teaching from the instruction of younger students where dictation was likely the norm. In any case, by 1452, further statutes at the University of Paris explicitly disregarded the earlier bans and dictation was the norm for early modern student notes, whether students were learning commentary on classical texts or courses in philosophy or other fields. Dictation remained common in French pedagogy in secondary school and beyond down to modern times, alongside regulations that increasingly sought to minimize it. We have evidence that students appreciated dictation across the centuries. In the Middle Ages, dictation spared students the expense of paying for a copy of the material being taught and as late as 1968 French students in post-secondary *classes préparatoires* valued dictation for conveying the most information in the least amount of time.[14] Indeed dictation was efficient, by conveying course material simultaneously to as many students as could hear the teacher and had sufficient space to write while doing so.[15]

An alternative method for generating student manuscripts was practicable only with small classes sizes, such as those of a minor colonial college on the periphery of Europe. At Harvard College in the English colony of Massachusetts, students made their coursebooks in logic and natural philosophy by copying in successive sections during a few months a manuscript exemplar (in English, now lost) by Charles Morton (1627–1698), a religious dissenter who emigrated to New England in 1686.[16] Some two dozen of these student manuscripts survive, made between 1686 and 1730; although Cambridge had a printing press, there were evidently too few students (twenty-two students in the class of 1690, thirty-seven in that of 1721) to warrant printing the text that was published only as a historical source in the mid-twentieth century (for a sample page see Figure 1.3).

In addition, pedagogues throughout early modern Europe and its colonies consistently insisted that writing out a text was an essential aid to retaining it in memory—presumably this applied whether the writing was done under dictation or by copying an exemplar.[17] Copying likely occurred now and then in courses transmitted by dictation, notably for the transmission of diagrams and drawings from teacher to students. An exemplar could be circulated on a sheet of paper or a slate; or in some cases the teacher might have had the use of a blackboard.[18] No doubt students also copied the notes of their peers occasionally, for example, after an absence. We learn from the French nobleman Michel de Marolles how he handled his absence when he fell sick in 1617 and missed the philosophy lectures of Jean-Cécile Frey at the University of Paris: "our professor gave me private lessons for the time I had lost and I had [someone] write under him those [lessons] which he dictated in public." Marolles was also proud to have provided his teacher with "figures which I had drawn up" for astronomy and geography and which Frey "used quite often and praised in public."[19] For taking dictation from Frey's lectures while he was sick, Marolles presumably relied on a skilled servant or *amanuensis*—and possibly also

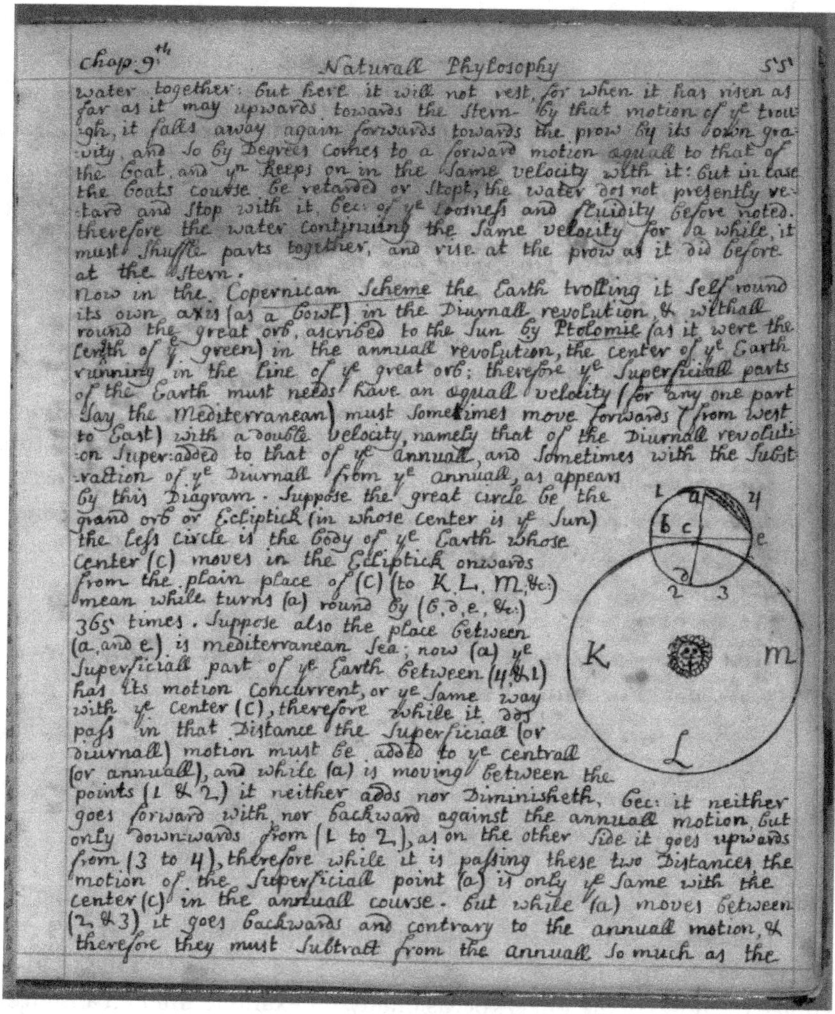

Chap: 9th Naturall Phylosophy 55
water together: but here it will not rest, for when it has risen as
far as it may upwards towards the Stern by that motion of ye trou:
:gh, it falls away again forwards towards the prow by its own gra:
:vity, and So by Degrees Comes to a forward motion equall to that of
the Boat, and yn keeps on in the Same velocity with it: but in case
the Boats course be retarded or Stopt, the water dos not presently re:
:tard and Stop with it, Bec: of ye looseness and fluidity before noted.
therefore the water continuing the Same velocity for a while, it
must Shuffle parts together, and rise at the prow as it did before
at the Stern.
Now in the Copernican Scheme the Earth trolling it Self round
its own axis (as a bowl) in the Diurnall revolution, & withall
round the great orb, ascribed to the Sun by Ptolomie (as it were the
Length of ye green) in the annuall revolution, the center of ye Earth
running in the Line of ye great orb; therefore ye Superficiall parts
of the Earth must needs have an equall velocity (for any one part
Say the Mediterranean) must Sometimes move forwards (from West
to East) with a double velocity, namely that of the Diurnall revoluti:
:on Super:added to that of ye annuall, and Sometimes with the Subst:
:raction of ye Diurnall from ye annuall, as appears
by this Diagram. Suppose the great circle be the
grand orb or Ecliptick (in whose center is ye Sun)
the less circle is the body of ye Earth whose
center (c) moves in the Ecliptick onwards
from the plain place of (C) (to K.L.M.&c:)
mean while turns (a) round by (b.d,e, &c:)
365 times. Suppose also the place between
(a, and e) is mediterranean Sea; now (a) ye
Superficiall part of ye Earth between (4&1)
has its motion concurrent, or ye Same way
with ye Center (C), therefore while it dos
pass in that Distance the Superficiall (or
diurnall) motion must be added to ye centrall
(or annuall), and while (a) is moving between the
points (1 & 2) it neither adds nor Diminisheth, Bec: it neither
goes forward with, nor backward against the annuall motion, but
only down:wards from (1 to 2), as on the other Side it goes upwards
from (3 to 4), therefore while it is passing these two Distances, the
motion of the Superficiall point (a) is only ye Same with the
center (c) in the annuall course. But while (a) moves between
(2 & 3) it goes backwards and contrary to the annuall motion, &
therefore they must Subtract from the annuall So much as the

Figure 1.3. Charles Morton, "Naturall philosophy. A system of physicks," 1706, in the hand of Samuel Phillips. The text explains how the diurnal rotation of the earth is added or substracted from the annual rotation of the earth around the sun. Phillips has likely used a compass only for the larger circle and the smaller one is more approximate. Houghton Library, Harvard University: MS Am 2535, seq. 63.

for drawing up those high-quality figures, notwithstanding his use of the first-person pronoun to describe making them.[20]

4. What can and cannot be learned from student notes

Student notes are invaluable sources for reconstructing the content and methods of teaching—they offer much more direct insight into the classroom than the sources that have been most used in the history of education: official curricular statutes and printed textbooks (see also Chapter 6). Student notes have brought to light how often early modern students were exposed to topics that were not in the official curriculum. This kind of exposure had different motivations. A course on a standard topic like Aristotelian natural philosophy could include discussions that Aristotle did not address (such as the cosmological options of heliocentrism and geoheliocentrism). Alternatively, teachers offered extracurricular courses on completely different topics, including, in the case of Frey's teaching in Paris in 1607–30, on methods of study, the arts of memory following Ramon Lull, the philosophy of the druids, or "curious propositions about the universe." Frey's extracurricular courses generated the same kinds of freestanding student manuscripts as the curricular ones; the latter manuscripts had higher production values (larger format, more careful layout and illustrations) than the former, but since different students were involved in making them the comparison is not a rigorous one (Blair 1993).

Nevertheless, dictated notes can hardly be taken as a record of everything that was said in the classroom, nor even as a complete record of what the students wrote there. One area of uncertainty is whether a given set of notes comprises first-order notes (*Mitschriften*) written directly as the teacher was speaking or second-order notes copied over from the first-order notes after the fact (*Reinschriften*). Notes copied from a manuscript or printed exemplar should likely be considered second-order too. Close attention to the material features of the notes can offer some clues: arguments in favor of a *Mitschrift* would be haste of handwriting, words crossed out and replaced in the flow of the line, and blanks left to be filled in later. A neat and regular script and careful layout, for example, with tapering at the end of paragraphs, and the presence of different ink colors are arguments for a *Reinschrift* (for some examples of both, see Figure 1.1). Some manuscripts combine both kinds of notes. In the *feuille classique*, interlinear paraphrase is presumably mostly first-order, while red ink used to highlight the words from the text being commented on would be added later, as suggested by the cases when this work was not completed.[21] We may also encounter third-order notes, especially when notes were prepared for publication, notably as a tribute to a deceased teacher by some of his students in a gesture that of course also brought attention to the students themselves.

In preparing notes for publication, students often worked together. This practice has been documented as early as the turn of the sixteenth century (Oosterhoff 2018: Chapter 4). Some 150 years later, the printed version of Frey's course on cosmography names two students (Antoine de Rocbine and Antoine Morand) who prepared it, presumably by collating their two sets of notes, neither of which survive. The printed text can be compared with one surviving manuscript from yet a third student on the same course (Charles Trainquard). The differences between the manuscript and the printed version are minimal, but include one correction of an aural misunderstanding—"Clavius" appeared in print where Charles Trainquard's manuscript version had "Labius."[22] While we cannot know if this error appeared in the manuscripts of the two Antoines from which the printed version was prepared, we can assume that working together from multiple sets of notes enabled those preparing notes for publication to avoid errors made at earlier stages of note-taking. We also know that early modern students were encouraged to study together in a variety of ways. In Jesuit colleges, students drilled one another orally on the lessons of the day in *reparationes* scheduled at the end of the day (Codina Mir 1968: 118–19). The Calvinist professor of philosophy Bartholomaeus Keckermann (1572–1609) recommended that students form groups of three who were well matched in level and skills and friendly with one another; the group would divide up the assigned reading among themselves and share their excerpts from it (see Blair 2010: 103).

Working together could prove especially valuable in taking notes from oral events that were not dictated but delivered at the usual rate of speech. Table talk of the late seventeenth century, the *Menagiana*, reports that the sixteenth-century French legal scholar Jacques Cujas "did not dictate but spoke his lessons with such clarity that his students and especially the German ones wrote down what they could and conferring together afterward found that little of what he said escaped them; they gave to the printers what they had drawn up in a clean copy."[23] The story dates from one hundred years after Cujas' teaching, so the veracity of its specifics may not be sound, but it speaks at least to a method of working that seemed noteworthy and plausible in the late seventeenth century—that students would pool their notes to reconstruct the whole lecture when it was not dictated and that the German students were particularly keen on doing so. At about the same time as the *Menagiana* appeared, August Hermann Francke (1663–1727) was implementing a method of writing down sermons through teamwork. He trained the orphans he was educating in Halle to take notes in a team of about ten students to each record in turn as much of the full spoken sermon as they could before the next member of team continued the task. The work generated a succession of sentence fragments that would be put together and copied to create a full written record of a sermon delivered at speed. This *Schreibechor* ("writing choir") generated hundreds of volumes of transcribed sermons; among them are two slips of the kind each note-taker would make listing numbered fragments of sentences that would then be combined with the other team members' sentence fragments to reconstruct the whole text. Those slips only survive for a section of one sermon because the others in the set were lost, preventing the usual complete transcription from them; so, when the system broke down momentarily, the first-order notes survive that usually would have been discarded when superseded by the second-order notes (Blair 2008: 59–62). The *Schreibechor* represents an explicit plan on the part of the speaker (in this case a preacher) to use listener notes to create a full text from an oral delivery. How often might teachers have relied on student notes from a previous iteration of their course in lecturing and by contrast how often did they go to class with more or less full notes of their own? Since the teacher was expected to dictate their course, it seems challenging (to us today at least) to do so without a full text, since dictating meant speaking slowly, without false starts, and with repetitions as needed. Yet this was evidently a skill that early modern professors mastered. Nicolas de Nancel, the biographer of the Paris professor Petrus Ramus (1515–1572), described Ramus' teaching method from his perspective as Ramus' assistant at the time: "[Ramus] made do with brief notes on a piece of paper which he held in his hand and glanced down at as he was speaking," and

> when he returned home he used to jot down *in shorthand* what he had lectured and commented on; after we [that is, Nancel] had copied out these notes in our own hand *in a beautiful script*, he kept them at home together with other far more numerous manuscripts with the intention of publishing them.[24]

On this account Ramus never had more than brief notes preceding the lecture, but a full text would be generated after the fact with the help of his assistant (who had also been a student of Ramus') and with the plan to publish in due course. Indeed, Ramus published multiple pedagogical texts, although to my knowledge we cannot compare them to relevant surviving manuscripts. Similarly, among the Frey manuscripts one volume containing four texts might well be autograph and one of those texts contains later corrections that indicate a plan to publish them, though this was never carried out.[25] In general professorial manuscripts survive rarely and even more rarely when their plans to publish the notes were carried out, since the printing process would often destroy the manuscript involved and was also considered to supersede earlier manuscript versions.

From the teacher's perspective the method of dictating each course afresh offered some advantages, including the opportunity to make changes from one iteration to the next. The seven surviving student manuscripts from the physics courses of Jean-Robert Chouet in Geneva (1642–1731) indicate that Chouet did make some changes from one iteration to the next between 1669 and 1685 but only minor ones, for example, in the examples offered or the ordering and titles of one or two subsections. In the main, the text (including the wording of sentences), and its presentation (for example, the order and titles of sections) remained quite consistent from one iteration to another. Perhaps that continuity was aided by Chouet's own professorial notes or by his reliance on student notes from an earlier iteration—sadly we have no specific evidence to shed more light on his teaching methods nor any autograph manuscripts (Blair and Goeing 2022).

It is not surprising that we have many more student manuscripts than professorial ones, given the typical teacher–student ratio of one to many. A further survival bias is likely introduced by the fact that whereas professorial manuscripts are functional but non-descript, some students devoted exceptional resources to their manuscripts—through personal or delegated effort and skill invested in both the text and illustrations. One of Chouet's students who went on to some fame as a close friend of Isaac Newton, Nicolas Fatio de Duillier (1664–1753), left an exceptional set of notebooks from the philosophy courses he took with Chouet in 1678–80. They feature painstaking calligraphy, additional paratexts not found in other student manuscripts from the time, including a table of contents, a Tree of Porphyry (representing the hierarchy of beings), and an ink-drawn frontispiece copied from the engraving in a book of 1640. The production values of these manuscripts surely motivated others to save them after Fatio de Duillier's

Figure 1.4. "Dialectica dictata a doctissimo domino D. Ioanne Corbion," Leuven, 1703. Houghton Library, Harvard University: MS Lat 481, seq. 105.

death, although sadly the physics volume is missing (possibly because Fatio took it with him to England rather than leaving it behind in his hometown of Geneva, but that is speculation; Blair and Goeing 2022: 190–7).

Even Fatio's skills in pen- and draughtsmanship pale in comparison with a manuscript from Leuven, a "Dialectica dictata a Doctissimo domino Ioanne Corbion Leodiensi" by Josephus Peeters of Antwerp in 1703. The Tree of Porphyry, the square of oppositions, Atlas carrying the globe, self-portraits of the young man at work with a paintbrush and praying in his room, and a vivid portrayal of the building of Trinity College Leuven, accompany a text regularly embellished with flowers (on headings and initials), drawings of pointing fingers or manicules to call attention to important passages and carefully managed ink washes that operate like a highlighter (see Figure 1.4).[26]

Joseph Peeters used the course notebook as much more than an opportunity to learn and keep a record of dialectic through writing the course under dictation and then perhaps again in second-order notes. This exceptional manuscript memorialized his student experience with great art and skill for the benefit, one hopes, of his later self and generations since then. Today it spreads admiration for the teaching and learning that happened in early modern Leuven from another continent, across the Internet.[27]

Notes

[*] I am grateful for excellent suggestions to Anja-Silvia Goeing, Philippe Schmid, and the editors of this volume.

[1] Heinrich von Friemar, *Quaestiones in Quartum librum sententiarum*: "Et istae Quaestiones sunt reportatae per modum notabiliorum, et non sunt positi tituli quaestionum in principio, quia reportans adhuc non habuit modum, et non potuit ita velociter scribere, quia lector non legebat ad pennam, sed cursorie, et ergo, si aliquid fuisset obmissum, quod non digne videatur, istud non est imponendum legenti, sed reportanti" (as cited in Meier 1954: 4). It seems that this work is that of the younger Heinrich von Friemar (c. 1285–1345); see Saack (2022: 352).

[2] Hamesse (1997: 419 *et passim*). On the many forms of note-taking in medieval universities, see Burnett (1994).

[3] On Boyle and other members of the Royal Society, see Yeo (2014). On the massive note collection of Joachim Jungius, see Meinel (1995).

[4] See Chapter 9 by Bielak and de Mûelenaere for more details on the visual aspects of student notes.

[5] See the contributions of Isabel Suzeau-Gagnaire, Gérard Freyburger, and Bastien Rissoan in Bénévent and Bisaro (2019: 127–70).

[6] These editions could contain brief printed words of summary in the margins or in an *argumentum* (summary) at the beginning of the text; another distinctive feature was the "double-spacing" of the printed classical text, which facilitated the interlinear insertion of Latin synonyms or paraphrases of the classical original.

[7] See, for example, Leonhardt (2008) for Leipzig; DaLeT (s.d.) for Leuven; and Compère, Couzinet, and Pédeflous (2009) for the French case, with the literature cited there.

8   Dainville (1940: 222–3); see also Nelles (2007).
9   On the teaching of Cartesianism, see Cellamare and Mantovani (2023). On Chouet, who introduced some Cartesianism into the Aristotelian curriculum at the Academy in Geneva, see Blair and Goeing (2022). On logic teaching in the seventeenth and eighteenth centuries, see Coesemans (2019). Student manuscripts from the University of Cervera, founded by the Jesuits in 1714, are now at the Biblioteca de Catalunya, Barcelona, including: Jaume Puig, "Tractatus in octo libros physicos Aristotelis," MS 1647 (1741–2); Joseph Vallesca, "Cursus aristotelicus," MS 2521 (eighteenth century); Josep Osset, "Philosophiae novo-antiquae institutiones," MS 602 (1779), all of which focused on Aristotelian physics. On the curriculum there, indebted to the Jesuit *Ratio studiorum* of 1599, see Clúa Serena (2001).
10 See the notes by Gabriel Hummelberg II (1530–82?) studied in Grafton and Leu (2013: 262).
11 This discussion relies on Hess (2003).
12 On commonplacing see Moss (1996).
13 See Drexel (1638: sig. [A8]r): "Quod si praeceptiones istae et Excerpendi leges non placeant, scribe tibi alias, pauciores, breviores, studiis tuis commodas, dummodo Excerpas. Hoc autem vere TUUM dixeris, quod in rem tuam cum judicio excerpseris." ("But if these prescriptions and rules for excerpting are not pleasing, write for yourself other rules that are fewer, shorter, adapted to your studies, as long as you make excerpts. But you could truly call this yours, since you judiciously excerpted it for your own good.") For more discussion of Drexel and note-taking manuals, see Blair (2010: 85 and Chapter 2 more generally).
14 Hajnal (1959: 135); Waquet (2003: 78). But students also demanded an end to dictation in 1789; see Brockliss (1987: 192–3).
15 Sadly, we know little about the setting in which lectures took place and students took notes. But for recent work on the material circumstances of English grammar schools, see Schrire (2021).
16 Coesemans (2019: 29–30) presents evidence that Leuven manuscripts called "dictata" may in fact have been copied, given that they present none of the aural errors found in the "annotata" manuscripts.
17 See Knoles and Zaucha Knoles (2003); Blair (2008: 57–9 [Harvard manuscripts], 63–5 [writing as retention]).
18 Blackboards have not yet been well studied. In the sixteenth century blackboards used in music teaching are known from inventories after death and from a few iconographical sources; see Owens (1997: 87). For use of the *pietra nera* by eighteenth-century Italian mathematicians, see Dooley (1984: 129). On methods of transmitting visual elements in the classroom, see Eddy (2016: 99, 107–109; 2023).
19 Marolles (1656: 35–6): "Nostre Professeur me donnoit des leçons en particulier pour le temps que i'avois perdu, et ie faisois escrire sous luy celles qu'il dictoit en public, où il méloit beaucoup de questions et recherches curieuses, tant de l'Astronomie, que du Sisteme du monde et de la Geographie, dont i'avois acquis desia quelque connaissance: et se servoit mesmes bien souvent des figures que i'avois dressées pour induire des preuves de cette science, lesquelles il recommendoit publiquement, et les faisoit beaucoup valoir."
20 On delegating handwriting, see Blair (2016).
21 For other examples of annotations comprising a mix of first-order and second-order notes, see Feys (s.d.).
22 Compare "Cosmographiae selectiora" in Bibliothèque municipale de Bourges, MS 343 (230 folios), p. 62, and as printed in Frey's *Opuscula* (1646: 131–320, 185), with the colophon at p. 320: "Excipiebant Antonius de Rocbine et Antonius Morand affines Donomarenses. 1629." I have not identified the place designated by Donomarensis; "excipio" is a verb that specifically means writing spoken words, as in "snatching" them from the air. So, this colophon reads: "Antoine de Rocbine and Antoine Morand, neighbors from Donomare (?), captured these words." For discussion, see Blair (1993: 96–7).

[23] Ménage (1694: 13–14), as discussed in Schuwey (2020: 93).
[24] "Hoc autem scire juvabit, hunc Ramo nostro morem fuisse, ut de re qualibet, vel Gorgiae in modum thesi posita dicturo sufficerent notae breves, quas in chartula gerebat, et obliquis oculis dicendo inspectabat." "Reversus domum, ex more, praelecta sibi aut enuntiata ταχυγράφοις exscribebat: quae singula, nostra manu notis καλλιγράφοις descripta, domi cum aliis longe plurimis monumentis premebat, eo quidem consilio ut ederentur." (Italics reflect code-switching to Greek.) See the edition and translation in Sharratt (1975: 194–5, 190–1) of Nancel (1599: 24, 21). On Nancel and Ramus more generally see Couzinet (2015: 228–300).
[25] Bibliothèque de l'Arsenal MS 1146: "De geographia tractatus" (138 folios), "In universam Politicen Praefatio" (63 folios), "Miscellaneorum ex selectis disciplinis aut lectorum aut noviter inventorum libellus" (30 folios), "Στεφανοπλόκος id est, ex diversis politioris litteraturae [sic] floribus corollae contextae" (21 folios). In "Miscellaneorum," the original title is crossed out and replaced with "Jani Caecilii Frey Parisiensis Hortus"; then Frey's prefatory exhortation to "adolescentes" is corrected to "posteritas," suggesting a change of audience from students to the readers of a published work. The marginal annotations modify the prose construction of the first chapter fairly densely, but then disappear abruptly. No such work was published.
[26] On the manicule and its history, see Sherman (2008: Chapter 2).
[27] The manuscript, recently acquired by Houghton Library at Harvard, is cataloged as MS Lat 481 and fully digitized. For these illustrations see ff. 5 (self-portrait), 17 (Atlas), 29 (tree of Porphyry), 54 (at prayer), 77 (square of oppositions), 103 (syllogisms), 105 (Trinity College Leuven).

Suggestions for further reading

Christine Bénévent and Xavier Bisaro 2019. A collection of 12 essays studying examples of humanist teaching in the 16th century, with many illustrations including some in color.

Blair 2004. A discussion of note-taking in general and its significance across many historical contexts.

Burnett 1994. A detailed and illustrated discussion of note-taking techniques in European universities in the 12th and 13th centuries.

Campi, De Angelis, Goeing, and Grafton 2008. A collection of 17 essays which offer insight into the pedagogy in different early modern European contexts and the roles of manuscript and printed course books.

Compère, Couzinet, and Pédeflous 2009. An authoritative and thorough discussion of the *feuille classique* form, with many valuable references.

Grafton 1981. Probably the first detailed study of a *feuille classique*, before that term was coined.

Waquet 2003. An innovative study of orality by an expert in the genres and forms of scholarly work down to the modern period.

References

Manuscripts and annotated prints

Dates of composition appear when they are known and mentioned in the chapters. Underlining indicates an annotated print. For bibliographical details about the early modern prints, one should consult the section "Early modern printed sources."

Barcelona, Biblioteca de Catalunya
  MS 602: Osset, Josep. 1779. "Philosophiae novo-antiquae institutiones."
  MS 1647: Puig, Jaume. 1741–2. "Tractatus in octo libros physicos Aristotelis."
  MS 2521: Vallesca, Joseph. Eighteenth century. "Cursus aristotelicus."
Bourges, Bibliothèque municipale de
  MS 343: Trainquard, Charles. "Cosmographiae selectiora" (teacher: Jean-Cécile Frey).
Cambridge, MA, Harvard University, Houghton Library
  MS Am 2535: Morton, Charles. 1706. "Naturall philosophy. A system of physicks."
  MS Lat 481: Peeters, Josephus. 1703. "Dialectica dictata a Doctissimo domino Ioanne Corbion Leodiensi."
  *<u>FC5.A100.B565v, seq. 52</u>: a *Sammelband* containing 26 imprints, including Virgil 1542 (student: Mallianus; teacher: M. Venegas S.J.; institute: Collège de Clermont; finished: January 1566).
Geneva, Bibliothèque de Genève
  MS lat 323: Livron, Abraham de. 1679. "In hoc libro continentur Metaphysica, Physica [...]" (teacher: Jean-Robert Chouet).
Paris, Bibliothèque de l'Arsenal
  MS 1146: Frey, Jean-Cécile. "De geographia tractatus" and other works.

Early modern printed sources

Drexel, Jeremias. 1638. *Aurifodina artium et scientiarum omnium; excerpendi sollertia, omnibus litterarum amantibus monstrata*. Antwerp: Johannes Cnobbarus' widow.
Frey, Jean-Cécile. 1646. *Opuscula varia nusquam edita, philosophis, medicis et curiosis omnibus utilissima*. [Edited by Antoine Morand.] Paris: Petrus David.
Marolles, Michel de. 1656. *Mémoires [...] contenant ce qu'il a vu de plus remarquable en sa vie, depuis l'année 1600*. Paris: Antoine de Sommaville.
Ménage, Gilles. 1694. *Menagiana ou bons mots, rencontres agreables, pensees judicieuses et observations curieuses de M. [Gilles] Ménage*. Amsterdam: George Gallet.
Nancel, Nicolas de. 1599. *Petri Rami vita*. Paris: Claude Morel.
Virgil. 1542. *Georgicon liber quartus*. Paris: Petrus Gromorsus.

Secondary literature (including online resources)

Bénévent, Christine, and Xavier Bisaro, eds. 2019. *Cahiers d'écoliers de la Renaissance*. Tours: Presses universitaires François-Rabelais.
Blair, Ann. 1993. "The Teaching of Natural Philosophy in Early Seventeenth-Century Paris: The Case of Jean-Cécile Frey." *History of Universities* 12: 95–158.
———. 2004. "Note-Taking as an Art of Transmission." *Critical Inquiry* 31: 85–107.

———. 2008. "Textbooks and Methods of Note-Taking in Early Modern Europe." In Campi et al. (2008: 39–73).

———. 2010. *Too Much to Know: Managing Scholarly Information before the Modern Age*. New Haven–London: Yale University Press.

———. 2016. "Early Modern Attitudes toward the Delegation of Copying and Note-Taking." In *Forgetting Machines: Knowledge Management Evolution in Early Modern Europe*, edited by Alberto Cevolini, 265–85. Leiden–Boston: Brill.

Blair, Ann, and Anja-Silvia Goeing. 2022. "Manuscripts as Pedagogical Tools in the Philosophy Teaching of Jean-Robert Chouet (1642–1731)." In *Teaching Philosophy in Early Modern Europe: Text and Image*, edited by Susanna Berger and Daniel Garber, 165–203. Cham: Springer.

Boodts, Shari, and Anthony Dupont. 2018. "Augustine of Hippo." In *Preaching in the Patristic Era: Sermons, Preachers, and Audiences in the Latin West*, edited by Anthony Dupont, Shari Boodts, Gert Partoens, and Johan Leemans, 177–197. Leiden–Boston: Brill.

Brockliss, Lawrence. 1987. *French Higher Education in the Seventeenth and Eighteenth Centuries: A Cultural History*. Oxford: Clarendon Press.

Burnett, Charles. 1994. "Give Him the White Cow: Notes and Note-Taking in the Universities in the Twelfth and Thirteenth Centuries." *History of Universities* 14: 1–30.

Campi, Emidio, Simone De Angelis, Anja-Silvia Goeing, and Anthony T. Grafton, eds. 2008. *Scholarly Knowledge: Textbooks in Early Modern Europe*. Geneva: Droz.

Cellamare, David, and Mattia Mantovani, eds. 2023. *Descartes in the Classroom: Teaching Cartesian Philosophy in the Early Modern Age*. Leiden–Boston: Brill.

Clúa Serena, José A. 2001. "Anotacions sobre l'humanisme classicista jesuític a la Catalunya del segle XVIII: La Universitat de Cervera." *Calamus Renascens* 2: 43–75.

Codina Mir, Gabriel. 1968. *Aux sources de la pédagogie des Jésuites, le "modus parisiensis."* Rome: Institutum Historicum S.J.

Coesemans, Steven. 2019. "Faculties of the Mind: The Rise of Facultative Logic at the University of Louvain." Unpublished PhD dissertation, Leuven: KU Leuven.

Compère, Marie-Madeleine. 2004. "Les 'feuilles classiques': Un support pour la prélection des textes latins et grecs (XVIe–XVIIe siècles)." Online article. Le cours magistral: Modalités et usages (XVIe–XXe siècles). April 6, 2004. http://rhe.ish-lyon.cnrs.fr/cours_magistral/expose_feuilles_classiques/expose_feuilles_classiques_complet.php.

Compère, Marie-Madeleine (†), Marie-Dominique Couzinet, and Olivier Pédéflous. 2009. "Éléments pour l'histoire d'un genre éditorial: La feuille classique en France aux XVIe et XVIIe siècles." *Histoire de l'éducation* 124: 27–49. https://doi.org/10.4000/histoire-education.2060.

Couzinet, Marie-Dominique. 2015. *Pierre Ramus et la critique du pédantisme*. Paris: Champion.

Dainville, François. 1940. *La géographie des humanistes*. Paris: Beauchesne.

DaLeT. Database of the Leuven Trilingue, edited by Raf Van Rooy, Xander Feys, Maxime Maleux, and Andy Peetermans. https://www.dalet.be/. Last accessed December 3, 2024.

Dooley, Brendan. 1984. "Science Teaching as a Career at Padua in the Early Eighteenth Century: The Case of Giovanni Poleni." *History of Universities* 4: 115–51.

Eddy, Matthew. 2016. "The Interactive Notebook: How Students Learned to Keep Notes during the Scottish Enlightenment." *Book History* 19: 86–131.

———. 2023. *Media and the Mind: Art, Science, and Notebooks as Paper Machines, 1700–1830*. Chicago: University of Chicago Press.

Fera, Vincenzo. 1983. *Una ignota* Expositio Suetoni *del Poliziano*. Messina: Centro di Studi Umanistici.

Feys, Xander, ed. S.d. "Nannius-Episcopius annotations on Vergil's *Aeneid* 12 (Latin, 1549)." Contr. Jan Papy, Andy Peetermans, and Raf Van Rooy. DaLeT: Database of the Leuven Trilingue. www.dalet.be. Last accessed December 3, 2024.

Grafton, Anthony. 1981. "Teacher, Text and Pupil in the Renaissance Class-Room: A Case Study from a Parisian College." *History of Universities* 1: 37–70.

Grafton, Anthony, and Urs Leu. 2013. "*Chronologia est unica historiae lux*: How Glarean Studied and Taught the Chronology of the Ancient World." In *Heinrich Glarean's Books: The Intellectual World of a Sixteenth-Century Musical Humanist*, edited by Iain Fenlon and Inga Mai Groote, 248–79. Cambridge: Cambridge University Press.

Hajnal, István. 1959. *L'enseignement de l'écriture aux universités médiévales*. Budapest: Maison d'édition de l'Académie des Sciences de Hongrie.

Hamesse, Jacqueline. 1997. "La technique de la reportation." In *L'enseignement des disciplines à la Faculté des Arts (Paris et Oxford, XIIIe–XVe siècles): Actes du colloque international*, edited by Olga Weijers and Louis Holtz, 405–21. Turnhout: Brepols.

Hess, Gilbert. 2003. "Fundamente fürstlicher Tugend: Zum Stellenwert der Sentenz im Rahmen der voruniversitären Ausbildung Herzog Augusts d.J. von Braunschweig-Lüneburg (1579–1666)." In *Sammeln, Ordnen, Veranschaulichen: Zur Wissenskompilatorik in der Frühen Neuzeit*, edited by Frank Büttner, Markus Friedrich, and Helmut Zedelmaier, 131–73. Münster: LIT.

Jeger, Isabelle. 2016. *Catalogue des manuscrits latins 1–376*. Genève: Bibliothèque de Genève.

Knoles, Thomas, and Lucia Zaucha Knoles. 2003. "*In Usum Pupillorum*: Student-Transcribed Texts at Harvard College before 1740." In *Student Notebooks at Colonial Harvard: Manuscripts and Educational Practice 1650–1740*, edited by Thomas Knoles, Rick Kennedy, and Lucia Zaucha Knoles, 7–88. Worcester: American Antiquarian Society.

Leonhardt, Jürgen. 2008. "Classics as Textbooks: A Study of the Humanist Lectures on Cicero at the University of Leipzig, ca. 1515." In Campi et al. (2008: 89–112).

Lepri, Valentina. 2022. "The Bees' Honey: Remarks on Students as Agents of Knowledge in Renaissance Europe through the Case of Simon Clüver (1540–1598)." *Mediterranea. International Journal on the Transfer of Knowledge* 7: 71–94.

Meier, Ludger. 1954. "Über den Zeugniswert der *Reportatio* in der Scholastik." *Archiv für Kulturgeschichte* 36: 1–8.

Meinel, Christoph. 1995. "Enzyklopädie der Welt und Verzettelung des Wissens: Aporien der Empirie bei Joachim Jungius." In *Enzyklopädien der frühen Neuzeit: Beiträge zu ihrer Forschung*, edited by Franz Eybl, 162–87. Tübingen: Niemeyer.

Moss, Ann. 1996. *Printed Commonplace-Books and the Structuring of Renaissance Thought*. Oxford: Clarendon Press.

Nelles, Paul. 2007. "*Libros de papel, libri bianchi, libri papyracei*: Note-Taking Techniques and the Role of Student Notebooks in the Early Jesuit Colleges." *Archivum Historicum Societatis Iesu* 76: 75–112.

Oosterhoff, Richard. 2018. *Making Mathematical Culture: University and Print in the Circle of Lefèvre d'Étaples*. Oxford: Oxford University Press.

Owens, Jessie Ann. 1997. *Composers at Work: The Craft of Musical Composition 1450–1600*. Oxford: Oxford University Press.

Saack, Eric Leland. 2022. *Augustinian Theology in the Later Middle Ages*. Leiden–Boston: Brill.

Schrire, Ray. 2021. "Shifting Paradigms: Ideas, Materiality and the Changing Shape of Grammar in the Renaissance." *Journal of the Warburg and Courtauld Institutes* 84 (1): 1–31.

Schuwey, Christophe. 2020. *Un entrepreneur des lettres au XVIIe siècle: Donneau de Visé, de Molière au Mercure galant*. Paris: Classiques Garnier.

Sharratt, Peter. 1975. "Nicolaus Nancelius, *Petri Rami Vita*: Edited with an English Translation." *Humanistica Lovaniensia* 24: 161–277.

Sherman, William H. 2008. *Used Books: Marking Readers in Renaissance England*. Philadelphia, PA: University of Pennsylvania Press.

Waquet, Françoise. 2003. *Parler comme un livre: L'oralité et le savoir XVIe–XXe siècle*. Paris: Albin Michel.

Yeo, Richard. 2014. *Notebooks, English Virtuosi, and Early Modern Science*. Chicago: University of Chicago Press.

CHAPTER 2

Getting a First Grasp of Student Notes

Raf Van Rooy and Xander Feys

1. Introduction

Student notes come in different shapes and the history of their making and remaking can be utterly varied, as Ann Blair has highlighted in the previous chapter. What makes many bodies of student notes difficult to process is what can be called their referentiality. Whereas a text written and published is usually intended for reading on its own, early modern student notes typically were not—they need to be read in reference to something else. Of course, even with a published text you often need the historical context in which it was created to understand it, especially if particular people, events, practices, or texts are mentioned or alluded to. Getting a grasp of a body of early modern student notes not only requires this historical and textual context, but also an insight into how they were made (see Chapter 1), which cognitive processes these notes reflect, and with which texts they interact. This chapter addresses the two last questions, to the extent possible, since research into the underlying cognitive processes is still in its infancy (see particularly Schrire 2021).

It is, however, clear that student notes reveal a process of intellectual consumption, of learning, in a particular historical setting, to which these sources refer in various ways. Modern scholars of these notes, therefore, have to read them in reference to something else, to which they do not necessarily have direct access any longer: especially the text commented upon (if any and if extant), the pedagogical setting in which the notes were taken (if known), and the method of note-taking adopted (if deducible or made explicit): *reportatio*, dictation, or some other method, for instance involving second-order revision or expansion of one's first-order classroom notes. This chapter offers guidelines on dealing with the referentiality of student notes, their provenance, as well as their form and contents, including their paleography, mostly offering examples from the Collegium Trilingue in Leuven during the period 1517–78. This means that this chapter is mainly based on the experience of its authors. Given the variegated nature of student notes, our experience may be of limited use for other scholars. Still, we believe it may help starting researchers who struggle with their corpus of student notes.

2. Referentiality, fragmentariness, and provenance

Many bodies of student notes cannot be understood without considering the text(s) on which they constitute a commentary or with which they interact in other ways, not unlike intertextuality in literary texts. These reference texts can be present in the document itself, in which case they are typically positioned centrally on the page of the manuscript or printed book, with the notes being relegated to the margins, the spaces between the lines, and interleaved pages (see Chapters 1, 3, and 4). This is, for instance, the case for many student notes surviving from the Collegium Trilingue, including those of Nicolaus Episcopius the Younger in 1549–50 (Feys 2024). In the case of manuscript-only notebooks, the text commented upon is often absent or only partly present in the form of lemmas. In such cases, one is often left to wonder which version of the text, either in manuscript (which copy?) or in print (which edition?), the students had in front of them, as with John Helyar's *reportatio*-style notes on the Hebrew text of *Genesis* from 1536/7. These notes must reflect Hebrew courses at the Leuven Trilingue where the student selectively wrote down the professor's explanations, paraphrasing them where he saw fit (Maleux 2023: 110–13). In case of dictation, professors typically prepared their own coursebooks that entered into dialog in various ways with other texts, for instance by authorities like Aristotle at the arts colleges of many early modern universities (cf. Geudens 2020) or other handbooks, as in the case of a grammatical introduction to Hebrew dictated by professor Andreas Balenus in 1553 and 1559 at the Trilingue (Maleux 2023: 99–103). In its final form, this dictated source refers systematically to a Hebrew grammar published in Cologne in 1557.[1] Even if a substantial share of early modern student notes deals with other texts, certainly not all of them do. Some corpora of notes offer a commentary not on other texts but on situations of perception, an approach typical for the more empirical fields of study, most notably medicine, taught in anatomical theaters or at patients' bedsides (see Chapter 6 for examples).

The method of note-taking reflected in a source can be mentioned explicitly. Dictated notes are frequently identified as such. For instance, in the Magister Dixit database containing manuscripts from the old university of Leuven, 62 out of 570 sources contain titles with forms of *dictat**, although Ann Blair has pointed out in the previous chapter that such self-identification tags may not correspond to reality.[2] Other cases require scrutiny to reveal whether they reflect *reportatio*, dictation, or some other method. Most notably, pedagogues devised tailormade methods for note-taking that students might adopt and adapt to their purposes. Only rarely does the source mark the adoption of such a method explicitly, as in the case of a young student in seventeenth-century Greifswald who compiled a massive reference work for his studies following the Antwerp Jesuit Jeremias Drexel's (1581–1638) method of note-taking.[3]

By their very nature, student notes are not only referential but also fragmentary, even in the case of dictated notes. Notes capture only a fraction of classroom interactions: mostly the words uttered by the teacher in the perception of the often-selective annotator, who could revise his notes after class and possibly transfer them to a commonplace book. In the case of dictation, it remains an open question what happened before or after dictating, or even during: to what extent did interactions occur in these moments? As to private studies, the precise process of note-taking can be gleaned only indirectly from the material object that survives as well as from occasional metaremarks on this process (cf. Chapter 1).

In addition to the text referenced and the note-taking method adopted, a third crucial piece of information is the historical setting in which notes were taken. Indeed, tracing the provenance of student notes arguably constitutes the single-most important initial step you have to take when confronted with a corpus of notes. Provenance can be gathered from various types of clues stemming either from the contents of the notes or from the material properties of the book as object (cf. Chapters 3–4 for more details). In an ideal scenario you are blessed with a provenance note, which supplies information on the course, the student, the professor, the location, and the time frame. For the Leuven Trilingue, there are several examples of rather extensive provenance notes, perhaps betraying a feeling of pride on the part of the students—for instance (see also Figure 2.1):

Sum Jo[hann]is Ægidij a[nno] 1543 Incepit D[ominus] Rutgerus Rescius 23 Octobris Louanij

I belong to Johannes Aegidius. In 1543, master Rutgerus Rescius started [these lectures on Homer's Odyssey] on October 23 in Leuven.[4]

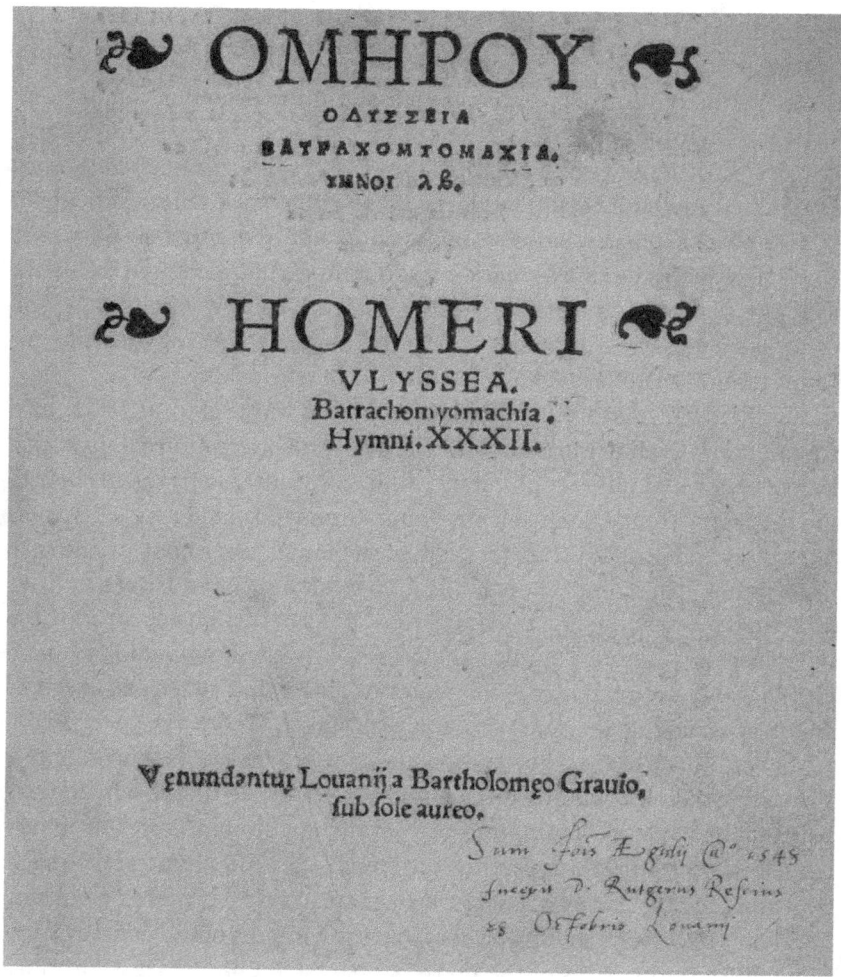

Figure 2.1. Detailed provenance note of Johannes Aegidius on the title page of his *Odyssey* textbook. Ghent, University Library, BIB.CL.00451.

The book speaks to the readers, informing them that it was in the possession of a certain Johannes Aegidius, otherwise unidentified, but potentially the same Johannes Aegidius who became city clerk of Antwerp in 1556, an office he held until his death in 1581 (Feys 2024). What can be deduced with certainty from the information offered is that he followed courses in the Brabant city of Leuven with Rutgerus Rescius (*c.* 1495–1545), who at that time was professor of Greek at the Trilingue, as is known from many other sources (see Van Rooy 2022 for a survey). Judging by the text in the book and the coverage of the student notes, the course concerned at least the first two-and-a-half books of the *Odyssey*, until 3.282, amounting to 1,160 lines of the *Odyssey* plus the three short summaries of each book that the professor also read and commented upon. If one may assume that Rescius discussed about twenty lines per lesson, like Trilingue professor Theodoricus Langius (died 1578) did in 1551 (Van Rooy and Van Hal 2018: 138), then it would have taken him about sixty lessons to arrive at *Odyssey* 3.282. As lessons probably took place almost daily, the course—or at least Aegidius' attendance of it—likely lasted for about ten weeks, roughly until late December 1543 or early January 1544. This calculation must, however, remain somewhat of a guess. The provenance note, therefore, allows you to identify the elements outlined above, as shown in Table 2.1, with information that we have been able to deduce from other historical sources between round brackets.

Table 2.1. Provenance information.

Course	Lectures on the Greek text of Homer's *Odyssey*, 1–3
Student	Johannes Aegidius (*c.* 1519–1581?)
Professor	Rutgerus Rescius (*c.* 1495–1545)
Location	Leuven (in the Trilingue building near the Fish Market)
Time frame	Started October 23, 1543 (Aegidius likely attended about sixty lessons, for a period of about two to three months)

For several Latin courses at the Leuven Trilingue, the researcher is likewise blessed with such explicit provenance notes (see the Exercise materials below). In other cases where such notes are lacking, closer scrutiny is required. Looking at the contents of the student notes may reveal the professor's name, leaving one to guess about the identity of the student and other elements like the time frame of the course. For instance, Xander Feys (2024) has found various bodies of student notes referring to Petrus Nannius, Rutgerus Rescius, and Theodoricus Langius in this way.[5] In other cases, certain features of the book, like its binding or the panels that cover it, provide a clue about the location where a book was used. For instance, the Spes designs on panels by Jacob Pandelaert (*fl.* 1534–55) and Jacob Bathen (*fl.* 1541/5–57), in combination with a Latin, Greek, or Hebrew textbook edition, can point to use at the Trilingue.⁶ In such cases, one can only roughly place the student notes in their historical setting.

The text of the notes can also help in this process to arrive at a rough estimation. As student notes reflect a learning process, they are prone to errors: the type of errors may reveal the level of teaching and also the geographic location or background of the student or professor. Even if we would not have known anything about the Vergil course that Petrus Nannius gave in 1549 in Leuven, we may have been able to guess that the student notes were taken shortly after publication of the book in 1549 in Dutch-speaking territory thanks to a peculiar mistake against Latin spelling found in the notes: "fagabundos" instead of "vagabundos," reflecting a typically Dutch pronunciation of the letter <v> as [f] rather than as [v], which the Swiss student had difficulties understanding.⁷

Finally, there can be cases where researchers have no decisive clues whatsoever, leaving them to conjecture about the notes' creation context. In this situation, the historical value of student notes is typically more limited but certainly not zero, as even anonymous notes can contribute to our understanding of early modern learning processes, albeit in a more general vein. Moreover, through paleographical analysis, one can often at least situate the notes in time and sometimes also in place, enabling a rough situation of the source. In ideal scenarios an identification of the student may be possible by comparing hands.

3. Paleography

Paleography refers to the study of older handwriting, which typically involves identifying the type of writing and its peculiarities, as well as deciphering abbreviations used and the properties of individual hands. Paleographic proficiency is a necessary skill for those venturing into the field of early modern student notes, and it is a skill best learned on the job. The ability to decipher and understand older handwritings is acquired over time through repeated practice and patient study. For the most part, early modern student notes are written in the so-called humanist cursive, though there is much regional and personal variation, with consequences for the readability of individual hands. For the history and development of this type of writing we refer to detailed discussions found in Berthold Ullman (1960) and more recently Cherubini (2019), as

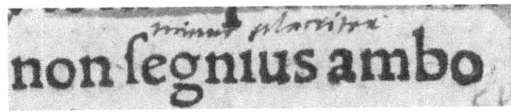

Figure 2.2. Detail of DaLeT Annotation ID 3062. Basel, University Library, Ba Va 28:1, fol. Civ^r.

well as Coulson and Babcock (2020).[8] In the present section, we want to offer some tips and tricks to get you started on your paleographic journey. While daunting at first, you will soon be able to unravel the intricacies of even the most strenuous hands. Since student notes are typically written in Latin, because of the set-up and nature of early modern education in large parts of Europe and beyond, we will focus on the peculiarities and idiosyncrasies of this language, looking at the shapes of certain letters in addition to abbreviations and ligatures.

First, a quick note about some letters of the Latin alphabet. Generally, the letters <v> and <u> are used interchangeably (for example, *vertex–uertex*). The same goes for <i> and <j>, especially at the end of a word (for example, *filii–filij*). The letter <s> is sometimes reproduced as a so-called *s longa* <ſ> and should not be confused with the letter <f>, as some text recognition services and even human transcribers are wont to do. Frequent ligatures include <æ> and <œ>, representing <ae> and <oe>, respectively. Additionally, one will frequently come across the *e caudata* (<ę>, "the tailed e") for <ae> (for example, *quę* for *quae*). Quite often, words containing a combination of any of the following letters <i>, <j>, <n>, <m>, <v>, or <u> are difficult to decipher, because these letters are generally written by means of one or more vertical pen strokes (cf. the word *minus* in Figure 2.2).[9] If you are unable to decipher a word and cannot infer it from the context, you can try to rule out certain letters by counting the pen strokes, reducing the amount of possible letter combinations. A great online aid for such matters is the website *Enigma*, which can generate lists of possible Latin words when provided with some letters that you can read.[10] With advances in technology, we expect tools like *Enigma* to become ever better in the future, although human revision will probably remain necessary.

A key feature of early modern student notes (and other forms of writing) is their numerous abbreviations, a trait they share with early printed books. These abbreviations are steeped in (late) medieval writing practices, which is why the researcher of early modern written sources

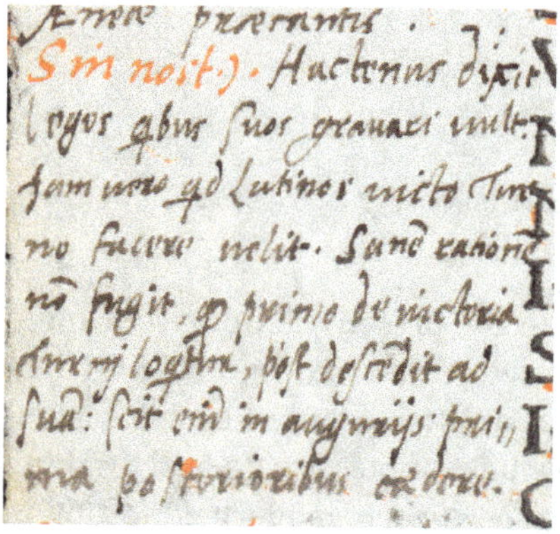

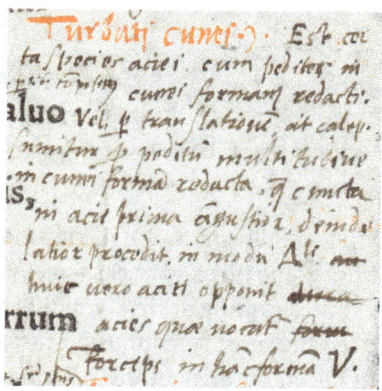

Figure 2.3. Episcopius 1.
DaLeT Annotation ID 2171.

Figure 2.4. Episcopius 2.
DaLeT Annotation ID 2379.

can still rely on Adriano Cappelli's useful dictionary of abbreviations, first issued in 1899 and also available online.[11] Here, let us focus on some abbreviations that you are most likely to run into. First up is the diacritic macron that indicates that an <n> or <m> is omitted, often, but not exclusively, at the end of a word (for example, *nā* for *nam* or *Nañius* for *Nannius*). At the beginning of a word, the symbol representing the number nine <9> stands for <con> or <com> (for example, *9cessus* for *concessus*). At the ending of a word, however, the same symbol is used to abbreviate the letters <us> (for example, *regi9* for *regius*). Passive or deponent verbs ending in <ur> are sometimes shortened by means of a superscript letter <r> or what resembles a superscript <2> (for example, *audiat^r* for *audiatur*). In addition, an <r> crossed with a line means that <rum> needs to be read (*quor* for *quorum*). The wealth of different abbreviations for such prepositions or prefixes as *per*, *pre*, *pro*, *prae*, the pronoun *qui*, *quae*, *quod* (and its many variations), as well as the enclitic *que* and adverbs such as *quam* are best learned via Cappelli. For now, consider the following examples taken from the student notes on *Aeneid* 12 by Nicolaus Episcopius the Younger (Figures 2.3 and 2.4).[12] Pay special attention to the different means of abbreviating words and other peculiarities discussed above (such as the ligature <æ> and the letter <j> at the end of a word).

Sin nost[rum] ·/· Hactenus dixit leges q[ui]bus suos grauari uult. Iam uero q[ui]d Latinos uicto Turno facere uelit. Sane[m] ratione[m] no[n] fugit, q[uod] primo de uictoria Turnj loq[ui]tur, post desce[n]dit ad sua[m]: scit eni[m] in augurijs prima posterioribus cædere.¹³

Turbati cunei ·/· Est certa species aciei cum pedites in cunei formam redacti. Vel, p[er] translatione[m], ait calep[inus], sumitur p[ro] peditu[m] multitudine in cunei forma[m] redacta, q[uæ] cuncta in acie prima a[n]gustior, deinde latior procedit, in modu[m] Δ^(li[tterae]) ~~ue~~ huic uero aciei opponit ~~dura~~ acies quæ vocat[ur] ~~forue~~ forceps in ha[n]c forma[m] V.

Handwritten Text Recognition (HTR) can be useful for automated transcription of early modern student notes, especially for dictates and linear texts, although it requires you to provide transcriptions of your own (at least around fifty pages) to train a model that can transcribe your handwritten documents in full, so you need paleographical skills anyhow. Several other caveats are in place. Often your document will be shorter or only slightly longer than fifty pages, making this effort superfluous. Even if your corpus is larger, an error rate remains, making it necessary to manually revise and correct the text if you want to publish it. Still, a partly faulty text can be very helpful in finding relevant passages or subjects in your corpus. For sources where a handwritten or printed reference text is accompanied by annotations and/or where multiple languages are used, HTR may get confused and cause problems, although some providers have lay-out analysis options to overcome this problem. Transkribus probably is the most widely known HTR service.¹⁴ Other useful software includes eScriptorium and Rescribe.¹⁵ HTR will no doubt improve significantly in the future in the wake of the artificial intelligence (AI) revolution we are currently experiencing.

Depending on the context of creation (*dictatio, reportatio*, revised notes and so on), the handwriting in which student notes are written can pose problems: their readability depends on factors such as the students' attention, diligence, and habit; their speed of writing; their mastery of the discipline and the language(s) used; the quality of their pen, ink, and paper; and the later fate of the book, which might involve water damage partly erasing the ink or trimming of the outer margins, thus compromising the readability of the notes.

Handwriting is very much an individual property, and as a researcher you always need to familiarize yourself with the handwriting of a specific corpus of student notes. Their readability can vary considerably: is the hand messy and quick (for example, reflecting *reportatio*), or neat and meticulous (for example, as a result of revision or careful dictation)? Are there many abbreviations or is everything spelled out in full? The speed with which you can familiarize yourself with a hand varies and depends on its peculiar properties. Justus Lipsius (1547–1606), professor in Leuven and Leiden, had a notoriously difficult hand, which can be read by only a few specialists (Figure 2.5). Fortunately, Lipsius is at the far end of the spectrum of paleographic difficulty, and most student hands can be mastered more easily. The best way to familiarize yourself with the script of a specific set of student notes is identifying the type of script, comparing similar hands with available transcriptions, and then trying your hand at your own particular source. If you are fortunate enough to have uncovered parallel sets—that is, notes taken by different students during the same course—it might prove useful to compare these sets to one another. If one student's handwriting is more readable than the other, putting both next to each other will undoubtedly enhance your grasp of the more difficult one.

If your student notes have no provenance, paleography can help give you a rough indication of the timeframe and, possibly, of the geographic location, next to codicological and book-historical indications (see Chapters 3–4) as well as their contents, which may include references to certain people, vernacular languages, events, and/or local practices. Each handwriting is unique, and it may prove useful to be aware of the defining traits of the hand(s) you study. For it might just happen that, while browsing through relevant sources, you recognize a certain hand, which in turn might reveal new information about provenance. For a concrete example of this, let us once more focus our attention on the Trilingue. In the Royal Library at Windsor Castle, we found an annotated copy of Homer's *Odyssey* printed by Rutgerus Rescius in Leuven in 1535. Even though the notes were similar to those of Aegidius who attended Rescius' 1543 course on the epic, it remained difficult to label the notes as relevant Trilingue material due to the lack of a provenance note or other convincing clues. However, before long, we realized that the handwriting of the anonymous student matched that of the unnamed *amanuensis* of Trilingue professor Petrus Nannius found in several other documents, at least two of which are dated March 1544. While the name of the student remains unknown, we were able to prove that the notes held at Windsor Castle were in fact taken at the Trilingue.[16] If we had depended solely on digital tools such as

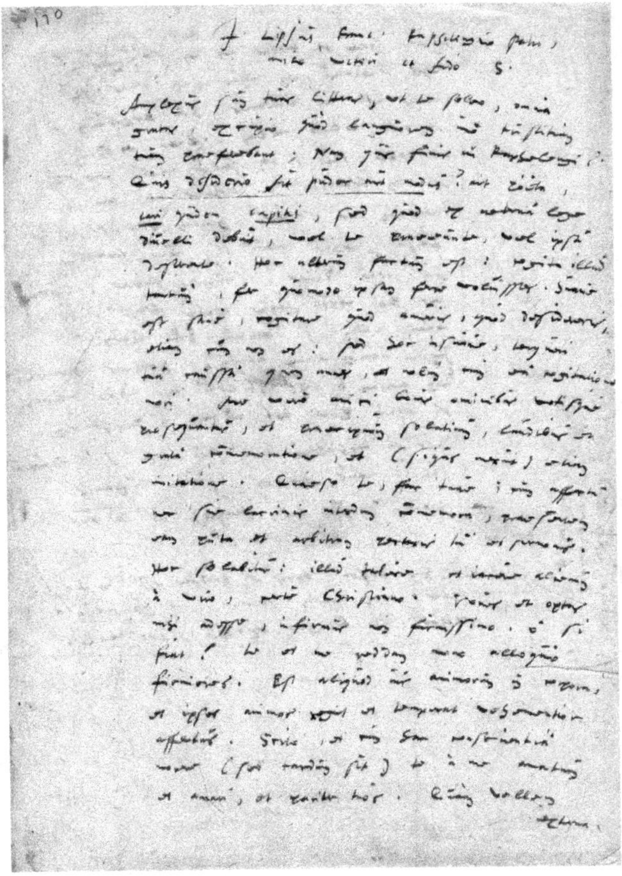

J. Lipsius Franc. Raphelengio patri,
amico veteri et fido S.

Amplexus sum tuas litteras, vt te soleo, omnia
gratas, excipio quod languorem imo tristitiam
tuam praeferebant. Nam quis finis mi Raphelengi?
<u>Quis desiderio sit pudor aut modus?</u> ait poëta,
<u>cari</u> quidem <u>capitis</u>, sed quod ex aeterna lege
diuelli debuit, vel te praeeunte, vel ipsâ
deserente. Hoc alterum factum est: cogita illud

Figure 2.5. Specimen of a letter by Justus Lipsius with partial transcription. Haverford College, Quaker & Special Collections, Charles Roberts Autograph Letter Collection, 170LipsiusA.

Transkribus without ever familiarizing us with the handwriting itself, we might never have come to this conclusion.

4. Drawing up a typology for student notes

How can you get a first grasp of the contents found in a newly encountered body of student notes? The obvious answer is to read the source in detail, but this might not be possible for various reasons. Next to poor preservation and paleographical difficulties, time might be an additional constraint for the researcher. A good first step would be to first read the initial pages and then probe the remainder of the source in order to assess the form, structure, and contents of the notes.

4.1. Form

What is the form of the notes? They can appear as a continuous running text in case of dictation (for example, the dictate in Figure 2.6, as mentioned in line 5 of the title); a fragmentary collection of notes that comment on a certain text or situation (for example, the note collection of John Helyar studied in Maleux 2023); a collection of notes reflecting a course or learning experience that may or may not be rigidly structured or copied in clean afterward (for example, commonplace book and *reportatio*-style notes in Toruń, University Library, Rps 152/IV). The notes can have various degrees of continuity and intensity, which correlates to some extent with the type of source you are confronted with. Dictated texts typically show considerable continuity and a more or less equal attention span throughout, whereas student notes accompanying a reference text may show gaps or a decline in intensity as a consequence of beginner's enthusiasm, apparently not an uncommon phenomenon in the early modern period (see, for example, Mazzon 2021: 314). Figure 2.7 shows a source that has a gap of almost sixty lines where the student seemingly missed several classes.

Another question to ask yourself is where student notes begin and end: how are these boundaries marked, if at all? Is there an incipit or explicit? Do the notes give an impression of being complete or do they not have a clear beginning or, as will happen in many cases, a clear ending, given that the notes peter out as they progress (for example, the Aegidius and Vossius notes in DaLeT)?

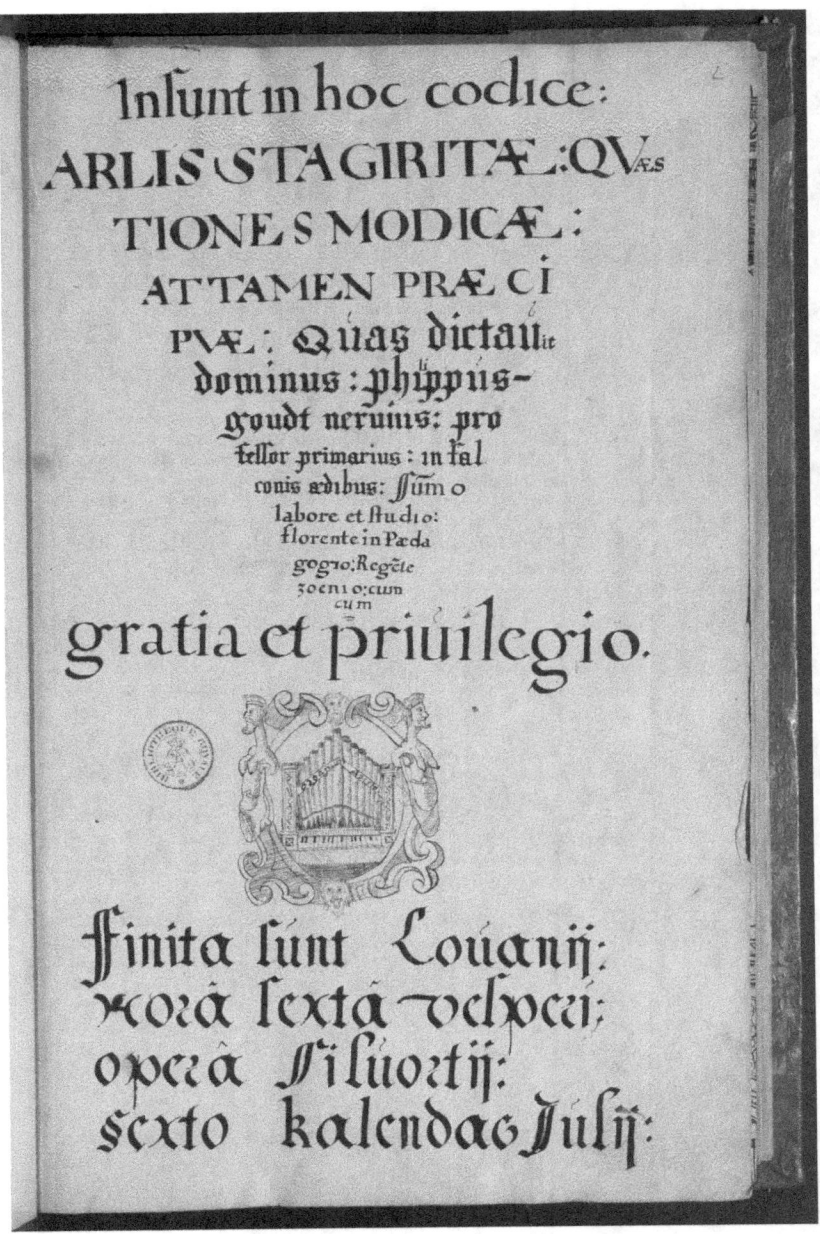

Figure 2.6. Brussels, KBR, MS 18373–4, *Physica* (1602–3).
Student: Joannes Sillevoorts/Professor: Philippus Goudt.
University of Leuven, Artes, Paedagogium Falconis.
Magister Dixit.

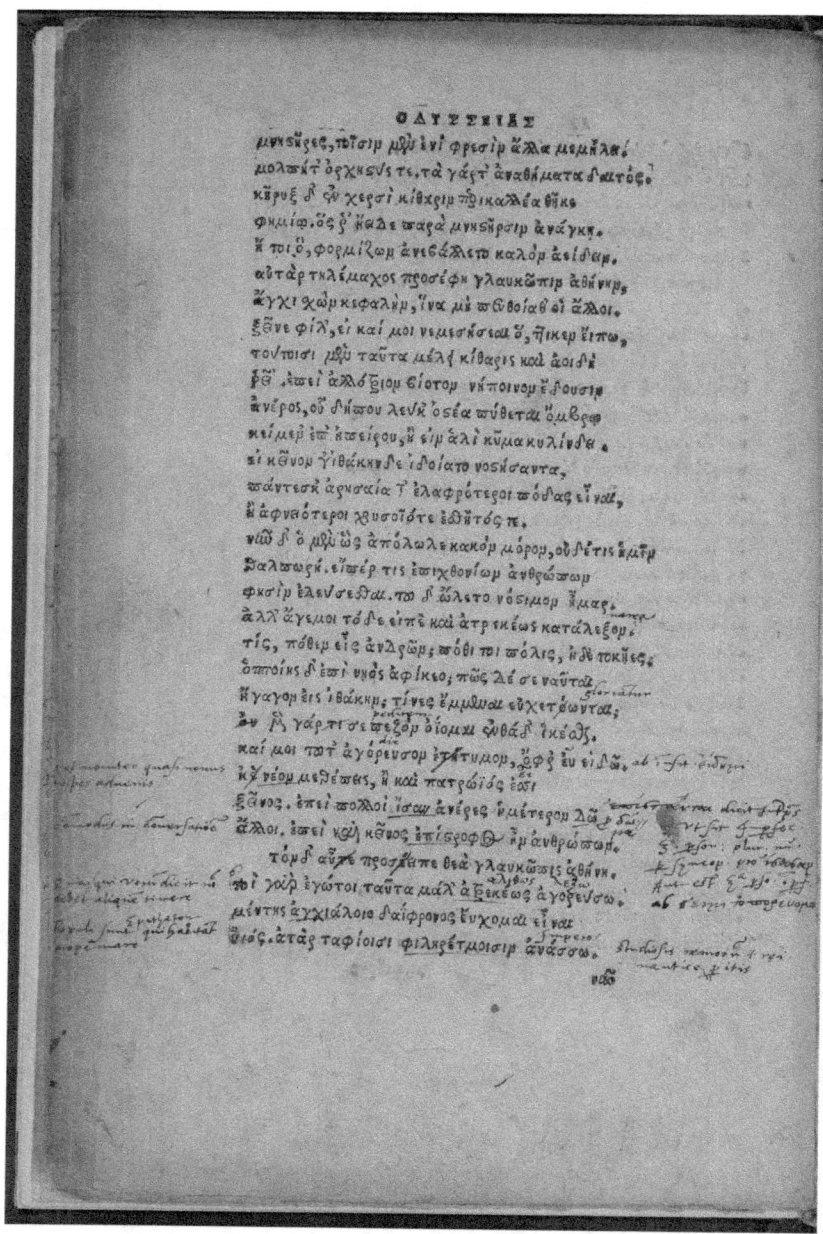

Figure 2.7. Johannes Aegidius' student notes skip certain blocks of text, probably indicating that he missed one or more classes. DaLeT (fol. A iv^r of DaLeT Copy ID 1).

The notes can take up three major forms, no doubt the most frequent one being text, often in Latin but as the early modern period progresses increasingly also in other languages, both learned (for example, Hebrew, Greek, or Arabic) and vernacular (for example, French, English, or Dutch). Textual notes can range from a single letter through words and sentences to entire essays and texts. The two other forms are of a visual and a diagrammatic nature. Drawings and symbols can be used as didactic support, taken over by the student from a master copy, or reflect student interests or distractions. Examples of visual notes include *maniculae*, drawings of little pointing hands attracting attention to a specific piece of information as a kind of visual "nota bene" (for example, Sherman 2008: Chapter 2) and other symbols conveying encoded information (for example, marking of non-standard language use in Homer by Aegidius in DaLeT Annotation ID 91 — see Figure 2.8), drawings of the objects of study (see Chapter 9), and student doodles, as in Figure 2.9, where the student inventively turned the Hebrew letter mem <מ> into a kind of smiley *avant la lettre*.[17] Diagrams combine, in fact, the two other types, as they consist of both text and image, forming a table, scheme, figure, flowchart, or other elements.[18]

4.2. *Structure*

When confronted with the notes, you might also want to figure out to what extent the notes reflect a specific structure. How are the contents structured in the case of a running dictated text or *reportatio*-style notes, for instance? Do the notes follow a specific model (for example, a work of Aristotle, a printed handbook, a question-and-answer format) or are they structured according to the teacher's or student's own liking and insight? In cases where a reference text is present in the source itself, you will be confronted with a plethora of ways in which student notes relate to it.

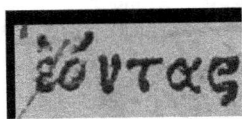

Figure 2.8. Strike marking a non-standard element in Homer's language, meaning "one would expect the form *óntas* [ὄντας] not *eóntas* [ἐόντας] in normal Greek." DaLeT Annotation ID 91.

Figure 2.9. The Hebrew letter mem turned into a smiley. DaLeT (fol. b 8.ᵛ of DaLeT Copy ID 21).

The most common relationship is interlinear and marginal annotation. On the one hand, short notes often occur between lines of printed text in manuscripts or printed works facilitating this, for instance the *feuille classique* format.[19] Longer notes, on the other hand, typically feature in the margins (see Figure 2.10 for the two types).

Other relationships tend to occur less frequently, but they are too often left out of consideration, which is why they deserve an explicit mention here. Notes can also be linear in that they cover the reference text: both intentionally, for instance to introduce a correction to the text (for example, Figure 2.11), and by accident, for instance in cases where the reference text is overwritten for lack of space. Notes commenting on the reference text can also be written on pages other than the one containing the relevant passage. In this case, the notes can be labeled either interleaved (or interfoliar) when they are found on interleaved pages or stray when they appear on other pages that are not necessarily in the vicinity of the passage they comment on.[20] For instance, for lack of space on the relevant page, Nicolaus Episcopius wrote various notes on the title page of his copy of Vergil's *Aeneid* 12. The professor's commentary on line 12.83 (sig. A iij^v in the source) appears in written form on the title page, some five pages apart.[21] Episcopius devised a reference system in his mostly second-order notes to guide his future self through this complex web of stray notes, showing a meta-awareness of the structure of his corpus of annotations. Even when handwritten notes are on the same page as the passage they comment, they can be linked by lines or other note-marking devices, called *appels de note* in French.

The different formal relationships outlined here (interlinear, marginal, etc.) often correlate to some extent with different types of contents, as interlinear notes frequently contain glosses, synonyms, or translations, whereas marginal annotations offer lengthier explanations. The positional classification outlined above, useful though it may be in assessing the structure of a collection of notes, does not always apply, most notably in cases where notes appear that bear no relationship to the reference text but somehow reflect the professor's course, for instance notes summarizing introductory remarks by the professor on the author.[22] In other cases, the full reference text may be absent, with the students instead offering lemmas on which they comment or quoting the text discussed in other ways.

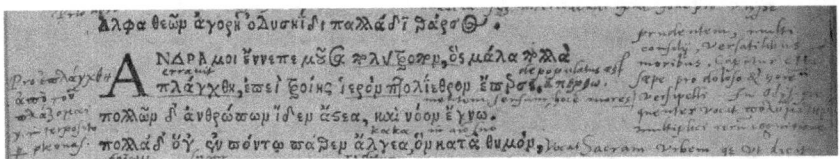

Figure 2.10. Interlinear annotations (between the lines of the printed text) and marginal annotations (next to the printed text). Fol. A ii^r of DaLeT Copy ID 1.

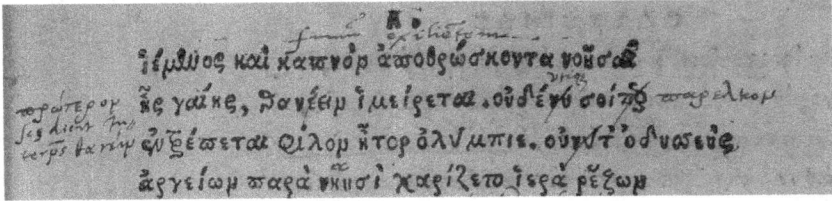

Figure 2.11. Examples of linear notes.
(Strikes over the printed text marking "uncommon" Greek.)
Fol. A iii^r of DaLeT Copy ID 1.

4.3. Contents

While assessing the form and structure of the notes, it is crucial to also get a grasp of their contents, and to do this on two levels. On the one hand, what is the overall subject of the course? On the other, what is the content of individual sections or notes? The former question will be the easier to answer generically. For instance, Vossius attended a course on the Hebrew book of Psalms that focused on textual comprehension (DaLeT Course ID 42), whereas Gijsbert Coeverincx noted down under dictation the grammatical explanations of his professor, followed by a grammatical analysis of Psalm 1 (DaLeT Course IDs 46–7). The latter question forces one to zoom in on the microlevel: what is the contents of a paragraph or note? To what extent can these contents be classified? It is clear that a universal typology of contents is at the moment unfeasible and will probably remain impractical in the study of early modern student notes, but it may be useful to develop a tailor-made typology for your collection of notes to get a firmer grasp of their contents. The utility of devising such a typology and systematically tagging each individual note with a label emerges from Figures 2.12–13, created and discussed by Feys (2024: Chapter 3) and

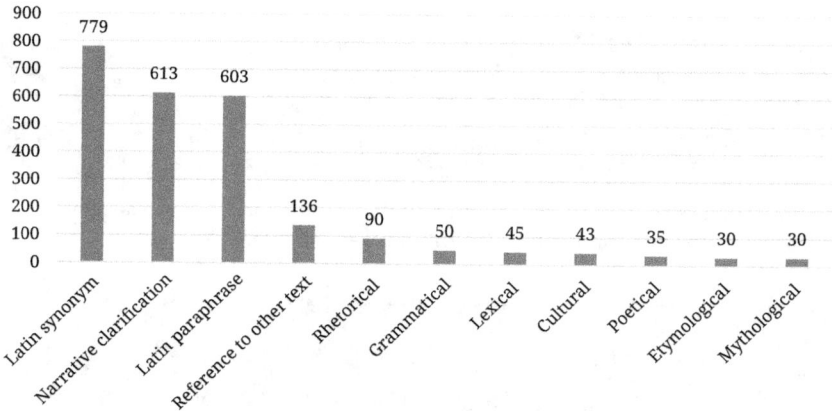

Figure 2.12. Most frequent content-related types in Episcopius' notes on Vergil's *Aeneid* 12.

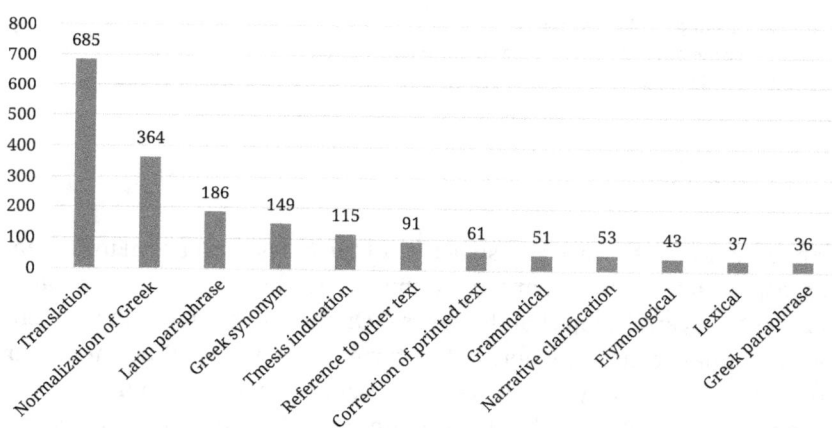

Figure 2.13. Most frequent content-related types in Aegidius' notes on Homer's *Odyssey* 1–3.

revealing in one glimpse the specific contents of these courses on Vergil's *Aeneid* 12 (Figure 2.12) and Homer's *Odyssey* 1–3 (Figure 2.13), respectively.

Another method to gauge the contents of student notes is to diligently transcribe and/or translate them, but whatever method you adopt in your pursuit to get a grasp of the notes' contents, the process will prove to be time-consuming but—as Part II aims to demonstrate—worth the effort.

5. Conclusion

A first confrontation with a body of student notes tends to be overwhelming, especially for the beginning researcher. Situating the notes in time and place is an important initial exercise to make, an exercise that may have to be preceded by a paleographic study of the handwriting in the source and other material characteristics (on which see Chapters 3–4). This initial step is crucial as understanding early modern student notes involves a lot of work to contextualize the notes and the ways in which they refer to the historical classroom situation and the knowledge discussed, typically in the form of texts or empirical observation (see also Chapter 6).

In sum, student notes offer access to an intellectual archive, comprising different ways of teaching, learning, and thinking in the past, each at a given time and place. As with other archives, it is good practice to indicate which component parts of documents you have read and analyzed as part of your methodological outline. Transparency is key for your readership to assess in what ways you have engaged with the form, structure, and contents of the sources and, possibly, how you have preceded in putting together a typology to analyze the notes and/or created a transcription or edition of the notes. Ideally, such a document would be publicly available online, whether or not accompanied by images, enabling your peers to assess the results and perhaps conduct follow-up research (see Chapter 5).

6. Exercise

What information can be deduced from the following provenance notes (Figures 2.14–5)? Write it down using Table 2.2 below. The last page of this chapter contains a transcription and a model solution, but try to find the key elements yourself by means of the images and goal-oriented searches on the Internet to identify the historical actors mentioned. We do not offer an English translation here since you are not typically in the possession of one when facing a source like this, but you can consult a translation through DaLeT in this specific case if need be. DaLeT offers further opportunities for training in transcription, as it offers images of student notes alongside a semi-diplomatic transcription.

Figure 2.14. Provenance notes on title page.
DaLeT Annotation IDs 1734–5.

Figure 2.15. Colophon note.
DaLeT Annotation ID 4133.

Table 2.2. Provenance information.

Course	
Student	
Professor	
Location	
Time frame	

The solution can be found at the back of this chapter, after the references.

Notes

1. DaLeT Edition ID 340.
2. https://www.kuleuven.be/lectio/magisterdixit/solr-search?q=. Search conducted on April 18, 2023.
3. Toruń, University Library, Rps 152/IV. Information by courtesy of Alicja Bielak. On Drexel, see also Chapter 1.
4. DaLeT Annotation ID 7.
5. See also the finding list in Van Rooy et al. (2023).
6. On Spes ("hope") panels, see Indestege (1956) and especially Fogelmark (1990).
7. See DaLeT Annotation ID 3289 and the comment there.
8. See, for example, also the very accessible website *Ad fontes* of the University of Zürich, which offers short introductions, exercises, and samples for various script types: adfontes.uzh.ch/en/tutorium/schriften-lesen/schriftgeschichte. Last accessed April 9, 2024. See especially the sections from "Humanistic Minuscule and Cursives" onward. In a similar vein, see also the online research guides offered by the Library of Congress https://guides.loc.gov/manuscript-facsimiles/deciphering-scribal-abbreviations and the Special Collections of the University of Nottingham https://www.nottingham.ac.uk/manuscriptsandspecialcollections/researchguidance/medievaldocuments/letterformsandabbreviations.aspx, both last accessed April 9, 2024.
9. Some students will use the diacritic breve ˘ to differentiate <u> (or <v>) from <n>.
10. Enigma, enigma.huma-num.fr. Last accessed April 9, 2024.
11. Cappelli Online, adfontes.uzh.ch/en/ressourcen/abkuerzungen/cappelli-online. Last accessed April 9, 2024. See also the supplement to Cappelli (1899) by Pelzer (1966).
12. On Nicolaus Episcopius the Younger, see Chapter 8 (with further references).
13. Read "Sane" instead of "Sane[m]"; Episcopius added a superfluous abbreviatory line. Also note the hypercorrected form "cædere" instead of "cedere."
14. Transkribus, https://readcoop.eu/transkribus/?sc=Transkribus. Last accessed February 23, 2024.
15. eScriptorium, https://www.sofer.info/, and Rescribe, https://rescribe.xyz/, both last accessed February 23, 2024. See also Chapter 5, Section 2.3.
16. Van Rooy and Feys (2024: 175); Feys (2024: ch. 2.4.6).
17. On the visual in student notes, see in more detail Chapter 9 by Bielak and de Mûelenaere.
18. See the Aristotelian diagrams in Chapter 7, Section 4.
19. On the *feuille classique*, see Compère, Couzinet, and Pédeflous (2009) as well as Chapters 1 and 4.
20. On interleaving, see Chapter 3. An example of an interleaved note is DaLeT Annotation ID 1929.
21. See DaLeT Annotation ID 1892.
22. For example, DaLeT Annotation ID 21.

References

Cappelli, Adriano. 1899. *Lexicon abbreviaturarum quae in lapidibus, codicibus et chartis praesertim medii-aevi occurrunt. Dizionario di abbreviature latine ed italiane usate nelle carte e codici specialmente nel medio-evo riprodotte con oltre 13000 segni incisi. Aggiuntovi uno studio sulla brachigrafia medioevale, un prontuario di sigle epigrafiche, l'antica numerazione romana ed arabica, i monogrammi, ed i segni indicanti monete, pesi, misure* Milan: Ulrico Hoepli.

Cherubini, Paolo. 2019. *La scrittura latina: Storia, forme, usi.* Roma: Carocci.

Compère, Marie-Madeleine, Marie-Dominique Couzinet, and Olivier Pédeflous. 2009. "Éléments pour l'histoire d'un genre éditorial: La feuille classique en France aux XVIe et XVIIe siècles." *Histoire de l'éducation* 124: 27–49.

Coulson, Frank T. and Robert Gary Babcock, eds. 2020. *The Oxford Handbook of Latin Palaeography*. Oxford: Oxford University Press.

DaLeT. Database of the Leuven Trilingue, edited by Raf Van Rooy, Xander Feys, Maxime Maleux, and Andy Peetermans. https://www.dalet.be/. Last accessed April 30, 2024.

Feys, Xander. 2024. "Language and Literature Teaching in the Sixteenth Century: Vergil and Homer at the Leuven Collegium Trilingue." Unpublished PhD dissertation, Leuven: KU Leuven.

Fogelmark, Staffan. 1990. *Flemish and Related Panel-Stamped Bindings: Evidence and Principles*. New York: Bibliographical Society of America.

Geudens, Christophe. 2020. "Louvain Theories of Topical Logic (c. 1450–1533): A Reassessment of the Traditionalist Thesis." Unpublished PhD dissertation, Leuven: KU Leuven.

Indestege, Luc. 1956. "De boekband in de zuidelijke Nederlanden tijdens de 16de eeuw." *De Gulden Passer: Tijdschrift voor boekwetenschap* 34: 40–71.

Maleux, Maxime. 2023. "The Teaching of the Old Testament Revolutionized? The Sixteenth-Century Low Countries and the First Institutionalized Hebrew Curriculum." Unpublished PhD dissertation, Leuven: KU Leuven.

Mazzon, Ottavia. 2021. "Bessarione lettore di Erodoto, Tucidide, Senofonte: Appunti sul ms. Venezia, BNM, gr. Z. 526 (coll. 776)." In *I libri di Bessarione: Studi sui manoscritti del Cardinale a Venezia e in Europa*, edited by Antonio Rigo and Niccolò Zorzi, 307–26. Turnhout: Brepols.

Pelzer, Auguste. 1966. *Abréviations latines médiévales: Supplément au Dizionario di abbreviature latine ed italiane de Adriano Cappelli*. Second edition. Leuven: Publications universitaires.

Schrire, Ray. 2021. "Shifting Paradigms: Ideas, Materiality and the Changing Shape of Grammar in the Renaissance." *Journal of the Warburg and Courtauld Institutes* 84 (1): 1–31. https://doi.org/10.1086/JWCI84010001.

Sherman, William H. 2008. *Used Books: Marking Readers in Renaissance England*. Philadelphia, PA: University of Pennsylvania Press.

Ullman, Berthold L. 1960. *The Origin and Development of Humanistic Script*. Rome: Edizioni di storia e letteratura.

Van Rooy, Raf. 2022. "In Rutger Rescius' Classroom at the Leuven Collegium Trilingue (1543–1544): His Study Program and Didactic Method." In *Trilingual Learning: The Study of Greek and Hebrew in a Latin World (1000–1700)*, edited by Raf Van Rooy, Pierre Van Hecke, and Toon Van Hal, 179–205. Turnhout: Brepols.

Van Rooy, Raf, and Toon Van Hal. 2018. "Studying Ancient Greek at the Old University of Leuven: An Outline in a European Context." In *The Leuven Collegium Trilingue 1517–1797: Erasmus, Humanist Educational Practice and the New Language Institute Latin – Greek – Hebrew*, edited by Jan Papy, 129–53. Leuven–Paris–Bristol, CT: Peeters.

Van Rooy, Raf, and Xander Feys. 2024. "Activating Greek at the Leuven Trilingue? Rescius' Use of Greek in his 1543 *Odyssey* Course." In *Reading, Writing, Translating Greek in Early Modern Universities and Beyond*, edited by Johanna Akujärvi and Kristiina Savin, 159–201. Lund: Lund University Press.

Van Rooy, Raf, Xander Feys, Maxime Maleux, and Andy Peetermans. 2023. "DaLeT, Database of the Leuven Trilingue: A New Method for Editing Annotated Prints." *Humanistica Lovaniensia: Journal of Neo-Latin and New Ancient Greek Studies* 71 (2): 103–21.

Transcription and model solution

Auspicatus est Duodecimu[m] Vergilij librum D[ominus] Petrus Nannius 24 Septe[m]bris A[nno] 1549. Louanij.

Est Nicolaj Episcopij Basiliensis

Finiuit hunc libru[m] D[ominus] Petr[us] Nanni[us] 5 Idus Dece[m]b[res] 9 Decem[bris] 1549.[1]

Table 2.3. Provenance information—model solution.

Course	Lectures on the Latin text of Vergil's *Aeneid*, 12 (952 lines)
Student	Nicolaus Episcopius the Younger (*c.* 1531–December 1565/January 1566)
Professor	Petrus Nannius (1496–1557)
Location	Leuven (in the Trilingue building near the Fish Market)
Time frame	September 24, 1549–December 9, 1549 (77 days)

---

[1] DaLeT Annotation IDs 1734–1735 and 4133.

CHAPTER 3

The Materiality of the Student Notebook

Jarrik Van Der Biest

1. Introduction

By now it has become clear that the student codex is not merely the written deposit of an oral-auditive process of knowledge transmission, through which we can unproblematically access the lecture hall. The difference between first-, second-, and third-order notes alone underlines this fact (see Chapter 1). Indeed, the lecture text as captured on its physical carrier—mostly paper—is more often than not the product of preparation and redaction before and after the ephemeral words uttered by a teacher. In other words, student notebooks are material objects in their own right, difficult to produce and often preserved for a reason: we should approach them as such. Two factors have an impact on the materiality of the manuscripts.

The first is that these notes only exist by grace of the student. Although the teacher articulated a text during class, it is the student who "encoded" this orally delivered (and thus ephemeral) text into the handwritten medium, making it a lecture text. As this chapter will demonstrate, codices were more difficult to produce than today's notebooks; a student's purpose thus informed the process of creating the manuscript. In other words, students were active agents in shaping the lecture text toward their own intellectual goals. These purposes could differ, bearing a different impression on the materiality of the text. For example, notebooks made by students preparing their teacher's lectures for publication often resemble printed works, complete with lavish title pages. Notes made to study for exams can contain a plethora of notes squeezed into the margins and any other free space the student found on the page. Other students could be preparing notes for their own teaching or preaching, including references on added leaves and other paratextual elements. Pupils applied the skills that circulated within their environment, like their monastery or their college, but also adapted such customs towards their own specific intentions. Such adaptations were also part of the learning process, as they required a good understanding of the course content and its application. In conclusion, the intellectual goals of the student are encoded in the materiality of the codex: the manuscript is to be read materially to uncover its broader cultural meaning. For example, Louvain arts students lavishly decorated their notebooks with engravings, drawings, and drinking songs and had them bound in precious leather bindings, as they were taken home to serve as a memory and perhaps unofficial proof of study. For the sixteenth-century Louvain theologians on the other hand, preserved manuscripts are not decorated, but do contain paratextual elements pointing to further circulation within monastic communities for use in preaching and teaching.

The second factor is the production process of the manuscript itself. Four moments are of importance in shaping a student notes codex as it is transmitted to us. The first stage is the preparation: raw materials had to be bought and passed through the hands of a myriad of manufacturers (papermakers, booksellers, printers, bookbinders, and so on) who left their mark on these products (think, for example, of watermarks and price notes). Copying and even dictation of the course text could be done before class as well; think, for example, of the *pecia*-system. Developed in thirteenth-century Paris, this dissemination method involved the separate circulation of quires holding sections of an authoritative text, to accelerate and streamline its copying among students (Destrez 1935; Pollard 1978: 147–8). During the second stage, the lecture itself, (first-order) notes were taken under dictation, *reportatio*, or a combination of teaching practices, which had an impact on the eventual student notes. Third, during the redaction phase, the student organized and wrote down the text on separate quires, added certain paratextual elements, notes from other lectures, and personal notes, and had them bound together, thus forming the codex. Lastly, the student might employ the notes in his future career, but certainly passed it down to other owners who might have left traces on the manuscript until, eventually, the codex was preserved in private collections or institutions who focus on conservation: typically, libraries, archives, and museums. All these stages have left their marks in the codex, from watermarks to mold damage. However, it is difficult to separate these phases: they have become entangled in the materiality of the codex, presenting the researcher with a complex puzzle to put together.

It is exactly these two factors that can provide insight into research questions about class practices, learning processes, and knowledge dissemination. However, we can often only access them through their physical remains. In other words, we cannot submit the manuscript to a "historical" analysis, in which its genesis is read in a chronological way. We must first take what can be called an archeological approach: take the codex as it is now and analyze its materiality. The methodology proposed here is to start with a mere description of the material characteristics of the manuscript, before any interpretation of its production is applied. The reverse movement would be to start from a chronological reconstruction of how the codex would be made and assess whether the physical traces line up with that. However, such a "historical" reading holds the danger of projecting incorrect conceptions of lecture and writing practices onto the codex, which often reflect contemporary notions of teaching and note-taking at universities. To provide the tools to uncover the different layers of the manuscript, this chapter will focus on the codicology of student notes. After a careful description of the codicological structure of the student manuscript, one can start interpreting its materiality according to a chronological schedule. One must be cautious with this interpretation: many insights given by the archeological reading are merely the most plausible hypothesis of how the manuscript came to be, unless students have left more explicit traces on how they produced their notebooks (for example, in colophons). Indeed, not all will become clear: the result will not be a continuous historical narrative of the educational process, but a fragmented archeological reading, including hiatuses and most plausible hypotheses.

The study of manuscripts as material *codices* rather than literary or textual *books* has grown into an entire field of inquiry, named codicology. The term was coined by François Masai to replace the use of the ill-fitting "paleography," which covered both the domains of what we now consider as the separate fields of codicology and paleography, and as a clear counterpart to the German *Handschriftenkunde* (Gumbert in Agati 2003: 9). This discipline, also aptly denominated as an "archeology of the book," develops its own terminology and handbooks to describe and analyze the physical characteristics and genesis of manuscripts (see bibliography; this chapter employs the terminology from Gumbert 2010). Venturing into its waters as part of your research into student notes can be quite daunting. A good grasp of the lingo and an understanding of how the codex was produced, however, are the best tools to unearth insights into the learning process of the student. Section 2 offers a short introduction to how early modern students produced the physical carrier of their notes, which was slightly more arduous than buying a Moleskine at the stationery shop. After that this chapter proposes a methodology to dig into the student notebook as it lies on the support pillow before you. Note, however, that my discussion merely grazes the surface of the possibilities offered by codicological analysis. Furthermore, although codicology generally concerns itself with entirely handwritten books, references to notes in printed books will also be made here. Lastly, aspects such as page lay-out and textual features—usually also part of a codicological study—have been summarily discussed in Chapter 2.

2. From paper mill to preservation

The first step in producing one's own manuscript was to procure the writing support: paper made from textile, often old rags. Paper increasingly replaced parchment during the early modern period as a much cheaper and easier to produce resource, allowing students to produce and stockpile notes on a large scale (Blair 2010: 309). Paper mills were usually located near a source of clear water (for example, in Troyes, or around Brescia and Bergamo in the Veneto), and produced paper in reams, units of about 480 sheets to be sold to printers and booksellers (Barrett 2012). Scholars of printing history have often asserted that paper was an expensive commodity—almost half the production cost of a printed book. However, according to Heather Wolfe (2018) this is mainly due to the large scale of the printing business itself: investing in these large quantities tied up an extensive part of the capital of printing houses, publishers, or authors. Indeed, at the bookseller or stationer, students could buy paper in much smaller amounts: single sheets, units of five sheets or twenty-four/twenty-five sheets (Bellingradt 2021: 20). It is certainly possible that colleges, pedagogies, monasteries, or maybe beadles of the faculties acted as intermediaries, purchasing larger quantities of sheets, but this is yet to be explored.

The large sheets were folded into smaller booklets of the desired size, that would serve as the building blocks of the codex: quires or gatherings. In codicological terms, these gatherings are composed of a number of bifolia (part of a sheet that folds into two leaves) arranged behind each other and folded along the middle. For example, a gathering of two bifolia is called a *binion*, and makes up four folios, of which the first and fourth folio, and second and third folio are part of the same sheet (or bifolium).

A *trinion* consists of three bifolia, a *quaternion* of four, and so on. Usually, manuscripts were written on a set of these loose bundles of leaves before they were bound together into a codex (Smeyers 2012: 74). This made personalization by the student possible: throughout the redaction process, one could make changes to the quires. For example, one could insert extra leaves in a quire in various ways, so-called interleaving with a bifolium or a hooked/stubbed leaf, a single folio with a stub where its bifolium counterpart is supposed to be (in other words, only a small strip of paper remains where the original leaf was). Moreover, the order of the gatherings could be changed, for example, to separate and group notes resulting from different parts of the lectures (for example, the *expositio textus*, the short commentary on the text, and the *quaestiones*). The trick to saving paper was to assess the right quire length based on a good estimate of how long the written text would be (Smeyers 1975: 251). When students did not succeed in matching the end of a quire with the end of the text, they would often cut the remaining folios out of the quire, leaving behind stubs at the end of the gathering. Sometimes, they simply left the remaining pages blank, or wrote something like *nihil deest* ("nothing is missing") for examinators or censors (Smeyers 2012: 76–7). That a manuscript was habitually written on loose quires is crucial for our codicological analysis: it implies a flexibility to form the codex to one's own desire.

After the redaction of the notes (before, during, and/or after class), the loose gatherings could be bound into a codex, by running a thread through the fold of each quire (attaching the bifolia) and stitching the quires together onto sewing supports. The free edges of the resulting text block were cut off so that their surface would be smooth and equal. During this operation, some written text could also be cut off. Examples of this are the catchwords and quire numerations or signatures—markings on each quire to signal their order while binding the book, which often did not survive trimming. Then, the binding was finished by attaching a parchment cover or boards covered with leather or other materials to the text block (through the slips at the end of the sewing supports). Finally, endpapers lining the boards (pastedowns) or serving as flyleaves tidied up the inside of the cover. The sophistication of the binding and the quality of the materials greatly varied, and depended on both the funds of the student and the value attached to the notes. Indeed, they range from provisional bindings barely holding together the codex, to parchment covers recycled from medieval manuscripts and even precious leather bindings with gold-stamped decoration (Cockx-Indesteghe 2012). As such, original bindings hold important clues to the intended function or value of the notebooks after the redaction process.

Was this complex final step in forming the codex carried out by the student? A letter-writing manual composed by Carolus Viruli in the 1480s suggests this possibility. The Louvain Arts professor includes a fictional letter in which a master writes to the father of one of his pupils that the latter bound his notes himself (*ligare sexternos*, binding quires of six bifolia; Smeyers 1975: 251). Another option was to have the notes bound by a bookbinder, a yet understudied profession at what historians often consider to be the lower end of the book trade (Day 2018: 5–8). These *bibliopegi* or *compactores librorum* did not usually sign their work: this often reduces them to the invisible hands of book production (Gialdini 2021b: 903). They did not only bind manuscripts but also printed books, which were usually sold as loose quires by the booksellers. In other words, printed textbooks too could be bound after a personalization process by the student, which for example could include interleaving the printed gatherings with blank leaves to make extra notes on. These interventions open up the annotated textbook for codicological study as well.

The process just described left a considerable amount of leeway for students to shape the material carrier of their notes toward their intellectual needs: buying the right paper, forming quires of the desired size and length, choosing the method and materials of the binding. There are also indications, however, that students did not always assemble their codex from loose gatherings. For example, a 1553 description of common teaching practices at Jesuit colleges relates that students were to take notes in *libri di carta bianca* during class, which seems to imply that these "blank (note)books" were bound before the lecture (Nelles 2007: 87). Venetian paper-retailers indeed sold pre-bound books of up to 400 leaves, which were often used for accounting or other commercial purposes, but could also have been bought by students (Gialdini 2021a: 38). Of course, such pre-bound codices would have lent themselves less to personalization. For example, extra leaves for additional notes would have had to be pasted to leaves already bound into the quires.

Although the act of binding was the final step in the formation of a student codex, it did not constitute the final material change to the carrier of the notes. Students and subsequent owners made changes to the paper: cutting out folios, pasting in extra leaves and engravings, adding notes to blank pages and so forth. The subsequent possessors also added marks of ownership in the form of handwritten notes, stamps and labels, usually on the pastedowns or flyleaves—we call these "provenances." A more drastic intervention was re-binding the book, in which the original cover was replaced and possibly also the entire sewing structure, for example by a nineteenth-century librarian with a penchant for half-leather bindings (see Graf 2015 for a thesaurus of bookbinding). Finally, the wear and tear of book usage and poor preservation conditions had an impact on the codex: mold, water damage, and ink corrosion are included in the many threats posed to a book's survival (to describe damage, see de Valk 2018). In short, the codex lying before you is the result of hundreds of years of material deposit, which the codicologist attempts to read in an archeological manner by uncovering the different strata of the manuscript.

3. Analysis

The above section has demonstrated how students habitually had a large hand in the progressive formation of the physical carrier of their notes: the codex is a molded object. This was a not an easy process—students had to choose the right paper (size), assess quire length based on a good estimate of how long the text would be, and so forth—but one allowing considerable flexibility to shape the manuscript to one's own needs. These codices are thus the material expression of different influences guiding the student's hands: teaching norms and dynamics; community practices of making manuscripts at the college, pedagogy, monastery, and so on; the individual skill of the student; and most importantly, the intended goals of confiding one's notes to the handwritten medium. In other words, forming the manuscript often was an integral part of the learning process of a student. The question is: how to disentangle all these factors and distinguish them from later material interventions, starting from the current state of the object?

The methodology proposed here is to map four types of structure within the codex, starting from a mere description of their characteristics: quire structure, distribution of watermarks, dates, and textual divisions. These four structures can give a glimpse into the genesis of the manuscript, but even more interesting is when the boundaries of two or more of these structures coincide in meaningful ways. When such intersections are the intentional product of the student, they provide insights into how the student shaped the codex toward their own intellectual goals. Larger groupings of such coincident structures could point toward what Johan Peter Gumbert (2004) has called codicological *blocks* and *units*. As always with archeological analysis, absolute certainty cannot be extracted from the material, therefore these clues should be cross-checked with others to improve the likelihood that their mark on the material was intentional rather than coincidental.

The next sections will briefly introduce how to assess quire structure, watermarks, dates, and textual divisions. Two manuscripts with similar notes but different codicological compositions will serve as an illustration: (1) State Archives of Belgium, Old University of Leuven, no. 3718 and (2) University Library of Utrecht, MS 434. Both contain notes from two cycles of lectures on the books of the New Testament, taught in the 1560s in the order of the Vulgate by Regius Professor of Sacred Scripture Michael Baius in Leuven. The first of these was produced by Baius' nephew Jacobus, a secular student who made notes during a first cycle of lectures from 1563 to 1567 and added notes from a second cycle to the margins.[1] The student of the second manuscript makes himself known in a series of colophons scattered throughout the codex. His name was Johannes Loemelensis, a Dominican friar who attended Baius' lectures somewhere at the end of the 1560s: he and Jacobus Baius probably were in the lecture hall together. How did these students from different backgrounds approach producing the physical carrier of very similar notes?

3.1. Quire structure

As gatherings are the basic building blocks of the codex, reconstructing the quire structure is the first step. This is done by finding the center fold of each quire, identifiable by the thread sewn through it, and counting the folios belonging to the same bifolium on each side of it (usually the sewing structure allows you to spot whether a folio belongs to the same quire or a different one). The first half of the quire should be the mirror image of the second half, containing the same number of folios. If that is not the case, leaves may have been added or removed. Often you will find a stub at the other side of the fold, signaling that a single folio has been added, or that the bifolium has been cut on that side to remove a single folio. Sometimes bifolia are added in such a way that both of their folios are on the same side of the fold (hooked or folded around, leaving no stub). These anomalies should be questioned, and perhaps visualized in a quire diagram. The entirety of the quire structure can also be summarized, for example in a collation formula (for a critical introduction, see Dorofeeva 2019). An exciting new option here is VCEditor, a DH tool developed by VisColl (Schoenberg Institute for Manuscript Studies, University of Pennsylvania) that allows you to edit, visualize, and export collation diagrams of your manuscript, both in the current state and theoretical past collations of

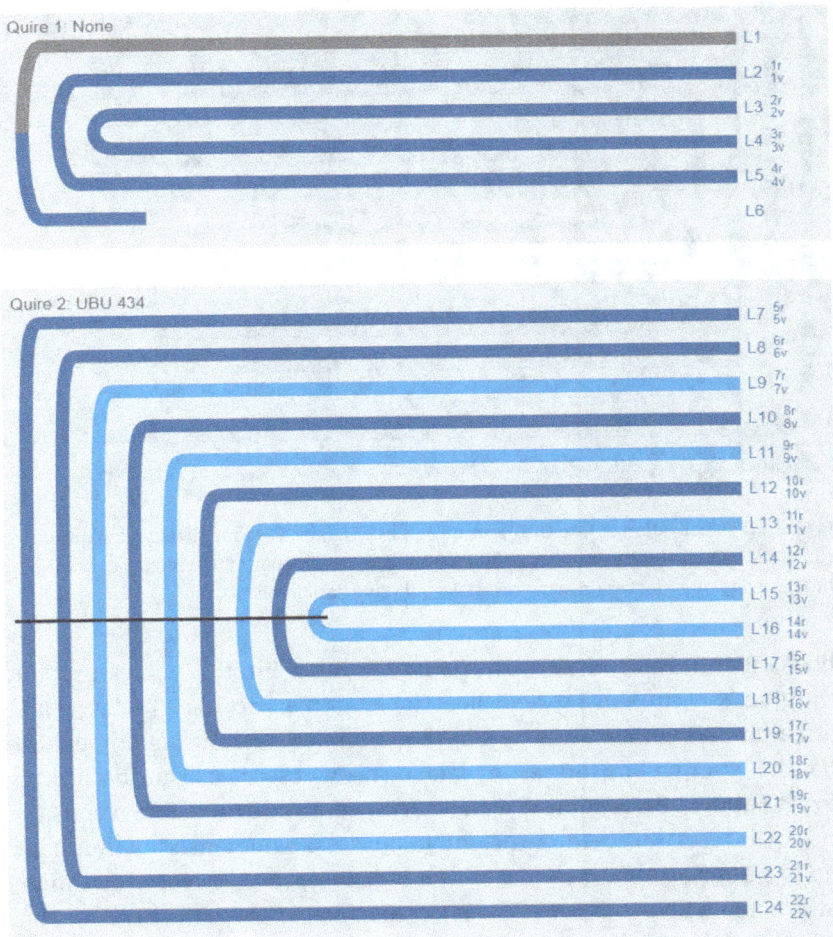

Figure 3.1. Visualization of UBU 434, quire 2 in VCEditor. Folio numbers are on the far right. The half-leaves are drawn in a lighter blue, and are part of the sewing structure of the quire.

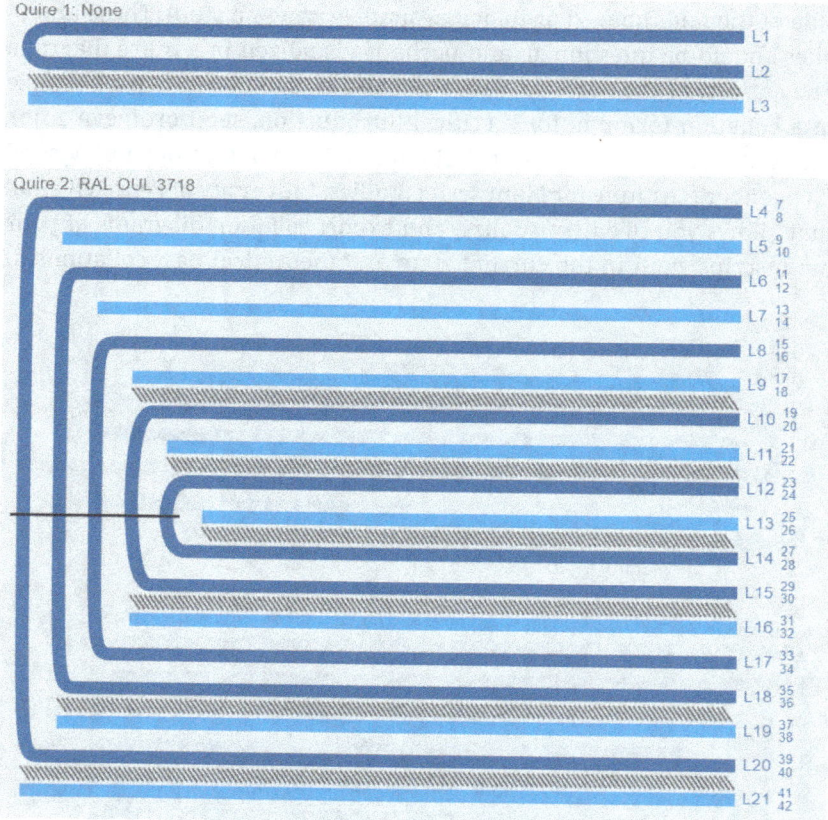

Figure 3.2. Visualization of RAL OUL 3718, quire 2 in VCEditor. Page numbers are on the far right. The half-leaves are drawn in a lighter blue: they are not part of the sewing structure, but pasted to other leaves (in some cases, the adhesive has dissolved).

books that have been disbound. If time is more limited, you can set out the quire structure in a spreadsheet (for example, Excel: see Tables 3.1 and 3.2), numbering the quires, adding folio numbers and the amount of bifolia (the latter will be interesting later). This will serve as your basic table to set out the distribution of watermarks, dates, and textual divisions.

An interesting case is that of Johannes Loemelensis' manuscript: he has interleaved his quires with half-leaves, so that every full folio is alternated with a half-folio. The latter alternately cover the head and tail of a full folio: this way, the book block has a uniform thickness.[2] Indeed, if he had only added leaves at the head half of the codex, the top of the book block would be much thicker and difficult to bind. In other words, the half-leaves are part of the sewing structure and thus were consciously added by Loemelensis before the book was bound. Whereas the full folios contain the commentary given by Michael Baius, the half-leaves contain extra references to the so-called Church Fathers. The latter have only been filled in for the first two-thirds of the codex, leaving the last third of the half-leaves blank (from fol. 331 onward). This suggests the following: Loemelensis had the idea of adding extra references to his written lecture text before binding his codex. He thus interleaved his quires with the half-leaves and had them bound, after which he started writing the references. However, he did not finish this task and left the last half-leaves blank. A very different approach is to be found in Jacobus Baius' manuscript: he also added leaves, but only a few (Gospel of John, pages 3–57). Moreover, these are not part of the sewing structure; he pasted them to some of the bound-in leaves with an adhesive. This points to an ad hoc approach: Baius could not fit his extra notes (on the second cycle of lectures) into the margins, so he decided to paste in some extra leaves.

3.2. *Distribution of watermarks*

Watermarks are witnesses to the production stage of paper: each sheet of handmade paper can be described as being its own birth certificate. Indeed, the line structure of thickness variations in the paper, visible through backlighting, is the imprint left by the molds used like sieves to pull the paper fibers out of the water containing them. It consists of finer wire-lines (also laid lines), thicker chain-lines perpendicular to the former and further apart, and the iconographic motif of the watermarks: this is the fingerprint unique to each mold. As these molds were intensively used for a couple of years and then replaced, their imprint can be employed to identify the producer and even estimate the years of production (Harris 2017). Various repertories can be used to identify and date watermarks according to their motifs, which range from flowers and animals to coats of arms and ecclesiastical insignia. The most well-known of these are the collections of Charles M. Briquet (1907, 1923, 1968) and Gerhard Piccard (1961–97), which are now also available as online databases, but there is also a range of more regionally focused repertories available.

One should be very careful when attempting to identify a watermark: an excellent knowledge of how paper was produced and a detailed observation of the watermark, chain- and wire-lines is crucial. The sheets have usually been folded into quires in such a way that only part of the watermark is visible, for example in the inner fold of the quire. A watermark and its countermark (on the opposite side of the sheet) can be confused as being two separate watermarks. Iconographic motifs could be reused at various points in time, even by different papermakers: there should thus be an exact match between your watermark and that from the repertory, but distances between chain-lines should also be measured to be certain. Lastly, the two papermaking colleagues—one pulling the mold out of the vat and the other sliding the paper onto the sheets of felt (the coucher)—employed two nearly identical molds for an efficient workflow. A stock of paper thus always contained twin watermarks, which are very difficult to distinguish (Stevenson 1951: 57–91; Harris 2017, under "Dillying and Dallying with Watermarks"). Successfully identifying and dating the watermarks of course offers limited insight into the student's practice. If no other clues are given about the date of redaction, the production date of the paper can give a *terminus post quem* (an earliest possible date), but there could technically still be years between the production of paper and its actual use (Agati 2017: 101–13; Harris 2017, under "Time-Frames, Case Books, and the Value of Paper as Evidence").

A more interesting approach is to set out the distribution of different watermarks throughout the codex against the quire structure. For example, Johannes Loemelensis' codex contains no less than five iconographic motifs in its watermarks, one of which consisting of at least two variants (a coat of arms containing three lilies and a hand with book descending from a cloud, with the letters "S Nivelle" underneath). This seems to imply that our student regularly re-supplied with relatively small bundles of paper. Moreover, in a single quire, the half-leaves contain different watermarks than those from the full bifolia: it strengthens the hypothesis that Johannes first formed the quires to contain the lecture text, and sometime afterward decided to interleave these with the half-leaves for references. Jacobus Baius' codex contains two watermarks, the second of which only features in quires 7–11 (of 21). This suggests a less "organic" approach in procuring paper, and could also point to a less gradual editing of the notes. However, it is unclear why only the middle of this codex would contain a different watermark, as it does not concur with other textual divisions or divisions related to dates. This demonstrates well how such material observations almost never tell a conclusive story.

3.3. Dates

Students often expressed their relief when finishing their notes on a certain section with colophons like *Finis coronat opus*. These sometimes contain a date. Other times, students included a date near the title (page) of a section. As many note collections are *Reinschriften*, written down sometime after the lecture, the question is whether these dates point to the lecture itself or the editing process of the notes. Sometimes the answer is stated explicitly: words like *inchoata, dictata, condita, repetit* with an ablative to point to the lecture, or *(ex)scripta, finis per me* to signal the redaction. The placement of the date near the title or professor's name, or near the colophon or end of the section can also be a clue. A cross-check with parallel lecture notes made by a different student or other sources can help determine lecture dates as well.

Jacobus Baius wrote down the date when his uncle started lecturing on a new book of the Bible next to the title of the book (*inchoata anno...*). In some cases, he added the date on which his professor lectured about a certain book for a second time. He did so in darker ink, like the rest of the marginal notes taken around that time. This allows us to reconstruct the two cycles of lectures on the New Testament of about 4.5 years and compare with the dates found in Johannes Loemelensis' manuscript (see Tables 3.1 and 3.2). At first sight, the latter do not hold a chronological line throughout the manuscript, and do not seem to agree with the dates reconstructed from Jacobus' codex. However, the placement of dates is important here: when a date is written next to the title, it seems to point to the lecture date and agrees with the reconstruction. The other dates are written in the colophons and suggest the editing date (for example, *finis per me, fratrem Joannem Loemelensem anno 1571*). This shows that there could be quite some time between the lecture and the editing of the notes. For example, Michael Baius started his lecture on *Philippians* on January 9, 1570 as can be gathered from Jacobus' notes, whereas Loemelensis finished his editing process around the end of August 1571. Furthermore, the year 1571 is found throughout the codex and is also the year Michael Baius concluded the Book of Revelation, the final book in the manuscript: this is probably when Loemelensis finished editing the notes and possibly also when he had the manuscript bound. The date "1571" can also be found on the half-leaves with references at the beginning of the codex, whereas we know that the commentary on the full leaves was taught around 1569. This strengthens the hypothesis that Loemelensis first wrote out the main commentary on the full leaves, and only decided to interleave the quires and add the references after having finished redacting the main commentary (and right before having the codex bound in 1571).

3.4. Textual divisions, codicological blocks

Setting out the textual divisions against the quire structure forms the capstone of this proposed method. It allows the codicologist to start interpreting the interplay between the four structures described here. More specifically, the key is to assess whether quire boundaries intersect with changes in the other structures in the codex. These points are caesuras that divide the manuscript in different blocks: for example, when the end of a chapter coincides with the end of a quire. This terminology was developed by Johan Peter Gumbert (2004) to accurately describe what he called the "stratigraphy" of codices. In this view, a codicological block differs from a codicological *unit*: a unit is "a discrete number of quires, worked in a single operation, containing a complete text or set of texts" (Gumbert 2004: 25). In other words, a collection of texts forms a *unit* if the writer(s) intended it that way when forming the codex, even if the content of the texts is widely different. By contrast, a collection of texts is a *composite* when it consists of more than one unit: for example, if a seventeenth-century student had the notes of two different sixteenth-century students (that is, two separate units) rebound into one codex. Thus, although students could work on their notes for several years, they still form a single unit if the student intended for them to become a single manuscript. Of course, this sometimes still leaves room for doubt: as we have seen, the archeological reading of the codex can rarely conclusively grasp the student's intent.

Although a student always produced a codicological unit, he did not necessarily compose it out of blocks: a unit is *articulated* when it contains several blocks, and *unarticulated* when this is not the case (Gumbert 2004). The presence or absence of these blocks is the material imprint of the students' choices in molding their codex; thus, identifying them allows the codicologist to move from a mere description of the object to a cautious interpretation of the student's activity. For example, analyses of the student notes from the Faculty of Arts in Louvain by Maurice Smeyers, Serena Masolini, and Christophe Geudens demonstrate that students created different codicological blocks for the textual exposition of the Aristotelian treatises and the *quaestiones* raised in class (Smeyers 1975; Geudens and Masolini 2016). These separate quire structures were written on in parallel and were completed progressively through the course of the year. The textual exposition was habitually written before class, probably through *dictamen*, whereas the *quaestiones* were dictated during class. The different codicological blocks were thus created to accommodate these two redaction moments, while simultaneously arranging the notes in an organized manner. After finishing the quire structures, the blocks with *quaestiones* were bound behind those containing the textual exposition, leaving the two separated in the manuscript. In other words, these notebooks consist of only one unit, but this unit is an articulated one: the quires containing the textual exposition and those containing the *quaestiones* are separated into different blocks.

A different approach was taken by Johannes Loemelensis and Jacobus Baius, who both followed Michael Baius' lectures at the Faculty of Theology (see Tables 3.1 and 3.2). Johannes Loemelensis clearly attempted to end the commentary on an epistle on the final page of a quire. When a commentary could fit on one quire, he slightly adjusted the quire length to accommodate it (for example, he used eleven bifolia for the block containing *Galatians* and only eight for the block containing *Colossians*). For other biblical books he even decreased the amount of bifolia in the final quire of the block. This required a good sense of how long the text would be before writing it down, and might point to the use of draft notes (perhaps a *Mitschrift*?) from which he copied the final text. Two blocks in the middle of the codex contain more than one epistle (*Thessalonians* to *Philemon* and *Hebrews* to *Jude*): these are very short commentaries, for which creating separate blocks might not have been worthwhile. In contrast, Jacobus Baius did not create separate blocks for most of the biblical books, only for the first three (Gospel of *John*, *Mark*, and the *Letter to the Romans*).[3] Two of these were not taught by Michael Baius, but by professor Thomas Gozaeus: perhaps that is why he initially wrote them out on separate quires.

To summarize, whereas the formation of codicological blocks by arts students was the result of shared practices, pointing to a "Louvain tradition," our two case studies from the Faculty of Theology suggest more individual strategies. Jacobus Baius seems to have had an ad hoc approach to his notes, writing them down in the chronological order of the lectures without taking the effort to create separate codicological blocks. He had to squeeze the notes on the second cycle into the margins and even paste in extra leaves. Johannes Loemelensis, on the other hand, took a more deliberate approach, creating separate blocks for each biblical book and had the foresight of interleaving his codex to add references. These approaches were not inspired by communal practices at the Faculty, but point to individual choices, to be interpreted through the background of the students. Loemelensis was a member of the Dominican Order, in which book ownership was communal (Thomas 1974: 424). In other words, he did not just write for himself, but also for his fellow Dominicans. This could explain why he molded his codex in a more premeditated way: to facilitate comprehensibility for future members of the order. Jacobus Baius was a secular student, writing mainly for himself, which is why his method of note-taking and the material imprint it left might be closer to how we take notes today. Of course, this interpretation is only a partial explanation: to interpret the students' approaches further, text, provenances, and historical context ought to be brought into dialog with codicological analyses like the one I have proposed in this chapter.

THE MATERIALITY OF THE STUDENT NOTEBOOK 89

Table 3.1. Codicological structure of UBU 434 (Johannes Loemelensis). Codicological blocks are separated by dotted lines—every quire within a block is represented by the number of bifolia it contains.

Folio nos	Book	Professor	Amount of bifolia per gathering	Date in Colophon	Date lecture (reconstructed)
2r-5r	Romans 1.9-3.26	Gozaeus	[added after binding]		?
6r-60v	Romans	Baius	9 – 10 – 9	1571 (on half-folio)	1568
61r-141r	1, 2 Corinthians	Baius	8 – 9 – 8 – 9 – 6	1571 (on half-folio)	1569
142r-161	Galatians	Baius	11	1569 (title)	1569
165r-183r	Ephesians	Baius	10		1569
183v-199r	Philippians	Baius	9	1571 (colophon)	1570
201r-217r	Colossians	Baius	8		1570
218r-232r	1, 2 Thessalonians	Baius	9 – 8 – 9 – 8		1570
241r-270r	1, 2 Timothy	Baius			1570
270v-279r	Titus	Baius			1570
282r-284v	Philemon	Baius			1570
285v-330r	Hebrews	Baius	11 – 8 – 9 – 8 – 9 – 8 – 9	1570 (colophon)	1570
330v-347v	James [A]	Baius		1573 (colophon)	?
350r-377r	1, 2 Peter	Baius		1571 (colophon)	1571
377v-394v	1, 2, 3 John	Baius		1571 (colophon)	1571
396r-401	Jude	Baius		1571 (colophon)	1571
409r-418v	James [B]	Baius	8 – 9 – 6		?
420r-452r	James [C]	Petri			?
455r-534v	Revelation	Baius	9 – 8 – 9 – 8 – 7	1571 (colophon)	1571
535v-537v	Romans 3.26-...	Gozaeus	[added after binding]	"Scripsi Insulis 1575"	?

Table 3.2. Codicological structure of RAL OUL 3718 (Jacobus Baius). Codicological blocks are separated by dotted lines—every quire within a block is represented by the number of bifolia it contains.

Page nos	Book	Professor	Amount of bifolia per gathering	Lecture date cycle 1	Lecture date cycle 2
1-58	John	Baius	5 – 3[+1]	11 Jan 1563	
59-99	Mark	Gozaeus	[1+]5 – 5	May 1563	
101-127	Romans	Gozaeus	4 – 3	1564	
129-161	1, 2 Corinthians	Baius	4 – 6 – 4 – 5 – 4 – 4 – 5 – 5 – [2]	June; 21 Sep 1564	18 Feb 1569
162-169	Galatians	Baius		4 Dec 1564	
169-177	Ephesians	Baius		21 Aug 1565	
177-182	Philippians	Baius		25 Oct 1565	9 Jan 1570
183-187	Colossians	Baius		1565	30 Jan 1570
187-191	1, 2 Thessalonians	Baius		Dec 1565; 15 Jan 1566	
192-200	1, 2 Timothy	Baius		22 Jan; 8 Feb 1566	29 May 1570
200-202	Titus	Baius		18 Feb 1566	
202-203	Philemon	Baius			
203-206	Hebrews	Baius		6 Mar 1566	
217-221	James	Baius		15 May 1566	
222-230	1, 2 Peter	Baius		10 June 1566	
230-235	1, 2, 3 John	Baius		1566	
235-236	Jude	Baius		Sept 1566	
237-253	Revelation	Baius		10 Sept 1566	
254-286	Matthew	Baius		8 Jan 1567	
287-320	Luke	Baius		4 Aug 1567	
323-340	Acts	Baius			

Notes

[1] This codex also contains some fragmented quires with a partial copy of a few distinctions from Michael Baius' classes on Peter Lombard's *Sentences*, bound after the biblical commentaries. For the sake of clarity, these will not be in focus for this manuscript. Fols 342–67 contain a partial commentary on Book II (dist 1–4), and a full commentary on Book I. However, the quires are bound in the wrong order: the section starts with the final page of Book I and continues with Book II, dist. 1–4, after which it reverts to Book I, dist. 3–48 and ends with a folio containing the introduction to Book I and dist. 1–3. Based on the note on this final page (366) ("composita circa annu[m] 1550, exscripta vero 1563"), these quires likely formed a separate codex, but were added to the biblical notes when they were rebound, probably in the nineteenth century.

[2] In contrast, the terminology "upper" and "lower" is generally used for terminology relating to respectively the front part of a book (for example, front cover) and the end part of a book (for example, back cover).

[3] The commentaries on the *Sentences* are written on different quire structures, which were taken apart when the codex was rebound in the nineteenth century. Since Jacobus Baius had not intended for the biblical notes and the notes on the *Sentences* to be bound together, the quires on the *Sentences* form a different codicological unit, even if they were written by the same hand.

Thematic bibliography

Handbooks for codicology

Agati, Maria Luisa. 2003. *Il libro manoscritto: Introduzione alla codicologia*. Studia Archaeologica 124. Rome: L'Erma di Bretschneider.

Agati, Maria Luisa. 2017. *The Manuscript Book: A Compendium of Codicology*. Studia Archaeologica 214. Rome: L'Erma di Bretschneider.

Clemens, Raymond, and Timothy Graham. 2007. *Introduction to Manuscript Studies*. Ithaca: Cornell University Press.

Lemaire, Jacques. 1989. *Introduction à la codicologie*. Publications de l'Institut d'études médiévales: Textes, études, congrès 9. Louvain-la-Neuve: Institut d'études médiévales.

Maniaci, Marilena. 2002. *Archeologia del manoscritto: Metodi, problemi, bibliografia recente*. I libri di Viella 34. Rome: Viella.

Codicological dictionaries

Gnirrep, W.K., J.P. Gumbert, and J.A. Szirmai. 1992. *Kneep en binding: Een terminologie voor de beschrijving van de constructies van oude boekbanden*. The Hague: Koninklijke Bibliotheek.

Graf, Klaus. 2015. Language of Bindings (LoB). https://www.ligatus.org.uk/lob/. Last accessed January 21, 2025.

Gumbert, Johan Peter. 2010. *Words for Codices: A Codicological Terminology in English*. Self-published, Ludwig-Maximilians-Universität München. https://www.cei.lmu.de/extern/VocCod/WOR10-1.pdf; https://www.cei.lmu.de/extern/VocCod/WOR10-2.pdf; and https://www.cei.lmu.de/extern/VocCod/WOR10-3.pdf. Last accessed January 21, 2025.

Maniaci, Marilena. 1996. *Terminologia del libro manoscritto*. Addenda: studi sulla conoscenza, la conservazione e il restauro del materiale librario 3. Rome: Instituto centrale per la patologia del libro.

Muzerelle, Denis. 1985. *Vocabulaire codicologique du français*. Rubricae: histoire du livre et des textes 1. Paris: Editions CEMI.

Denis Muzerelle's influential 1985 dictionary is in French. It can be consulted online, together with a translation of the terms in French, Italian, Spanish, English, and Arabic:

Institut de recherche et d'histoire des textes. 2011. Codicologia. http://codicologia.irht.cnrs.fr/. Last accessed January 21, 2025.

Ostos, Pilar, Maria Luisa Pardo, and Elena E. Rodriguez. 1997. *Vocabulario de codicología*. Instrumenta bibliologica. Madrid: Arco/Libros.

Printed books

Gaskell, Philipp. 1995. *A New Introduction to Bibliography*. 3rd edn. New Castle: Oak Knoll Press.

Werner, Sarah. 2019. *Studying Early Printed Books 1450–1800: A Practical Guide*. Hoboken, NJ: Wiley.

Paper and watermarks

Barrett, Timothy. 2012. "European Papermaking Techniques 1300–1800." Paper through Time: Nondestructive Analysis of 14th- through 19th-Century European-style Papers. http://paper.lib.uiowa.edu/european.php#raw. Last accessed on January 21, 2025.

Bellingradt, Daniel. 2021. "The Paper Trade in Early Modern Europe: An Introduction." In *The Paper Trade in Early Modern Europe: Practices, Materials, Networks*, edited by Daniel Bellingradt, 1–27. Library of the Written Word 89. Leiden: Brill.

Briquet, Charles M. 1968. *Les filigranes: Dictionnaire historique des marques du papier dès leur apparition vers 1282 jusqu'en 1600. A Facsimile of the 1907 Edition with Supplementary Material Contributed by a Number of Scholars*. Edited by Allan Stevenson. 4 vols. Amsterdam: The Paper Publications Society. See also the 1907 and 1923 editions, and the online database: Bernstein: The Memory of Paper. Last modified May 14, 2021. https://www.memoryofpaper.eu/BernsteinPortal/appl_start.disp.

Gialdini, Anna. 2021a. "Selling Paper in Early Modern Venice: Paper-Retailers and the 'Libri da carta bianca'." In *The Paper Trade in Early Modern Europe: Practices, Materials, Networks*, edited by Daniel Bellingradt, 31–54. Library of the Written Word 89. Leiden: Brill.

Harris, Neil. 2017. "Paper and Watermarks as Bibliographical Evidence." Institut d'histoire du livre. http://ihl.enssib.fr/paper-and-watermarks-as-bibliographical-evidence.

Nelles, Paul. 2007. "*Libros de papel, libri bianchi, libri papyracei*: Note-Taking Techniques and the Role of Student Notebooks in the Early Jesuit Colleges." *Archivum Historicum Societatis Iesu* 76: 75–112.

Piccard, Gerhard. 1961–97. *Die Wasserzeichenkartei Piccard im Hauptstaatsarchiv Stuttgart*. 17 vols. Stuttgart: Verlag W. Kohlhammer.

Stevenson, Allan H. 1951. "Watermarks are Twins." *Studies in Bibliography* 4: 57–91.

Wenger, Emanuel, and Frieder Schmidt. "Printed Watermark Repertories." International Association of Paper Historians. Last modified February 22, 2021. http://www.paperhistory.org/Watermark-catalogues/.

Wolfe, Heather. 2018. "Was Early Modern Writing Paper Expensive?" The Collation: Research and Exploration at the Folger. https://collation.folger.edu/2018/02/writing-paper-expensive/.

Codicological structure

Destrez, Jean. 1935. *La Pecia dans les manuscrits universitaires de xiiie et du xive siècle.* Paris: Vautrain.

Dorofeeva, Anna. 2019. "Visualizing Codicologically and Textually Complex Manuscripts." *Manuscript Studies* 4 (2): 334–60.

Gumbert, Johan Peter. 2004. "Codicological Units: Towards a Terminology for the Stratigraphy of the Non-Homogeneous Codex." *Segno e testo* 2: 17–42.

Pollard, Graham. 1978. "The Pecia System in the Medieval Universities." In *Medieval Scribes, Manuscripts and Libraries: Essays Presented to N. R. Ker*, edited by M.B. Parkes and A.G. Watson, 145–61. London: Scolar Press.

Smeyers, Katharina. 2012. "De student aan het werk: Hoe collegedictaten tot stand kwamen." In *Ex Cathedra: Leuvense collegedictaten van de 16de tot de 18de eeuw*, edited by Geert Vanpaemel, Katharina Smeyers, An Smets, and Diewer van der Meijden, 73–89. Leuven: Universiteitsbibliotheek.

Smeyers, Maurits. 1975. "Een collegeschrift van de oude Leuvense Universiteit (1481–1482): Een codicologisch en iconografisch onderzoek." *Arca Lovaniensis* 4: 243–303.

Other

Blair, Ann. 2010. "The Rise of Note-Taking in Early Modern Europe." *Intellectual History Review* 20: 303–16.

Cockx-Indesteghe, Elly. 2012. "Een beschermend omhulsel voor de collegedictaten." In *Ex Cathedra: Leuvense collegedictaten van de 16de tot de 18de eeuw*, edited by Geert Vanpaemel, Katharina Smeyers, An Smets, and Diewer van der Meijden, 91–106. Leuven: Universiteitsbibliotheek.

Day, Matthew. 2018. "Deceit, Self-Interest, and Censorship: Problems at the Bookbinders in Early Modern England." *The Papers of the Bibliographical Society of America* 112 (1): 1–25.

De Valk, Marijn. 2018. *Library Damage Atlas: A Tool for Assessing Damage.* Armarium: Publicaties voor Erfgoedbibliotheken 5. Antwerp: Vlaamse Erfgoedbibliotheek.

Geudens, Christophe, and Serena Masolini. 2016. "Teaching Aristotle at the Louvain Faculty of Arts, 1425–1500: General Regulations and Handwritten Testimonies." *Rivista di filosofia neoscolastica* 108 (4): 813–44.

Gialdini, Anna. 2021b. "Bookbinders in the Early Modern Venetian Book Trade." *The Historical Journal* 65 (4): 901–21. https://doi.org/10.1017/S0018246X21000728.

Thomas, A.P. 1974. "Boekenbezit en boekengebruik bij de Dominikanen in de Nederlanden vóór ca. 1550." In *Studies over het boekenbezit en boekengebruik in de Nederlanden vóór 1600*, 417–76. Archief- en bibliotheekwezen in België: Extranummers 11. Brussel: Vereniging van archivarissen en bibliothecarissen van België.

DH tools

VCEditor, <https://viscoll.org/help/>. Last accessed February 29, 2024.

CHAPTER 4

Book History:
The Basics with Two Case Studies

Natasha Constantinidou, Dieter Cammaerts, and Violet Soen

1. Introduction

The invention of moveable type in about 1450 (and its combination with the handpress) had a profound impact on society and education, as from then onwards scribal and print culture co-existed. The invention increased the number of books available, sped their production, and resulted in lowering the cost of books. At the same time, a new type of artisan, the printer, emerged, while a transition was also noticeable within bookshops, because *librarii*, or local booksellers, started to sell printed books in addition to handwritten manuscripts. The result of this proliferation of books meant that early modern students and scholars who strolled the streets of university cities in Europe, its overseas colonies, or its satellite states would have come across many print or book shops. This business of books was most often located in quarters close to the faculties of the local university or to other secular or clerical institutions of higher learning. Students frequently visited these book and print shops to browse through catalogs or to purchase printed items for their own use. On some occasions, they could even venture and take more active roles, through participating in the editing and the editorial strategies of publishing houses. Just like other groups in early modern society, students and scholars were intensively exposed to products of the printing press. At the same time, they seized the opportunities created by this technology to exchange knowledge and information: from textbooks to dissertation sheets, from newsletters to learned epitomes, from announcements to regulations, as soon as the handpress was introduced, so-called printed matter accompanied all stages and moments of intellectual communities and of early modern learning.

This chapter examines the relationship between students and books issued by handpress, as a way of understanding how they engaged with the final product of the printing press. Today, these printed works are qualified as rare books, a term for books printed between 1501 and 1820, as opposed to incunables, namely the early books printed between 1450 and 1500. At the same time, it aims to offer a series of points and parameters that one should consider to analyze early modern printed matter and to place these publications in their historical and intellectual context. The interdisciplinary field of book history at its core has a mission to examine how to make sense of printed matter as an artefact, and especially, to understand how these printed specimens functioned within their cultural, social, and intellectual setting.[1] This chapter will introduce briefly some of the key concepts used in the study of early modern printing, as a way of understanding the surviving artefacts, as well as their users' and students' traces. This entails considering the technological infrastructure and institutional context in which these printed books originated and circulated, as well as tracing the circuits and networks in which they were disseminated, also known as the sociality of publishers and printers, booksellers and authors, readers, and audiences. We conclude by discussing examples of editions as well as extant copies of a standard textbook in Leuven and Paris, as a way of illustrating some of the main issues upon which we touch.

2. An increasingly interdisciplinary field

The introduction of the printing press in the middle of the fifteenth century relied on three combined technologies (the production of texts by movable type, the wine and textile press transformed to a handpress, and the production of suitable ink to stick to the type), and it is still considered one of the chief media revolutions in history (Eisenstein 1993). Early discussions highlighted how Johannes Gutenberg and his presses mounted in Mainz in about 1450 revolutionized the world by providing the premises for mass media and thus for the homogenization of news and information on a global scale (McLuhan 1962). Contrary to triumphalist perspectives of the innovative nature of the printing press for Europe or its colonies, in many other parts of the world, especially in Middle Eastern or Asian cultures, mechanic printing had been invented or introduced many centuries to even a millennium earlier. Equally, preceding Gutenberg's technological changes in about 1450, the revolution in paper production and distribution (rather than the time-consuming and expensive production of parchment) had been named as a catalyst in these developments, as it had created a higher demand for information (Febvre and Martin 1976). In the last decades, however, we have come to understand that the printing press changed forever how news and knowledge were created and transferred.

The history of the book is an increasingly interdisciplinary field. An inquiry into the materiality of printed books still counts as the "core" of book history, although new analytical concepts are emerging rapidly. A very influential interpretation provided by Robert Darnton has steered the current crossover between history, literary studies, bibliography, and typography. The American book historian proposed the "communication circuit" in which books originate and survive (Darnton 1982: 68), making a basic distinction between the production, distribution, and reception of books. Within this circuit, he also identified important agents, such as the papermaker, printer (the craftsman with an operating printing press), and publisher (financer of the print run). As such, Darnton's model decentered the authors and/or editors of a book and embedded them within a complex chain, which included printers, publishers, booksellers, and audiences.

Other book historians like Donald Francis McKenzie have similarly argued that book history should incorporate research beyond the study of the material object so that book-historical studies identify the actions of what may be called book people, and the collaborations between them (McKenzie 1985). After all, every book has a specific lifecycle, meaning it passes through certain stages and through the hands of numerous people. Moreover, the Renaissance learned book was always the result of collaborations between individuals of different social, and sometimes regional, backgrounds, who were driven by different motives. More recently, the concept of sociality has been added to that of Darnton's circuit, placing more emphasis on the reconstruction of the intertwined networks of printing and scholarship (Bellingradt and Salman 2017: 4–8). In contrast to bibliographical approaches, sociality focuses on people, meaning it is a concept that researches human agency, as well as interactions and collaborations during the production, distribution, and consumption of books. Through the study of the people involved in these networks, and through refining this approach scholars have also become more aware of the multiple roles that each person could take on at the same time.

These important insights contribute to a book history today where the printed artefact remains the focal point of inquiry, but is embedded within cultural, social, and economic investigations into its contexts of

production, dissemination, and use. Broadly speaking, studies in the history of the book adopt four different approaches.
- First, researchers study books from a literary point of view, as an extension of textual scholarship, and with a primary focus on authors and texts.
- Second, some book historians focus on the book as a commercial product, and thus emphasize the economic aspects of the production and circulation of the book market.
- Third, a longstanding approach investigates books as cultural artefacts, imbued with meaning reflecting the culture of their creators and users.
- Finally, a different strand of book history examines handpress publications from the perspective of bibliography, focusing primarily on the material aspects of the book, such as format, paper, and collation.

Recent studies are often the result of cross-fertilization of these four perspectives, which will be at the heart of the next sections.[2] Especially useful for the purposes of this volume, is to insert students into the "communication circuit" and understand their particular role in the production, circulation, and reception of books.

3. Production and distribution of printed books

Many book-historical studies have assessed, and continue to do so, the production side, and its economic dimension. Moveable type meant that workers in the Renaissance printshop could cast new word orders every time, making an infinite number of texts possible. Loose letters could be flexibly used and reused and give a standardized impression, as opposed to carving out woodblocks for each page they wanted to reproduce. This ability of the printing press to produce texts faster and in larger quantities certainly stood out in comparison to the production of a single copy of handwritten codex, on commission from a client, and often enshrined as it was contained in more expensive materials such as parchment. The rise in the production of printed matter coincided with a rise in education, as witnessed by the numerous schools, colleges, universities, grammar schools, and new academies that appeared throughout Europe in the sixteenth century, together with an increase in the numbers of students taking classes of secondary and/or higher learning. Within Renaissance institutions of education, the new technology of the printing press was gradually embraced, both for scholastic and humanist disciplines. These developments contributed to a shift in the printing industry, as from the end of the fifteenth century printers turned to more commercial publications. In addition to the commentaries and scholastic texts, printers issued books required for teaching, such as grammars and textbooks, as well as broadsheet ordinances, and small devotional works for particular religious institutions (Pettegree 2010: chs. 3–4; Ashworth 1988).

This expanse in the production of printed textbooks had also led some earlier scholars of the book to assertions about the standardization of book production and the text (Eisenstein 1979), which also entailed the risk of fossilization of knowledge. However, even when two students bought a printed book from the same print-run, the two copies could look different. This was due to the artisanal, collaborative, and time-consuming printing process. The early modern handpress always relied on manual and physical labor, from inking the balls through rubbing the fonts to drying the paper sheets, from casting the text to correcting it, in several rounds if need be. Mistakes could be made and consequently corrected, hence, the potential difference in copies of an edition. Producing books was a craft, one in which fingers got dirty, and printing remained a capital and labor-intensive industry throughout the early modern period (Grafton 2020). Typically, printed books were sold as loose quires (folded leaves), meaning that binding these together was a decision of the reader. Many types of binding existed, which will be discussed in the next section. Likewise, the success of the new technology heavily depended on a series of artisans discerning its commercial potential. As a result, both within the European continent and through its colonial conquests, these artisans helped to create a book market catering to the need for printed matter.

By focusing on the persons behind the handpress, scholars have also started paying attention to the gendered aspects of the production process, as the many activities of women on the work floor, in the bookshops, and in the multiple other sources of income behind printing businesses have long been obscured. This silent elimination is above all evidenced in the rare books themselves: even when the print shop was legally in the hands of a woman, she often was referred to as "widow X or Y" on the title page or in the colophon, thus making women the invisible hands and reinforcing the typical patriarchal norms of the early modern world.

In fact, students would see male and female faces when buying books, as women often were responsible for the book counter (Jimenes 2018; Wyffels 2021; Watson et al. 2025).

The Renaissance witnessed the emergence of a subtype of a printer who may have originally started out as a scholar: book historians refer to them as "humanist printers" or "scholar-printers" (Bénévent et al. 2012). These erudite men possessed an excellent knowledge of Latin (sometimes, also Greek and/or Hebrew), and in addition to being printers, they also authored books or edited classical texts. In that sense, like other humanists, they dedicated themselves to producing accurate text editions, premeditated on the advances of the new media technology. Well-known names are, among others, Aldus Manutius (c. 1450–1515) in Venice, Josse Bade (1461/2–1535) and Robert Estienne (1503–1559) in Paris, and Rutgerus Rescius (c. 1495–1545) in Leuven. The latter was a professor of Greek at the Collegium Trilingue, and a producer of printed Greek textbooks intended for use by his own students. Other similar overlaps or collaborations between teaching institutions and printing houses include those of, in Paris, printer Chrestien Wechel (c. 1494–1554) with the royal professor of Greek Jacques Toussain (1499?–1547), and the professor appointed as royal printer Adrien Turnèbe (1512–1565), as well as in Geneva, the professor Franciscus Portus (1511–1581) with the printer Jean Crespin (c. 1520–1572) (Constantinidou 2015, 2018, 2022; Feys 2024).

When not competent themselves, or when they needed extra hands (and eyes), printers would hire students or aspiring scholars. Such a preoccupation also allowed students to consolidate their knowledge of classical and biblical languages, and even operated as a first step in their own ambition to become scholars. Before his appointment to the professorship of Greek, for example, the afore-mentioned Rescius had worked for the printer Dirk Martens, as a corrector in the print shop. Sometimes, students collaborated with their professors in editions of books. Alternatively, cohorts of students honored a deceased teacher by preparing his lecture notes in print, fashioning his intellectual legacy and memory.[3] Occasionally, lecture notes even appeared in print without the consent of the teacher, as happened to the *quodlibetica* of Adrian of Utrecht (1459–1523) printed in Leuven in 1515, when he had already moved out of the university city being appointed as the new grand-inquisitor in Castile.[4]

Even if the circulation of knowledge through print was more intensive, rapid, and wide than ever before, book historians recognize now that the production of books was heavily regulated, and that the circulation of ideas in print was certainly never free or unbounded. The most generic form of institutionalization and corporatism occurred on the level of the craft guild. For instance, a printer in Antwerp enrolled into the guild of Saint Luke, while a colleague in London became a member of the Stationers' Company—there were not only controlling labor conditions but also post-publication censorship and disciplinary enforcement (Blayney 2013; Wyffels 2021). As members of European craft guilds, printers were artisans, obligated to learn, as well as teach, the necessary skills on the shop floor. Through an apprenticeship, every printer acquired prescriptive knowledge or an understanding of what was required, in order to produce a book of high quality. At the end of his training, every apprentice needed to complete a master's test, which, when successful, offered proof of possession of the necessary skills. These credentials were important, as, for instance, in the Low Countries, guild documents were required in order for the Council of Brabant to grant permission to open up a print shop (Adam 2017). Another form of institutionalization occurred at the level of universities. Printers in Leuven and Cologne were not eligible to open a print or books shop without the recognition of the local universities, meaning they were obligated to become members of these institutions through matriculation. As a result, in the *impressum* (imprint) of their books, authorized printers who often referred to themselves as *typographus juratus* ("sworn typographer"), or in the case of an academic printer, *typographus academiae* ("academic typographer").

Given that printing was a craft and industry that at its core aimed at generating profit, a strong business plan that centered on the ability to effectively appraise the book market (be it local, regional, or international) was necessary. Academic printers fit this description, since connections with institutions of higher learning encouraged them to pursue specialization as a business strategy (Kirwan and Mullins 2015). In smaller university cities, printers survived primarily because of these connections, when they issued *Hochschulschriften* (university writings), such as dissertation sheets and theses. Moreover, they catered to the institutions' needs through the production of official documents. These sources were often broadsheets, or texts printed on one single page, making them cheap print and, therefore, a useful addition to other types of books that printers produced and sold in their shops (Pettegree 2017, especially part V). Printing thesis sheets offered a certain cash flow, as students needed to prefinance their printed matter. In a university city like Douai, widow printers would often continue the printing house of their late life and business partners, empowered by the secure income generated by printing thesis sheets (Wyffels 2021; Fantoli and Soen forthcoming). Although academic printers are to be found in most the European university towns, their role was not always formally established in the same way throughout, sometimes operating on commission or, occasionally, on a salary. In Leiden, for instance, Plantin's son-in-law Franciscus Raphelengius became the official academic printer of the new university, with a yearly salary of 200 guilders. At the same time, Raphelengius acted as professor of Hebrew, and head of the local Plantin satellite office from 1585 to 1597 (Hoftijzer 1990–1).

Another example of specialization was the production of Greek and Hebrew literature and grammars, as the growing interest among scholars and students for both these languages led to the creation of a specific audience in the European book market. However, the printing of Greek and Hebrew texts was a difficult enterprise, as it required special typefaces, and experienced and educated editors and proofreaders. Notwithstanding these difficulties, several printers, like Manutius, Rescius, and others mentioned above, acknowledged the potential benefits and chose to cater for this newly created audience. Some printers specialized in the production of textbooks intended for use within a specific university faculty. This was the case with Charlotte Guillard (late 1480s–1557), who printed editions of the *Corpus juris civilis* and *Corpus juris canonici* for the Sorbonne faculty of law. Others decided to print numerous editions of a book from a specific author. The catalogs of Richard Pafraet and Jacobus of Breda, both printers in the city of Deventer, provide evidence of this type of focused printing. Both men produced numerous copies of Petrus Hispanus' *Summulae logicales* for the students of the local Latin school in the first two decades of the sixteenth century. Another similar example comes from Paris, in the case of Jacques Lefèvre d'Étaples and the mathematical textbooks that printer Henri I Estienne was producing for him and his circle of students (Oosterhoff 2018, 2022).

Along with the institutionalized permissions for printers to start their business, books were also produced under other restrictions. The most current and known form was a privilege that was given to a printer, and the phrase *cum privilegio* is a distinctive feature that one often encounters on early modern title pages. This form of regulation was at its core a tool that printers used to first request and then receive protection against reprints of a certain edition, making it especially efficient for printers catering to a particular segment of the book market. Through a privilege, they obtained the printing monopoly for a specific book during a fixed period, usually from four to twelve years. As a result, every reprint of this book by other printers was considered a pirated edition, and numerous sources preserved in archives across Europe provide evidence of printers being punished for these types of infractions. After a request, civic authorities (be it at the local or state level) granted a privilege; although this was prestigious, a privilege also came with the accompanying disadvantage that its lawfulness was bound within the jurisdictional limits of the authorizing instance. In any case, privileges were difficult to impose and control within and beyond borders. This meant a French book was not protected against reprints in the Low Countries or the Holy Roman Empire and vice versa (Soetaert 2019: 96). This was a real disadvantage for printers who produced the *editio princeps* (first edition) of a European best-seller, typically in the lingua franca Latin, and transported it across Europe. Indeed, some cities like Geneva thrived on producing cheaper versions of expensive editions. As a result, printers living and working outside a prescribed geographical confinement were able to produce cheaper reprints without any danger of being punished; this led to the early modern book market being flooded with pirated editions. This pirate market benefited students, as they could buy a cheaper reprint in a local print shop, instead of an imported and, therefore often, more expensive book.

Already before the start of the Reformation, but certainly, afterwards, students were only supposed to consult books under the regime of censorship, a distinctive early modern feature across regions and confessions. In Catholic regions, this occurred through the use of approbations or other forms of preventive censorship exerted by clerical instances. The clerical judgment was about the text of the author, or the edition concerned, yet also figured in the paratext of a book. For instance, in the Habsburg Low Countries, every edition needed to be approved by a (mostly clerical) censor to be considered legal. This was the reason why printers included these approbations in their editions, as they informed the reader that the book had been through the censorship process according to existing laws (Grendler 1977; Soen et al. 2017). On the other hand, religious and civic institutions employed repressive book censorship, meaning they had to ban books already circulating on the local or European book market. The most famous example of this type of censorship was the indexes or lists of forbidden books, such as the Papal and Roman-Catholic *Index librorum prohibitorum* updated from 1559 until 1966. Other institutions also issued similar catalogs: Leuven and the Sorbonne had famously condemned Luther's works in 1519 and 1520, respectively, and the theological faculty of the University of Leuven drew up a list of "forbidden" books in 1546, 1550, and 1558 (see the editions provided by de Bujanda). Additionally, book razzias were repeatedly organized by state, university, or urban institutions. This occurred, for instance, in 1543, in Leuven, when the bookshop of Hieronymus Cloet was raided, and his entire inventory of books was confiscated. In Protestant regions, censorship took more post-factum control, yet it also entailed the removal of books causing unrest, especially those from Catholic authors, or those from contending Protestant churches. Similarly, the Tudor monarchy forbade the import and circulation of continental reforming books that did not suit its confessional stance during each particular turn that their ecclesiastical policy took in the sixteenth century. Needless to say, no single system of censorship in the early modern era was efficient. Rather, the legal pluralism in many countries opened up spaces for bargain and smuggling, illicit trade and reprinting, and serving clandestine communities; fake imprints were often a means to escape censorship, as the English Catholic community would pretend that their locally, yet clandestinely produced books, were published legally in Habsburg Douai in the continent. Illicit printing undercut competition, and had a significant impact on the international trade, or in upholding clandestine religious minorities.

4. From production to consumption: An inquiry into material objects

Sustained attention to the material aspects of the book, for a long time the purview of bibliography, has indeed changed the way we think about printed books in the transfer of early modern knowledge (Gaskell 1995; Tanselle 2009). Printing houses and their products, together with the market for which they were intended, are at the heart of this consideration. It is important to note at the outset, therefore, that the nature of this market was by definition a conservative one, since it traded in well-known texts and authors, habitually used throughout many centuries for teaching in a scholastic way. Thus, in the production of material books for the academic book market, "preservation of a past model was a virtue, while innovation could be perceived as a form of corruption" (Valleriani and Ottone 2022: 8).

In many ways, it is in the context of this fierce competition and specialization in the academic textbook market that we have to approach the material production of printed manuals. When discussing the printed products themselves, two main aspects should be addressed: the *mise en livre* and the *mise en page*. The *mise en livre* denotes the physical appearance of a book, such as the format and the binding, as well as the content. The latter refers to layout, typography, and the appearance of the printed text (Vanautgaerden 2012: 6). The format of a book is the most immediate and obvious aspect of its materiality. The format is the ratio of the number of printed leaves to the sheet of paper and was often dependent on the number of times a printed sheet was folded to create a smaller surface (Walsby 2021; Werner 2019: 42, 174). The folded sheets were signed with the same mark and "gathered" together in groups of four, eight, etc. quires or gatherings to physically compose the book. Different formats were intended for different purposes and uses, the most common ones being folio (2°), quarto (4°), octavo (8°), and sexto-decimo (16°).[5]

When considering student books, there are difficulties in attempting to make assertions on the relationship between format and use, due to geographical differentiations, distinctions on the basis of subject taught, as well as changes that came with time—notably, a gradual shift from bigger to smaller formats throughout the sixteenth century (Walsby 2020a: 49). It is fair to say, however, that as books printed in folio format were "bulky objects," they were intended to "be consulted in one place" (Richardson 1999: 125–8; Walsby 2021: 82). In a scholarly context, they could be reference works or textbooks, as we will see later for a Leuven edition produced for students of the Arts faculty. Editions in quarto and in octavo, which were cheaper and more practical to use, can more readily be identified as textbooks. Manutius described his octavo editions as manuals (*encheiridia*), that is, books that could be carried around in one's hand making these easily transportable (Aldine catalog of 1503, as cited in Richardson 1999: 127). If one considers, for example, editions of Aristotle's *Topica* printed in Latin and Greek in the sixteenth century, these were mostly in quarto or octavo format, while published commentaries of the same work can also be found in folio format. A different example can illustrate similar perspectives: out of about 400 Latin editions of Galen in France in the sixteenth century, 130 were produced in octavo, 115 in sexto-decimo, and 48 in quarto, while the remaining 100 appeared in folio. These numbers corroborate the existence of a large number of editions in small formats, which a physician could also carry with him during office, and a significant number of editions that could be used chiefly as reference works.

Turning to the *mise en page* and the layout of the page itself, some elements of early modern textbooks are distinctive. This has been traditionally the purview of the study of typography, which is the art of arranging type and text into a visually convincing and clear manner. A most obvious feature is the spacing of the text on the page: textbooks were usually printed with wide margins, to allow for note-taking during lessons, and many indeed survive with these annotations. In other cases, such as language learning, textbooks often also featured interlinear spacing, which would allow some room for students to write down notes on vocabulary, such as paraphrases and synonyms, as well as the translation of the text taught.[6] Professors' or editors' commentary or annotations notes were sometimes printed and included on the same page as the main text, in smaller font, either below, on the side, or surrounding the text, in the style of a "frame commentary," often in a typeface of different (smaller) format (Abbamonte 2018: 166). Examples include a Paris edition of Euripides' *Hecuba* (Jean Loys, 1545) and a Paris edition of Aristotle's *Topica* with comments by Augustino Nifo (Chrestien Wechel, 1542).[7] The feature of different texts arranged on the same page also introduces the point of languages, as sometimes the original text may be in one language and the commentary in a different one (for example, Greek for the main text and Latin for the commentary). In any case, all these examples of types of mixed letter sizes laid out on a page indicate a variation in intended use, and perhaps an attempt to aid learning and replace the need for written student notes.

As mentioned above, the physical appearance of printed textbooks evolved since the invention of printing in the middle of the fifteenth century. This was also the case with the gradual change in the layout of textbooks, which became more generous through spacing between paragraphs and lines, even in smaller paper and page sizes. The use of larger font for titles, subtitles in the margins, or the paragraph mark earlier in the sixteenth century were all utilized as mnemonic devices, to increase the visual impact of the printed page and enhance the learning process (Ciccolella 2008: 56–8, 65). Further developments in the scholarly apparatus of a book included the addition of tables, indexes, or diagrams to existing texts; these were considered innovations and contributed to more attractive editions. Examples of this sort are the diagrams that were included in editions of Sacrobosco's *Sphaera* (originally composed in the thirteenth century), or tables in grammar books depicting noun declensions and verb conjugations. From a publisher's or a bookseller's point of view, this was beneficial as newly incorporated textual and visual elements enabled them to sell their books as "new" and therefore also potentially protected by a new privilege. From the point of view of teachers and students, these innovations made textbooks more readable, and the knowledge contained in them more palatable, and thus more accessible.

The materiality and physical appearance of the book also encompass the series of paratexts contained in a book, such as a title page, a possible dedication or prefatory letter, liminary epigrams, additional texts like commentaries, and indices (Genette 1997; Bossuyt et al. 2008; Julhe 2014; Duncan and Smyth 2019; Duncan 2022; Tholen 2021). Lengthy and impressive title pages, which may have included engravings, often listed the names of contributors, editors, or translators and advertised the new elements of the edition ("newly translated", "newly collated", "newly commented" and so on); all these features were clearly aimed at making an impression and persuade the buyers. Taken together, all paratexts deliver information about the development and production of the specific book, the people involved in the process, but also on how the printer and/or publisher intended to market it, and how the printer, publisher and author, intended it to be used and read.

The cheapest version of student textbooks was the one that included merely the main text, without any paratexts whatsoever. As booksellers and editors competed, however, as to who would issue the most successful edition, they introduced some diversity, through different translations, commentaries, notes, or combinations of texts. Thus, establishing the contents of a book and dissecting the works into "text parts" (Valleriani and Ottone 2022: 2), or "information units" (Proot 2015: 47) is important, as editions of the same texts were not necessarily intended for the same purpose. As such, paratexts added to the prestige and marketability of an edition, aspects that were important in a traditional market such as the academic one, which traded in the same textbooks for many subjects for centuries.

The physical appearance of a book can be studied on two levels. Every book is the result of a print run, during which the printer issued numerous copies and therefore it is possible to study general material characteristics on the level of the edition, as the previous paragraphs have explained. However, it is also possible to explore the specificities of one copy of an edition. During a print run, printers often corrected mistakes in the text, which means that the text of not every copy was in fact identical (Fogelmark 2015). As a result, book historians pay attention to copy specificities, as a way, for instance, to study typesetting mistakes made during the printing process and how these were corrected, or to understand the intended audience, as sometimes a copy may display differences in paratextual materials, such as the inclusion or omission of a dedicatory letter.

Additionally, specific copies provide interesting evidence regarding the manner in which a copy was read and used by its owners' marks, be they ownership marks, reading annotations, or indeed student notes, if they were textbooks. Additional information regarding ownership, localization, and use of a book can come from examining a book's binding, another crucial aspect of a book's materiality. A book could be bound either soon after it was bought, or at a later stage—only in rare cases would the bookseller bind it before he sold it. Student texts survive individually bound, in a binding contemporary to the book's production, or bound later, in some cases together with other copies of editions with texts of similar subjects, perhaps after a student had finished his studies as a way of preserving his textbooks. The binding depended on the format of the book (the bigger the size, the bigger the need for a sturdy binding), the intended use, and the financial ability of the owner. As students typically had fewer financial means, we often find textbooks "solid stitched," namely lightly sewn together with thread going through the whole block of sheets; these could then be wrapped in paper, with a limp parchment, with little or no decoration (Pickwoad 1995, 2012, 2020: vol. 1, 111–27; Werner 2019: 71–7). In this way, student books could also be sold as uncovered sewn book blocks before boards and covers were added to them at a later stage. For a book to be later sewn into more solid binding, gatherings were sewn onto supports (normally thongs or cords running vertically) with the thread passing through the centre of the fold and then wrapping around the support (Werner 2019: 74). On such books, we may find more expensive binding materials, such as vellum, or decorative elements (toolwork), such as (gold) stamps. A final aspect that relates to binding is the practice of interleaving. Books used by students often include blank sheets of paper that were bound with the text; this gave space to the student to keep notes, write the translation of the text and so forth. As a result, the binding can provide clues as to the use of the book by the buyer, whether, for example they wanted it to be a valued display copy, or whether they intended it for frequent use. Moreover, different sewing and binding techniques were used or were popular in different parts of Europe and at different points in time. Assessing the binding, therefore, and reflecting upon these points generates important insights about where the book was bound and used (sometimes away from its place of publication), when it was used, how it was used, how it was regarded by its owner, and so forth.

Additional traces, first and foremost provenance marks, and handwritten annotations, can also be crucial in understanding how a book was ultimately used, received, and recycled.[8] The most basic form of a mark a reader would leave on the text would be his or her name. This feature, together with other questions regarding the use of texts, have also given rise to studies on the provenance in rare books, which traces the genealogy of books' owners based on mentions like ex libris ("from the books of") or other notes revealing the owner's identity.[9] In the case of humanistic books, we also find the name of the owner, together with the indication *et amicorum*, a sign that a book was used by the circle of the specific humanist. Identifying provenance can often be a hazardous enterprise, as both manuscript and printed matter frequently changed hands and owners, whether during or just after completing the curriculum, whether by exchange, heritage, sale, auctions, or donations—as a result, we frequently find more than one name noted down in a book.

The importance of annotations is the principle focus of this volume. From a book history point of view, handwritten student or scholars' annotations can help in charting the evolution of editions, as they could be the first step in the production of a new version. A number of surviving copies contain annotations by scholars whose hands have been identified, and who used a printed edition for the preparation of their own one. In other cases, professors read with their students a specific text before (or while) they prepared a new edition for it. Thus, these notes reflect the teaching and processing of a work by a scholar or student who could later be involved in the creation of another edition. Similar observations can be made with regards to functional paratextual material, such as indices or tables of contents. The annotations of lexicographers such as Estienne or Budé, for example, give us a glimpse in the process of compiling their respective dictionaries (Furno 2021). Understanding how early modern students read, understood, and used the printed book is a particularly difficult exercise. Handwritten annotations in printed textbooks offer tangible evidence that manuscript and print never functioned apart, nor as substitutes of each other, but merged into the same multimedial web of learning and knowledge (McKitterick 2003).

As with provenance, it can often be difficult for a researcher to ascertain when handwritten notes were added, and thus to determine whether these are student or reader notes. This becomes even more complicated when notes survive in more than one hand, with no obvious differences in the dating, which could mean either two students using a text successively or even simultaneously, or an educated person acquiring or inheriting and annotating the same book at a later stage. This appropriation of printed matter, whether by annotations or an ex libris, turned the readers or users of the printed book into authors again, endowing different meanings and appendices to existing texts, thus opening up a text for further critical engagements. As Darnton would phrase it, readers turning authors "closed the initial communication circuit," thereby sparking a whole new cycle of creations, appropriations, and audience behaviors.

5. Analyzing printed text editions: Aspects of book history in practice

We want to conclude this chapter by applying some of the above concepts and insights from book history of two different printed versions ("bibliographical units" in book history) of the same text destined for student use. Our two case studies relate to editions of Porphyry's *Isagoge*; this was a text that served as an introduction to Aristotelian thought, the basis of the curriculum in the arts. The first Porphyry edition under consideration here was printed in Leuven in 1509–10, by Dirk Martens (c. 1446–1534); the second stems from Paris and was printed in 1547 by Jean Loys (*fl.* 1535–1547). In addition to discussing two early modern printed textbooks used in university education in Leuven and Paris, we also analyze the role and relationship of students to these editions.

The first example demonstrates the importance of studying the materiality of extant copies and reconstructing the sociality of a book, especially in combination with archival research. Through archival sources, in this case the board decisions of the Leuven Faculty of Arts (the so-called *acta*

Figure 4.1. Title page: Aristotle and Porphyrius, *Isagoge Porphirii Phenicis in Cathegorias Aristotelis*, Antwerp, Dirk Martens, 1509, 20. © Bibliothèque nationale du Luxembourg: L.P. 4165.

facultatis), we learn that, during 1509 and 1510, this educational institution decided to print Porphyry's *Isagoge* and a number of Aristotelian texts (*Categoriae*, *De interpretatione*, *Analytica priora*, *Analytica posteriora*, *Topica*, and *De sophisticis elenchis*).[10] Together, these works constituted the full course on logic that Leuven students followed in the early modern period (Geudens and Masolini 2016). The board of the faculty engaged as printer Dirk Martens, who then ran a print shop in Antwerp. As a result, Martens printed three textbooks on commission or at the faculty's expense, with the faculty thus acting as publisher. The three textbooks were long considered to be lost books, which refers to editions of which no known copies survive (Bruni and Pettegree 2016). Many early modern textbooks fall into this category due to the intensive use they were subjected to. However, during the redaction of this very chapter, a copy of the three Leuven textbooks, bound in a convolute or a *Sammelband*, was identified in the collections of the Bibliothèque nationale du Luxembourg: see Figure 4.1.[11] Through a collective typographical inquiry of book historians and library curators, the edition gave material proof to information in the archival sources.

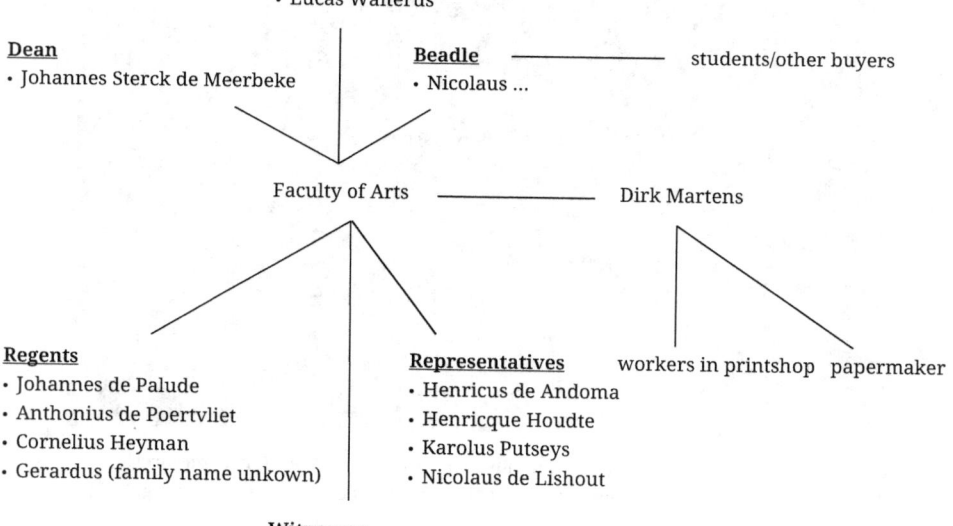

Figure 4.2. "Sociality" behind the production of the 1509 *Isagoge Porphirii*... (based on Cammaerts 2024).

A consultation of this retrieved copy in combination with existing archival sources reveal much about the role of print in teaching practices at the beginning of the sixteenth century. The production of the 1509–10 editions was entrusted to several members of the board of the faculty, both its ordinary professors and its lecturers (cf. Figure 4.2; Dauwe 1972). In total, twelve people decided on the content and physical appearance of the textbooks. The faculty board ordered no less than 1,200 copies, which Martens delivered to the beadle, a secretary to the dean who performed administrative tasks, and who became authorized to sell it to interested parties. This means that members of the faculty acted as the publishers of the print runs, as well as the sellers of the copies. Moreover, the beadle needed to sign the copies, confirming that no contradictory doctrines were present in the textbooks, by way of preventive censorship. Students and lecturers served as consumers, acquiring copies of these editions as reference texts used in public lectures, as well as during personal study in preparation of their exams and disputations.

The same archival sources give insight into the materiality and the intended use of the textbooks, confirmed by a typographical study of the edition. The members of the board of the faculty had three specific requests for Dirk Martens. First, Martens was asked to print the textbooks in folio. Even though this large format seems peculiar for a textbook, as it was not easily transportable, in Leuven students followed the lectures on logic in a pedagogy in which they also resided, meaning they did not have to carry their copies for a long distance. Second, Martens had to use high-quality paper that was easy to write on. Third, the printer was to provide wide margins around the text, allowing students to write in their books. Martens accomplished this in the three editions by means of a type area set to thirty-five lines per page and measuring 190 x 140 mm, with a relatively small interlinear space of only 3 mm (cf. Figure 4.3).

Through the archival sources it becomes clear that all the texts were produced during three separate print runs in 1509 and 1510. A cross-check with the remaining copies shows which texts were combined into one textbook. In 1509, Martens printed the *textus veteris artis* or *logica vetus*, that is, Porphyry's *Isagoge* together with Aristotle's *Categoriae* and *De interpretatione*. In 1510, he printed the *Topica* as well as a textbook that consisted of the *Analytica priora*, *Analytica posteriora* and *De sophisticis elenchis*. The sequence proves that the Faculty of Arts did not produce one textbook containing all the necessary texts for the course on logic.

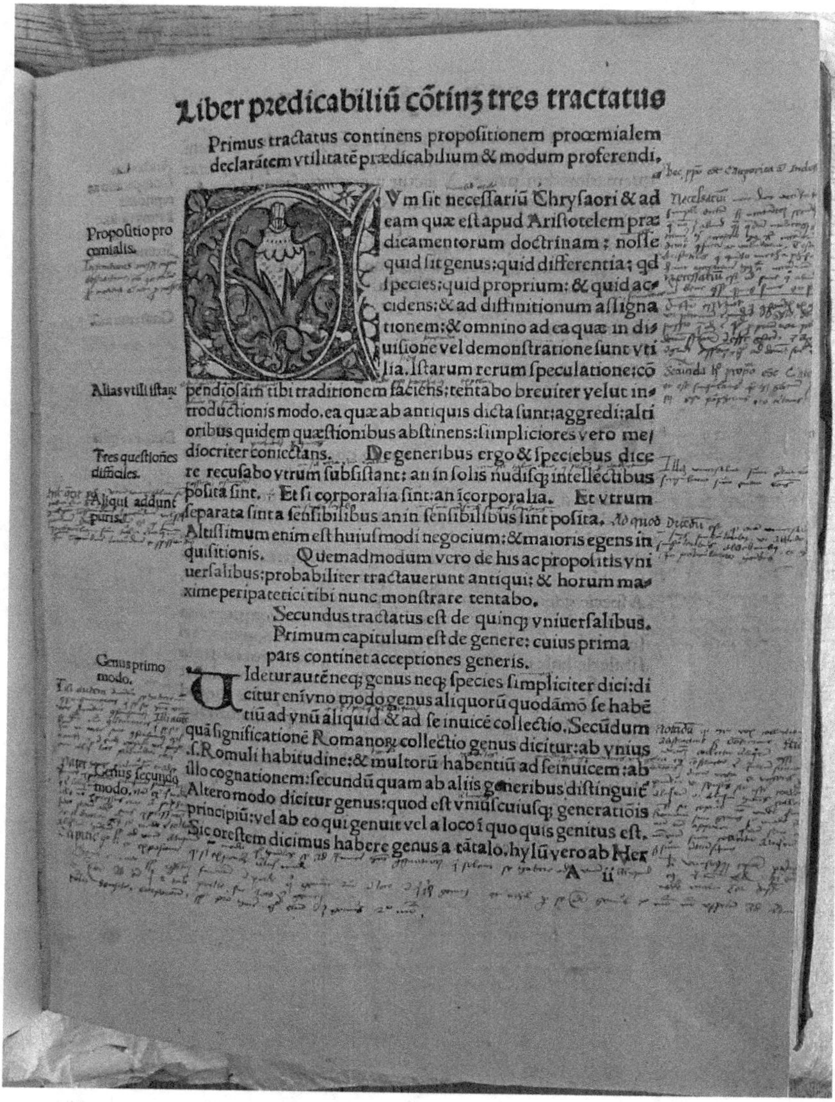

Figure 4.3. Page of Aristotle and Porphyrius, *Isagoge Porphirii Phenicis in Cathegorias Aristotelis*, Antwerp, Dirk Martens, 1509, 20., Aiir © Bibliothèque nationale du Luxembourg: L.P. 4165.

Rather, it offered students the opportunity to acquire all the texts through printed versions of individual text collections, which they then put (or had bound) together themselves, compiling a *Sammelband*, as was indeed the case with the copy in the Bibliothèque nationale du Luxembourg.

Our second example concerns another extant printed artefact, a copy of an edition that carries particularly interesting material features as well as many student annotations. This second examination focuses on a similar Latin edition of Porphyry's *Isagoge*, produced in Paris by Jean Loys in 1547, and today part of a private collection (Figure 4.4).[12] The book was printed in a much smaller format than its Leuven counterpart: in quarto, as was typical for textbooks in the French capital in that period. Similar to the Leuven edition, its layout provided wide margins for note-taking. Moreover, as with the Leuven edition, the physical copy under discussion is today part of a convolute (*Sammelband*), together with some other printed Aristotelian textbooks on logic.

The imprint also gives the potential buyer the address of the printshop: "apud Ioannem Lodoicum Tiletanum, è regione Collegii Remensis" ("at Jean Loys from Tielt, from the area of the College of Reims"). Jean Loys from Tielt in Flanders was a printer who often provided textbooks for the University of Paris as well as for the Collège Royal, the French version of a trilingual college, founded under the auspices of King Francis I in 1530. Even if only the title page of this book would have survived, the name of the printer, the information in the title on the text itself, and the location of the print shop in the vicinity of the Collège de Reims already point to its status as a textbook.

An examination of the binding can help us find out at which point in time these texts were bound together (whether, namely, they were put together in the same volume in the sixteenth century, or much later by those who inherited, purchased, or collected the book). In this case, the binding dates back to the sixteenth century, as evidenced by the volume covers bound in limp parchment, and by the type of sewing of the books and the quires. Despite missing endbands[13] and a back, the binding is quite strong, as it is sewn right through all leaves with double stitching. This strong binding underlines that the owner either held the contents of the volume in high esteem, or knew he was going to use it intensely and thus needed it to keep the volume together, and therefore invested in a more expensive binding. Apart from the 1547 edition of Porphyry, the convolute includes three editions from 1559/60 by Thomas Richard,

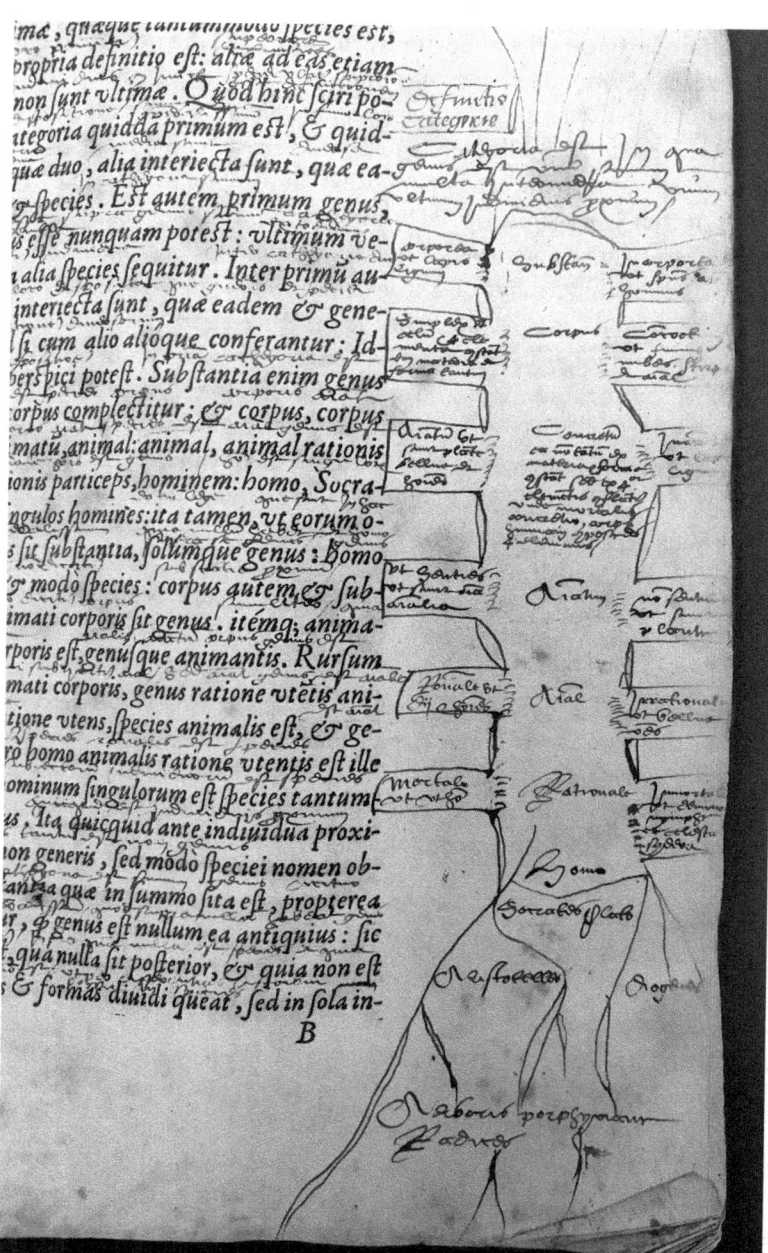

Figure 4.4. Page from Porphyrius, *Communium quinque vocum, sive praedicabilium liber*, in *Aristotelis dialectica eisagoge*, Paris, Jean Loys, 1547. © Malcolm Walsby.

who succeeded Jean Loys at the printshop. After the *Isagoge* we find a 1560 edition of Aristotle's *Categoriae*, followed by the 1560 *Topica*, also by Richard, and then the *Introductio in terminorum cognitionem, in libros logicorum Aristotelis* by Josse (Jacques) Clichtove, also printed in 1560.[14] These editions also indicate the location of the printing shop on the imprint: "sub Bibliis aureis, è regione Remensis" ("under the [sign of] the golden Bibles, from the area of [the college of] Reims").

The convolute contains notes taken by the same hand throughout the different editions, suggesting they were made and bound by the same person. Even with the wide margins provided by the book's layout, some of the texts in the volume are also interleaved to provide more space for additions by the users. The paper in these books is divided into columns. As a result, student notes are contained both in the margins of the printed pages and on the extra leaves. We also encounter various marks and mnemonic devices, such as asterisks and manicules. The annotations, moreover, include a hand-drawn tree of logic. Further research into the watermark(s) of the paper used for the interleaving would give us more clues as to when and where the book was bound.[15] Both the contents of the works, as well as the material evidence of this copy, point to the fact that it was a student book, which was possibly even bound with the other texts during the reader's years as a student, rather than at the end of his studies. This is also corroborated by the fact that some of the interleaving has remained blank, which perhaps could be explained by an incomplete coverage of the text during lectures, or possible absences of the student. Concerning the sociality of this *Sammelband*, several people involved in its production have been mentioned already: the printer Jean Loys; Thomas Richard, the heir to Loys' printshop who possibly also sold the book; and Josse Clichtove as editor of one of the texts. Further research is required to find out the outer circles of the book's social network. Closer dating of the handwritten notes, the binding, and the paper used may help us identify the lessons that this student attended.

In sum, the two examples examined here serve as illustrations of the significance of the material book as a cultural artefact and the insights the material book can provide into early modern intellectual, social, and economic life, especially that of the students and their circles.

6. Conclusions

Throughout their prolonged—but often interrupted—time of study in one or more of the many university cities in early modern Europe and beyond, students participated in the book trade in various capacities, yet most regularly as buyers and consumers, readers and manual annotators of printed books. Most generally, students only attended the bookshop of a publishing house, which was to be found on the entrance, separated from the actual printing presses located in the print shop. In the bookshop, they would purchase or even exchange books, based on the printer's catalog, the demands of their chosen curriculum, or their own bibliophile tastes and collector's interests. Taking books to their colleges, residences, and homes, they would use them as textbooks or as library objects to self-fashion themselves as learned, seeking intellectual and social promotion in society with a university matriculation. In the concluding phases of their study, then, students would often need to work with printers(-publishers) to have their dissertation sheets printed and publicly posted for defense. In that phase, university officials and administrators would proceed to production on their press in the university building. Only a smaller section of the student population became tangibly involved in the process of printing and publishing books, as a means of financing their studies or as a first engagement with scholarly life. In these roles of correctors, assistants, or compilers, they accessed the work floor of the publishing house, where typographers, (manual) printers, and other collaborators got "inky fingers" (cf. Grafton 2020). Understanding and appreciating the multiple roles of students, therefore, and their multifaceted connection with the world of books is essential in trying to approach and analyze handwritten student notes or annotations to printed books. To this end, we have demonstrated among early modern students the role of books as cultural artefacts, which cannot be understood without taking into consideration the complex background of their production, circulation, and eager consumption.

Notes

1. Although book history is gradually encompassing manuscript studies and codicology as well, the scope assumed here limits itself to items produced by handpress printing. On codicology, see Chapter 3.
2. For a concise overview of the historiography, see Walsby (2020b: 9–14).
3. See Part I, Chapter 1 for examples.
4. Adriaan of Utrecht, *Quaestiones quotlibeticae* (Leuven, 1515) [USTC 400344], following the interpretation of Reusens (1862). A so-called *oratio quodlibetica* is a rhetorical exercise recited in public.
5. https://manual.stcv.be/p/List_of_Bibliographical_Formats, accessed 29 February 2024.
6. For example, Reverdin (1984); Letrouit (1999); Suzeau (2001); Compère (2004); Compère, Couzinet, and Pédeflous (2009).
7. Euripides, Ἑκάβη. *Euripidis Ecuba*. Μετὰ σχολίων ἀξιολογωτάτων (Paris: Jean Loys, 1545) (USTC 206707); Euripides, Μήδεια, μετὰ σχολίων ἀξιολογωτάτων. *Euripidis Medea, cum scholiis eruditissimis* (Paris: Jean Loys, 1545) (USTC 160187); Agostino Nifo, *Commentaria in octo libros Topicorum Aristotelis* (Paris: apud Oudin Petit, 1542) (USTC 195167); joint edition with two other printers: Ambroise Girault (USTC 206141) and Pierre Regnault (USTC 206142).
8. Cf. Chapter 2 on the relationship of annotations to printed text.
9. Pearson (2019). On the importance of tracing the origin of a corpus of student notes, see Chapter 2.
10. Leuven, State Archives, *Old University of Leuven*, nr. 712: fol. 277r, 292r, 298rv, 299rv, 1509–10.
11. Cammaerts (2024); Walsby (2024). Aristotle and Porphyry, *Isagoge Porphirii Phenicis in Cathegorias Aristotelis*, Antwerp, Dirk Martens, 1509–10, 20 (BNL: L.P. 4165). Convolute and *Sammelband* are terms referring to copies of different editions bound together: see the Multilingual Glossary at the end of this research companion.
12. Porphyrius, *Communium quinque vocum, sive praedicabilium liber, in Aristotelis dialectica eisagoge*, Paris, Jean Loys, 1547. 40 (USTC 195945). The authors wish to thank the owner of this book, Malcolm Walsby, for his kind permission to discuss the volume and to publish the images.
13. Components that are found at the head and tail of the spine of a bookblock, which are either sewn with thread or thongs to the head and/or tail edges of the spine of a bookblock (sewn endbands) or attached by adhesive only (stuck-on endbands); source: LB (Language of Binding), ligatus.org.uk, http://w3id.org/lob/concept/2370. Last accessed on January 21, 2025.
14. Aristotle, *Categoriae* (Paris: Thomas Richard, 1560) (USTC 138993); Aristotle, *Topicorum libri VIII* (Paris: Thomas Richard, 1560) (no USTC reference); Josse Chlichtove, *Introductio in terminorum cognitionem, in libros logicorum Aristotelis* (Paris: Thomas Richard, 1560) (USTC 152843).
15. Cf. Chapter 3 on codicology, and watermarks, in particular.

Thematic bibliography

This thematic bibliography includes suggestions for further reading.

General overviews on the history of the book

Grafton, Anthony. 2020. *Inky Fingers: The Making of Books in Early Modern Europe*. Cambridge, MA: Harvard University Press.
Levy, Michelle, and Tom Mole. 2017. *The Broadview Introduction to Book History*. Peterborough: Broadview Press.
Pettegree, Andrew. 2010. *The Book in the Renaissance*. New Haven–London: Yale University Press.
Raven, James. 2018. *What is the History of the Book*. Cambridge, UK–Medford, MA: Polity Press.
Walsby, Malcolm. 2020a. *L'imprimé en Europe occidentale, 1470–1680*. Rennes: Presses Universitaires.

The study of printed/rare books

Bellingradt, Daniel, and Jeroen Salman, eds. 2017. *Books in Motion in Early Modern Europe: Beyond Production, Circulation and Consumption*. Cham: Palgrave Macmillan.
Bowers Fredson. 1949. *Principles of Bibliographical Description*. Princeton: Princeton University Press.
Darnton, Robert. 1982. "What is the History of Books?" *Daedalus* 111: 65–83.
Gaskell, Philipp. 1995. *A New Introduction to Bibliography*. 3rd edn. New Castle, DE: Oak Knoll Press.
Glossary of Early Modern Print. <https://popular-print-glossary.sites.uu.nl/>. Last accessed February 29, 2024.
Harris, Neil. 2004. Analytical Bibliography: An Alternative Prospectus. http://ihl.enssib.fr/analytical-bibliography-an-alternative-prospectus/introduction. Last accessed July 12, 2023.
McKenzie, Donald. 1985. *Bibliography and the Sociology of Texts*. London: British Library.
Pearson, David. 2019. *Provenance Research in Book History: A Handbook*. 2nd edn. Oxford–New Castle, DE: The Bodleian Library and Oak Knoll Press.
Tanselle, Thomas G. 2009. *Bibliographical Analysis: A Historical Introduction*. Cambridge: Cambridge University Press.
Wagner, Bettina, and Marcia Reed, eds. 2010. *Early Printed Books as Material Objects: Proceedings of the Conference Organized by the IFLA Rare Books and Manuscripts Section Munich, 19–21 August 2009*. Berlin–Boston: De Gruyter.
Werner, Sarah. 2019. *Studying Early Printed Books 1450–1800: A Practical Guide*. Hoboken: Wiley.

Impact of the printing press

Eisenstein, Elizabeth. 1979. *The Printing Press as an Agent of Change: Communications and Cultural Transformations in Early Modern Europe*. Cambridge: Cambridge University Press.
Eisenstein, Elizabeth. 1993. *The Printing Revolution in Early Modern Europe*. Cambridge: Cambridge University Press.
Febvre, Lucien, and Henri-Jean Martin. 1976. *The Coming of the Book: The Impact of Printing 1450–1800*. London: N.L.B.

Johns, Adrian. 1998. *The Nature of the Book: Print and Knowledge in the Making.* Chicago–London: The University of Chicago Press.

McLuhan, Marshall. 1962. *The Gutenberg Galaxy: The Making of Typographic Man.* Toronto: University of Toronto Press.

Book privileges

Armstrong, Elizabeth. 1990. *Before Copyright: The French Book-Privilege System 1498–1526.* Cambridge: Cambridge University Press.

Publications associated with the "Early Modern Book Project: An Evidence-Based Reconstruction of the Economic and Juridical Framework of the European Book Market" led by Angela Nuovo (accessible at https://emobooktrade.unimi.it/. Last accessed January 21, 2025).

Witcombe, Christopher L.C.E. 2004. *Copyright in the Renaissance: Prints and the Privilegio in Sixteenth-century Venice and Rome.* Leiden–Boston: Brill.

Book binding

LB, Language of Binding. <www.ligatus.org.uk>. Last accessed February 29, 2024.

Pickwoad, Nicholas. 1995. "The Interpretation of Bookbinding Structure: An Examination of Sixteenth-Century Bindings in the Ramey Collection in the Pierpont Morgan Library." *The Library* 6: 209–49.

Pickwoad, Nicholas. 2012. "An Unused Resource: Bringing the Study of Bookbindings out of the Ghetto." In *Ambassadors of the Book: Competences and Training for Heritage Librarians*, edited by Raphaële Mouren, 83–94. Berlin–Boston: De Gruyter.

Pickwoad, Nicholas. 2020. "Bookbinding." In *A Companion to the History of the Book*, edited by Simon Eliot and Jonathan Rose, 2 vols, 111–27. Hoboken–Chichester: Wiley-Blackwell.

Book censorship

Adam, Renaud. 2020. *Le théâtre de la censure (XVIe et XXIe siècles): De l'ère typographique à l'ère numérique.* Bruxelles: Académie Royale de Belgique.

De Bujanda, Jesus Martinez, ed. 1986. *Index de l'Université de Louvain: 1546, 1550, 1558.* Sherbrooke–Genève: Éditions de l'Université de Sherbrooke—Droz.

De Bujanda, Jesus Martinez, ed. 1991. *Index de Rome: 1557, 1559, 1564.* Sherbrooke: Université de Sherbrooke, Centre d'études de la Renaissance.

De Bujanda, Jesus Martinez, ed. 2002. *Index des Livres Interdits, Index Librorum Prohibitorum 1600-1966.* Sherbrooke–Montréal–Geneva: Éditions de l'Université de Sherbrooke–Médiaspaul–Droz.

De Bujanda, Jesus Martinez, Francis M. Higman, and James K. Farge, eds. 1985. *Index de l'Université de Paris 1544, 1545, 1547, 1549, 1551, 1556.* Sherbrooke, Québec: Éditions de l'Université de Sherbrooke.

Fragnito, Gigliola, ed. 2001. *Church, Censorship and Culture in Early Modern Italy.* Translated by Adrian Belton. Cambridge: Cambridge University Press.

Grendler, Paul F. 1977. *The Roman Inquisition and the Venetian Press, 1540–1605.* Princeton: Princeton University Press.

Higman, Francis M. *Censorship and the Sorbonne: A Bibliographical Study of Books in French Censured by the Faculty of Theology of the University of Paris, 1520–1551*. Geneva: Droz.

Soen, Violet, Dries Vanysacker, and Wim François, eds. 2017. *Church, Censorship and Reform in the Early Modern Habsburg Netherlands*. Turnhout: Brepols.

Other

Abbamonte, Giancarlo. 2018. "La terra di mezzo del commentario umanistico ai testi classici." *Annali dell'Istituto Universitario Orientale di Napoli* 40: 156–96.

Adam, Renaud. 2017. "The Profession of Printer in the Southern Netherlands before the Reformation. Considerations on Professional, Religious and State Legislations (1473–1520)." In *Church, Censorship and Reform in the Early Modern Habsburg Netherlands*, edited by Violet Soen, Dries Vanysacker, and Wim François, 13–25. Turnhout: Brepols.

Ashworth, Jennifer E. 1988. "Changes in Logic Textbooks from 1500 to 1650: The New Aristotelianism." In *Aristotelismus und Renaissance*, edited by Eckhard Kefler, Charles H. Lohr, and Walter Sparn, 75–87. Wiesbaden: Otto Harrassowitz.

Bénévent, Christine, Anne Charon, Isabelle Diu, and Magali Vène, eds. 2012. *Passeurs de textes: Imprimeurs et libraires à l'âge de l'humanisme*. Paris: Publications de l'École nationale des chartes.

Blair, Ann. 2010. *Too Much to Know: Managing Scholarly Information before the Modern Age*. New Haven: Yale University Press.

Blair, Ann. 2021. *L'entour du texte: La publication du livre savant à la Renaissance*. Paris: BnF éditions.

Blayney, Peter W.M. 2013. *The Stationer's Company and the Printers of London, 1501–1557*. Cambridge: Cambridge University Press.

Bossuyt, Ignace, Nele Gabriëls, Dirk Sacré, and Demmy Verbeke, eds. 2008. Cui dono lepidum novum libellum? *Dedicating Latin Works and Motets in the Sixteenth Century. Proceedings of the International Conference Held at the Academia Belgica, Rome, 18–20 August 2005*. Leuven: Leuven University Press.

Bruni, Flavia, and Andrew Pettegree, eds. 2016. *Lost Books: Reconstructing the Print World of Pre-Industrial Europe*. Leiden: Brill.

Cammaerts, Dieter. 2024. "*Manuale Lovaniense*: Een sociaaleconomische en typografische studie van het gedrukte academische handboek in de vroegmoderne Leuvense universiteit (1474–1650)." Unpublished PhD dissertation, Leuven: KU Leuven.

Ciccolella, Federica. 2008. *Donati Graeci: Learning Greek in the Renaissance*. Leiden: Brill.

Compère, Marie-Madeleine. 2004. "Les 'feuilles classiques': Un support pour la prélection des textes latins et grecs (XVIe–XVIIe siècles)." In *Le Cours magistral: Modalités et usages (XVIe–XXe siècles)*. www.inrp.fr/she/cours_magistral/index.htm. Last accessed June 1, 2023.

Compère, Marie-Madeleine, Marie-Dominique Couzinet, and Olivier Pédeflous. 2009. "Éléments pour l'histoire d'un genre éditorial." *Histoire de l'éducation*, 124. https://doi.org/10.4000/histoire-education.2060. Last accessed June 1, 2023.

Constantinidou, Natasha. 2015. "Printers of the Greek Classics in the 16th Century and Market Distribution: The Case of France and the Low Countries." In *Specialist Markets in Early Modern Europe*, edited by Richard Kirwan and Sophie Mullins, 275–93. Leiden–Boston: Brill.

Constantinidou, Natasha. 2018. "Constructions of Hellenism through Editorial and Teaching Choices: The Case of Adrien de Turnèbe (1512–65)." *International Journal for the Classical Tradition* 25: 262–84.

Constantinidou, Natasha. 2022. "Chrestien Wechel (c. 1495–1554) and Greek Printing in Paris: Education, Networks and Questions of Orthodoxy." In *Trilingual Learning: The Study of Greek and Hebrew in a Latin World (1000–1700)*, edited by Raf Van Rooy, Pierre Van Hecke, and Toon Van Hal, 137–78. Turnhout: Brepols.

Dauwe, Jozef. 1974. "Een kontrakt tussen Dirk Martens en de Leuvense Artesfakulteit in 1509." *Het land van Aalst* 26 (6): 355–7.

Duncan, Denis. 2022. *Index, A History of the: A Bookish Adventure from Medieval Manuscripts to the Digital Age*. New York: W. W. Norton & Company.

Duncan, Denis, and Adam Smyth, eds. 2019. *Book Parts*. Oxford: Oxford University Press.

Fantoli, Margherita, and Violet Soen. Forthcoming. "Computing Women's Centrality in an Academic Book World: Widow-Printers Spanish Habsburg University Town of Douai (1559–1659)." In *Digital Approaches to Historical Women's Book Culture*, edited by Alicia Montoya and Lieke van Deinsen. Leiden–Boston: Brill.

Feys, Xander. 2024. "Language and Literature Teaching in the Sixteenth Century: Vergil and Homer at the Leuven Collegium Trilingue." Unpublished PhD dissertation, Leuven: KU Leuven.

Fogelmark, Staffan. 2015. *The Kallierges Pindar: A Study in Renaissance Greek Scholarship and Printing*. 2 vols. Köln: Jürgen Dinter.

Furno, Martine. 2021. "Robert et Henri Estienne, lexicographes, lecteurs de Budé, lexicographe." In *Les Noces de Philologie et de Guillaume Budé: Un humaniste et son œuvre à la Renaissance*, edited by Christine Bénévent, Luigi-Alberto Sanchi, and Romain Menini, 469–84. Paris: École nationale des chartes.

Genette, Gérard. 1997. *Paratexts: Thresholds of Interpretation*. Translated by Jane E. Lewin. Cambridge: Cambridge University Press. [Original French edition from 1987, entitled *Seuils*.]

Geudens, Christophe and Serena Masolini. 2016. "Teaching Aristotle at the Louvain Faculty of Arts, 1425–1500: General Regulations and Handwritten Testimonies." *Rivista di Filosofia Neoscolastica* 108 (4): 813–44.

Hoftijzer, Paul G. 1990–1. "De 'belabbering' van het boekbedrijf: De Leidse Officina Raphelengia, 1586-1619." *De Boekenwereld* 7: 8–19.

Jimenes, Rémi. 2018. *Charlotte Guillard: Une femme imprimeur à la Renaissance*. Tours: Presses universitaires François-Rabelais.

Julhe, Jean-Claude, ed. 2014. *Pratiques latines de la dédicace: Permanence et mutations, de l'Antiquité à la Renaissance*. Paris: Classiques Garnier.

Kirwan, Richard and Sophie Mullins, eds. 2015. *Specialist Markets in Early Modern Europe*. Leiden–Boston: Brill.

Letrouit, Jean. 1999. "La prise de notes de cours dans les collèges parisiens au XVIe siècle." *Revue de la Bibliothèque nationale de France* 2: 47–56.

Maclean, Ian. 2009. *Learning in the Marketplace: Essays in the History of Early Modern Books*. Leiden–Boston: Brill.

Maclean, Ian. 2021. *Episodes in the Life of the Early Modern Learned Book*. Leiden–Boston: Brill.

McKitterick, David. 2003. *Print, Manuscript and the Search for Order, 1450–1830*. Cambridge: Cambridge University Press.

Oosterhoff, Richard J. 2018. *Making Mathematical Culture: University and Print in the Circle of Lefèvre d'Étaples*. Oxford: Oxford University Press.

Oosterhoff, Richard J. 2022. "Printerly Ingenuity and Mathematical Books in the Early Estienne Workshop." In *Publishing Sacrobosco's* De Sphaera *in Early Modern Europe: Modes of Material and Scientific Exchange*, edited by Matteo Valleriani and Andrea Ottone, 25–59. Cham: Springer.

Pettegree, Andrew, ed. 2017. *Broadsheets: Single-Sheet Publishing in the First Age of Print*. Leiden–Boston: Brill.

Proot, Goran. 2015. "Mending the Broken Word: Typographic Discontinuity on Title-pages of Early Modern Books Printed in the Southern Netherlands (1501–1700)." *Jaarboek voor Nederlandse Boekgeschiedenis* 22: 45–59.

Reusens, E.H., ed. 1862. *Syntagma theologiae Adriani Sexti, Pont. Max.* Leuven: Vanlinthout.

Reverdin, Olivier. 1984. *Les premiers cours de grec au Collège de France ou l'enseignement de Pierre Danès d'après un document inédit*. Paris: Presses Universitaires de France.

Richardson, Brian. 1999. *Printing, Writers, and Readers in Renaissance Italy*. Cambridge: Cambridge University Press.

Soetaert, Alexander. 2019. *De katholieke drukpers in de kerkprovincie Kamerijk: Contacten, mobiliteit & transfers in een grensgebied (1559–1659)*. Leuven–Parijs–Bristol: Peeters.

Suzeau, Isabelle. 2001. "Le cahier d'écolier de Beatus Rhenanus: L'étude de Virgile (Sélestat, 1499)." In *Beatus Rhenanus (1485–1547), lecteur et éditeur des textes anciens: Actes du colloque international tenu au Strasbourg et au Sélestat, 13–15 nov. 1998*, edited by James Hirstein, 21–32. Turnhout: Brepols.

Tholen, John. 2021. *Producing Ovid's "Metamorphoses" in the Early Modern Low Countries: Paratexts, Publishers, Editors, Readers*. Leiden–Boston: Brill.

Valleriani, Matteo and Andrea Ottone, eds. 2022. *Publishing Sacrobosco's* De sphaera *in Early Modern Europe: Modes of Material and Scientific Exchange*. Cham: Springer.

Vanautgaerden, Alexandre. 2012. *Érasme typographe: Humanisme et imprimerie au début du XVIe siècle*. Genève: Droz.

Walsby, Malcolm. 2020b. "Les étapes du développement du marché du livre imprimé en France du XVe au début du XVIIe siècle." *Revue d'histoire moderne & contemporaine* 67: 5–29.

Walsby, Malcolm. 2021. "Le format et le livre imprimé aux xve, xvie et xviie siècles. " In *Le monde de l'imprimé en Europe occidentale (vers 1470–vers 1680)*, edited by Joëlle Alazard, Céline Borello, Camille Desenclos, and Fabien Salesse, 77–91. Levallois-Perret: Bréal by Studyrama.

Walsby, Malcolm. 2024. "The Book and the Text: Defining the *Sammelband*." In *Perdite e sopravvivenze del libro antico: Il ruolo delle miscellanee*, edited by Amandine Bonesso, 17–37. Udine: Forum.

Watson, Elise, Nora Epstein, and Jessica Farrel-Jobst, eds. 2025. *Gender and the Book Trades*. Leiden–Boston: Brill.

Wyffels, Heleen. 2021. "Women and Work in Early Modern Printing Houses: Family Firms in Antwerp, Douai, and Leuven, 1500–1700." Unpublished PhD dissertation, Leuven: KU Leuven.

CHAPTER 5

How to Make Student Notes Accessible

Raf Van Rooy

1. Introduction

There are several good reasons for wishing to publish your source materials or at least make them accessible in some form. Making your transcription available would be good practice in an increasingly data-oriented humanities landscape that moreover puts great emphasis on reusability of data. It may be emphasized here that systematically disclosing transcriptions of student notes would counterweigh the focus there has been on authoritative voices in early modern education, especially those of humanists and professors (for example, Poliziano 2019; Polet 1936 for Petrus Nannius; Weaver 2022 for Melanchthon). Student notes, however, perhaps because of their often fragmentary and referential nature, have often been studied merely eclectically.[1] Scholars have tended to cite bits and pieces of their source without presenting a full or partial transcription that many of them make during their research (for example, Ellis 2020 among many other examples). This eclecticism is understandable in a research ecosystem where publications of papers are more highly valued than making your data findable, accessible, interoperable, and reusable—FAIR, in short—although this seems to be slowly changing. The present chapter offers general insights on how one may go about providing a transcription. Concomitantly, this chapter encourages the researcher to publish their data, in order to make their conclusions falsifiable and to increase the source basis for student notes research, enabling larger-scale investigations of this type of materials. Ideally, you would make a full transcription accessible, but this will often not be feasible in the frame of a research project that is bound to time constraints.

2. Choose wisely from the start

In view of making your source texts available, it is advisable to make some initial choices before transcribing that ensure you have a text that can be reused relatively easily by fellow scholars. This means first and foremost that you make the sources' transcription available digitally, as a txt or xml-file or another widely used and flexible format (csv, for instance).[2] If you are not in a position to make a transcription of your text, it is crucial to at least have a digital reproduction of the source and ideally make it available online for your colleagues to use and reuse. In what follows, I focus on questions of transcription and edition.

2.1. Diplomatic and semi-diplomatic transcription

For student notes, it is advisable to transcribe the text as much as possible as it is, conveying in detail the state of the text in the source. Standardizing texts would mean a loss of information about the students' learning processes and the errors they made. The faithful replication of the text is also known as diplomatic transcription or, if you expand abbreviations and do not mark line breaks, semi-diplomatic transcription, the latter being the principle followed in DaLeT: Database of the Leuven Trilingue (see Figure 5.1, where the abbreviations are expanded between square brackets).[3] A better, though much more time-consuming option than a (semi-)diplomatic transcription would be a transcription in XML following TEI principles, which allows you to record everything as it is found in the source text (that is, fully diplomatically), together with the intended forms, that is, in a standardized orthography.

2.2. XML

XML means Extensible Markup Language and allows the transcriber to encode a long list of features of a text. These features have been internationally standardized following the Text Encoding Initiative (TEI).[4] This labor-intensive option has the advantage that you can encode non-textual materials better and that you can register more variants of a text in a systematic way, for instance a (semi-)diplomatic rendering alongside a standardized version. Creating such a double text version increases search and visualization options and makes study and reuse more efficient for

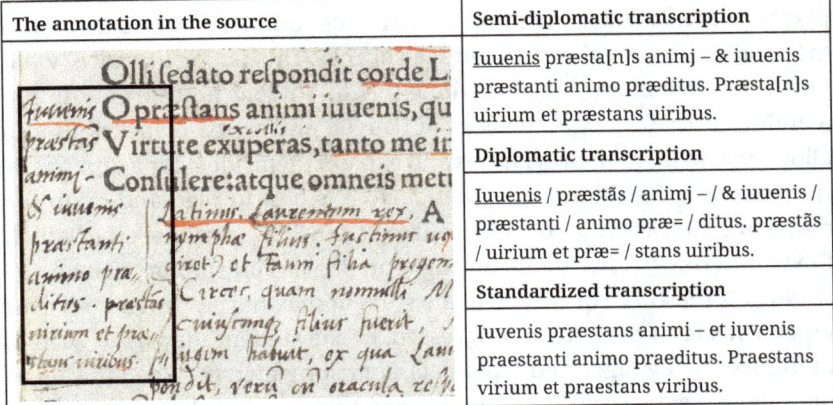

Figure 5.1. Source and transcription modes. DaLeT Annotation ID 1748.

other scholars than a simple (semi-)diplomatic edition. Many tools (free or not) are available for XML encoding, like the Oxygen XML Editor, or allow XML exports, like the transcription tool Transkribus.[5] Making an XML/TEI version of your student notes is, however, often unfeasible within the framework of a single project, especially since expertise typically needs to be acquired or hired, and since student notes typically show many non-standard forms.[6] What is more, funders are often reluctant to finance projects that solely want to make sources available, as they typically want a valorization of the newly generated data as well.

2.3. The act of transcribing: Benefits and tools

Which of the available transcription formats you choose may depend also on the nature and length of a source. For a linear text, XML may seem less daunting than in cases where students have annotated printed books and relationships between textual elements are complex (see Chapter 2). Whether you choose one option or the other, the very act of making a transcription itself can be rewarding also for interpreting a source. Transcribing requires you to read more slowly and triggers you to read and reread a passage, a fact that can lead to insights that would otherwise not be reached (see Van Rooy et al. 2023a for this argument).

Alternatively, instead of transcribing from scratch, you might train a transcription model for your source, for instance through the user-friendly platform Transkribus, based on a portion of your transcription, and use the model to transcribe your entire source.[7] This is, for instance, what Jarrik Van Der Biest (2024) has done for his student notes from the sixteenth-century faculty of theology at Leuven university. Transkribus also allows you to mark abbreviations and expand them, ideal for a diplomatic transcription. To attain a gold standard, it is best to read and clean the automatic transcription of your source as much as possible, especially if the handwriting is not stable throughout. The lack of stability can be due to various reasons. For instance, the student may have written with ever greater haste as the course progressed, or the student may have written in different languages and alphabets, some of which they had mastered only imperfectly, resulting in odd-shaped letters that the AI model has difficulty recognizing. But even if a student had a good command of various alphabets, their combination often confuses transcription software, giving a further reason why human inspection and correction remains of paramount importance, although models are getting increasingly better at recognizing different languages and alphabets. Other AI-driven transcription software that may be useful for tackling your sources are eScriptorium, focused on manuscripts and hence ideal for student notes, and Rescribe, useful in the first place for early modern prints.[8]

2.4. *Good practices*

Relatively few examples of good practices are available. We single out a number of source bodies that may provide inspiration for other student notes researchers, although we realize that they require greater investment in digital assistance than humanities projects typically can afford. A crucial first step is, whatever the nature of your text, to have a digital reproduction of the source, not only because this is less labor-intensive than providing accurate transcriptions, but also because it is useful to give easy access to the images for scholars wanting to check the accuracy of transcriptions provided. A pioneering project in this regard is *Magister Dixit*, a database started in the early 2010s and currently hosting metadata and images of 570 manuscripts with student notes—typically dictates—from the old university of Leuven.[9] The next step of this project is to develop a Handwritten Text Recognition (HTR) model for these sources, automatically transcribe them, and correct them as much as possible, making them available following FAIR-principles, that is, making the data findable, accessible, interoperable, and reusable on sustainable open access platforms.[10] For a substantial corpus of running texts, like the one in *Magister Dixit*, this modus operandi makes a lot of sense. If you aim to disclose one delimited corpus of student notes, a disclosure in print is moreover a possibility, ideally publishing the data openly in digital form as well. For instance, Maleux (2023: 313–30) offers a semi-diplomatic transcription of an ensemble of two dictates from sixteenth-century Hebrew classes from Leuven.

If the student notes take the form of annotations on a text, it will be much harder to make the source corpus accessible in a transparent and meaningful way. In recent years, researchers have had the good reflex to think about digital solutions that can help them in editing notes of this kind. An early attempt by Miriam Bräuer, who worked on no less than sixteen parallel sets of student notes from two installments of the same lecture, is recorded by Leonhardt (2017), although the platform mentioned in the paper seems to be no longer online, if it ever was. Leonhardt (2017: 204) is in any case right in stating that a digital presentation "renders the relationship between 'text' and 'annotation' legible as well as rendering possible the comparative reading of various individual notations." A second endeavor of note is the platform *Annotated Books Online* (*ABO*), which is identified on its website as a "digital archive of early modern annotated books."[11] The platform is broader than student notes alone and is conceived as a collaborative tool where people can contribute transcriptions of notes in printed books. This "virtual research environment for scholars and students interested in historical reading practices" currently holds images of 110 copies, a share of which is accompanied by standardized transcriptions of the notes.[12] These transcriptions are linked to markings (in various colors) on the digital image representing the original source. After creating an account, scholars can add their own transcriptions and English translations of the notes, or correct those of others.

Third, DaLeT, Database of the Leuven Trilingue, offers a gateway to, among other things, semi-diplomatic editions of student notes in printed copies of sixteenth-century editions.[13] Along with the editions, DaLeT offers digitized images of the sources and metadata regarding individual annotations. This editing method allows for a detailed typology of the notes (see the results in Maleux 2023; Feys 2024), but is also rather labor-intensive and necessarily requires a certain amount of funding. Hence, it is not freely available like *ABO*, although all data have been made accessible online and can be reused.[14] The notes are edited using relational database software (FileMaker), converted to a website using MySQL. The edition of the notes starts from the reference text: every note is linked to the printed text portion it has bearing on, if any. This approach means that DaLeT offers semi-diplomatic transcriptions of both the printed text and the handwritten notes. For the handwritten notes, an English translation is offered, in addition to metadata regarding each individual note, including its position on the page (interlinear, marginal, linear, interleaved, stray) and its contents (variable for each source, for example: translation, synonym, paraphrase, grammatical note, narrative clarification, etymological explanation). The digital presentation allows the researcher to consult the notes and their metadata by hovering over passages in the printed text that are rendered in bold, which indicates that they carry an annotation.[15]

3. Conclusion

In short, there are various ways of dealing with student notes as data. Ideally, the scholarly community moves from conducting case studies based on an eclectic reading of the sources to a more systematized approach, offering full-blown or partial transcriptions of the data in order to make scholarly conclusions falsifiable. This ideal approach typically requires a team effort. If full or partial transcription turns out to be impossible, research would benefit from generous sharing of digital reproductions among scholars, an endeavor that requires the involvement and cooperation of the GLAM institutions holding student notes.

The best approach to make student notes available as data depends on their nature. In the case of largely linear texts, transcriptions can be straightforwardly made available as a running text, ideally with some kind of mark-up (XML/TEI). If student notes take the form of annotations accompanying a reference text, the relational nature of this type of source requires a more complex and dynamic form of editing, for instance through a database and resulting website. In both cases, it may be stressed that open access availability of student notes is of crucial importance, as much as possible following the FAIR-principles and offering a transparent assessment of the provenance of the student notes as part of the source's metadata.

Notes

1. A rare exception is the student notebook disclosed and discussed in Margolin, Pendergrass, and Van der Poel (1991). Also interesting is the recent study of Núñez González and Fuente Cornejo (2023), who have studied preparatory notes by the sixteenth-century professor Pedro Juan Núñez and compared them with those of his students.
2. On digital editing, see, for example, Driscoll and Pierazzo (2016).
3. dalet.be, accessed April 30, 2024.
4. tei-c.org/, accessed February 5, 2024.
5. oxygenxml.com/, accessed February 5, 2024. On Transkribus, see Section 2.3.
6. To our knowledge, no substantial amounts of student notes have been made available in XML format at the date of publication of this research companion.
7. transkribus.eu. Last accessed April 30, 2024. Cf. Chapter 2.
8. sofer.info; rescribe.xyz, both last accessed April 30, 2024. See also Chapter 2, Section 3.
9. kuleuven.be/lectio/magisterdixit/solr-search. Last accessed April 30, 2024.
10. FAIR disclosure of the 570 student notes is an important goal of the STUDIUM.AI research infrastructure, which more generally aims to release a database of the old university of Leuven, funded by the Research Foundation—Flanders (Dutch: Fonds voor Wetenschappelijk Onderzoek—Vlaanderen [FWO]).
11. annotatedbooksonline.com. Last accessed April 30, 2024. The project is led by Arnoud Visser (Utrecht University).
12. Ibid.
13. dalet.be. Last accessed April 30, 2024. See Van Rooy et al. (2023a) for details.
14. Van Rooy et al. (2023b).
15. See, for example, notes from Petrus Nannius' Latin classes at the Trilingue, which can be consulted through dalet.be/bookpage/47. Last accessed April 30, 2024. Clicking on a passage in bold pins the note and its metadata on the right-hand side of the screen. There is also an option to compare different notes in one and the same copy.

References

Driscoll, Matthew James, and Elena Pierazzo, eds. 2016. *Digital Scholarly Editing: Theories and Practices*. Cambridge: Open Book Publishers.

Ellis, Anthony. 2020. "Greek History in the Early-Modern Classroom: Lectures on Herodotus by Johannes Rosa and School Notes by Jacques Bongars (Jena, 1568)." In *Receptions of Hellenism in Early Modern Europe: 15th–17th Centuries*, edited by Natasha Constantinidou and Han Lamers, 113–40. Leiden–Boston: Brill.

Feys, Xander. 2024. "Language and Literature Teaching in the Sixteenth Century: Vergil and Homer at the Leuven Collegium Trilingue." Unpublished PhD dissertation, Leuven: KU Leuven.

Leonhardt, Jürgen. 2017. "Annotation between Formation and Information." *International Journal of Humanities and Arts Computing* 11 (2): 199–211.

Maleux, Maxime. 2023. "The Teaching of the Old Testament Revolutionized? The Sixteenth-Century Low Countries and the First Institutionalized Hebrew Curriculum." Unpublished PhD dissertation, Leuven: KU Leuven.

Margolin, Jean-Claude, Jan Pendergrass, and Marc Van der Poel. 1991. *Images et lieux de mémoire d'un étudiant du XVIe siècle: Étude, transcription et commentaire d'un cahier de Latin d'un étudiant néerlandais*. Paris: Guy Trédaniel.

Núñez González, Juan Mª, and Toribio Fuente Cornejo, eds. 2023. *Ars conscribendi epistolas Petri Ioannis Nunnesii Valentini*. Valencia: Institució Alfons el Magnànim.

Polet, Amédée. 1936. *Une gloire de l'humanisme belge: Petrus Nannius (1500–1557)*. Louvain: Librairie Universitaire.

Poliziano, Angelo. 2019. *Appunti per un corso sull'Odissea*. Edited by Luigi Silvano. 2nd edn. Alessandria: Edizioni dell'Orso.

Van Der Biest, Jarrik. 2024. "An Augustinian Revolution in the Lecture Hall? Michael Baius (1513–1589) as Regius Professor of Theology in Leuven." Unpublished PhD dissertation, Leuven: KU Leuven.

Van Rooy et al. 2023a = Van Rooy, Raf, Xander Feys, Maxime Maleux, and Andy Peetermans. 2023. "DaLeT, Database of the Leuven Trilingue: A New Method for Editing Annotated Prints." *Humanistica Lovaniensia: Journal of Neo-Latin and New Ancient Greek Studies* 71 (2): 103–21.

Van Rooy et al. 2023b = Van Rooy, Raf, Maxime Maleux, Xander Feys, Andy Peetermans, Tom Gheldof, and Frédéric Pietowski. 2023. DaLeT datasets (1.0.0-beta). Zenodo. doi.org/10.5281/zenodo.8305741.

Weaver, William P. 2022. *Homer in Wittenberg: Rhetoric, Scholarship, Prayer*. Oxford–New York: Oxford University Press.

Student Notes Toolkit

When first encountering a body of student notes, it is key to historically contextualize this source and the historical actors involved. The toolkit below may serve as a detailed checklist to do so but is by no means intended to be exhaustive. The table offers a starting point that individual researchers can tailor to their own purposes.

Type of information		Direct evidence and its properties	Auxiliary disciplines and skills
Provenance	Student?	Ex libris Course note Other notes …	Biography Comparative study with parallel sets of student notes History of universities Paleography Book history Codicology (filigranology) History of education and science
	Professor?		
	Institute?		
	Location?		
	Date?		
	Subject?		
Material aspects	Support?	Parchment—Paper—Wax …	Codicology Book history
	Format?	Manuscript—Print—Hybrid	
	Handwriting?	Secretary—Humanist—Baroque …	Paleography

Type of information		Direct evidence and its properties	Auxiliary disciplines and skills
Typology of notes	Language?	Latin (vernaculars, for example, Italian, German) (other learned languages, for example, Greek, Hebrew)	Linguistics Historical sociolinguistics Grammar History of language studies
	Source?	Listening (selective *reportatio*) Dictation (more exhaustive) Copying from an exemplar	Paleography Textual comparison
	Reference text?	Yes Full Fragmentary Paraphrased No	Textual history and transmission
	Form?	Text Images Diagrams	Book history Codicology Paleography Iconography
	Structure?	Linking refence text and notes? Position notes in relation to reference text?	
	Contents?	Linguistic notes (grammar, lexicon) Clarifications (synonyms, paraphrases, narrative explanations …) Encyclopedic notes (geography, biology …)	History of education and science
Edition	Available?	In print In digital form	Mastery of secondary literature
	Desirable?	Yes If so, how? Linear or non-linear? No	Editorial techniques

PART II
The Potential of Student Notes Research

CHAPTER 6

History of Education

Daniel Gehrt and Michael Stolberg

1. Introduction

Student notes hold the potential to greatly enrich our knowledge of Renaissance and early modern academic education. Bearing witness to the real practice of teaching in institutions of higher learning, they make it possible to move beyond an analysis of statutes, lists of required reading, and similar normative sources. They shed light on the knowledge and skills students acquired, on the lectures and topics they found particularly "noteworthy," on the methods and practices of teaching that were employed, and on differences and changes across disciplines, places, and times. Moreover, they are indispensable for reconstructing the subjects actually offered by schools and universities and for ascertaining at what educational stages specific subjects were commonly dealt with and in what relation to one another. They also allow researchers to better detect the introduction of new subjects into the curriculum, for instance, Ancient Greek in German Latin schools in the fifteenth century (cf., for example, Bodemann and Dabrowski 2000: 34).

Hundreds of student notebooks from the Renaissance and the early modern period have come down to us. Yet research on the history of universities and academic teaching has so far made only very limited use of this rich body of sources. This is, however, gradually changing, and in recent decades several case studies have been published.[1] In-depth investigations of student notes represent an urgent desideratum since they enable, among other things, an approach to educational history that goes beyond norms and ideals to also focus on methods and practice as well as real-life circumstances and conditions.

In this chapter we will explore this largely untapped potential by examining student notes taken in Germany and Italy from the fifteenth century to the seventeenth. The first part will focus on those pertaining to the liberal arts, the humanities, theology, and other fields of basic academic study. It will highlight, in particular, the fluid boundaries between the teaching provided by Latin schools and by universities and the considerable degree to which students could determine their course of studies to suit their specific interests. The second part will look at various types of notes, particularly those of students of medicine, as an example of one of the three higher disciplines. In this field, verbatim lecture notes were increasingly complemented by notes on anatomical demonstrations, bedside visits, and similar practice-oriented types of teaching. The chapter will end with some general conclusions and suggestions for future research.

2. The diversity and flexibility of basic academic education

Two extraordinarily extensive and highly insightful collections of student notes in late medieval Germany have recently been reconstructed. One consists of forty manuscript volumes scattered throughout historical libraries in Germany, Austria, Switzerland, Italy, and France containing notes taken by students at the Latin school in the imperial city of Ulm, one of the most prominent schools of its time (Bodemann and Darbrowski 2000). The other comprises notes from Stephan Roth's (1492–1546) studies at various educational institutions.[2] They constitute a significant part of the comprehensive literary estate of this town clerk preserved at the Council School Library of Zwickau. Both collections point to the manifold parallels between early modern Latin schools and universities that have long been overlooked. Born in the flourishing silver mining town of Zwickau, Roth could have prepared himself adequately for university studies at the widely renowned Latin school in his hometown (Ross 2015). However, his notes reveal that from the ages of thirteen to twenty he attended several Latin schools in Central Germany, including those in Glauchau, Chemnitz, and Dresden, before enrolling at the University of Leipzig in 1512. When embarking on this seven-year *peregrinatio academica*, Roth was already well versed in Latin. Accordingly, the collection does not contain any notes on Latin grammar for this stage of his education. The various Latin schools in the region presumably employed individual teachers with distinct knowledge of specific academic fields who could help Roth significantly expand upon his learning experience in Zwickau. Thus, his collection of notes suggests that some sixteenth-century students considered it advantageous not only to study at various universities—as is well known—but also to attend various Latin schools prior to university enrollment (cf. Fasbender 2016: 66–9). It reflects the flexibility of these educational institutions that allowed students to enter and leave at different times of the year and to advance to a higher class or level of study according to individual progress instead of age or prescribed time periods (cf. Ridder-Symoens 1992: vol. 2, 289). This facilitated student mobility.

In general, it is crucial to recognize that schools and universities of the past were not as institutionalized as they are today.[3] Class schedules were not always set in stone. The curricular profile of an educational institution was often determined in part by the interests, knowledge, and personal skills of its teachers. They often responded to the individual progress and needs of their students, and students themselves, especially those at universities, could choose to a significant degree what private and public lectures and seminars they attended. Finally, Roth's collection of notes clearly indicates that the quality of education in many schools was surprisingly high, challenging the common belief that the educational system was in poor, dilapidated condition before the Renaissance and Reformation (cf. Fasbender 2016: 63–6).

The collections related to Ulm from the thirteenth century to the fifteenth and from Stephan Roth in the early sixteenth both attest to the fluid curricular boundaries between schools and universities in the German Renaissance (cf., for example, Grendler 1995: 776–88). Whereas the curriculum of many Latin schools transcended the trivium, universities and institutions affiliated with them also offered introductory courses related to this and other areas of study. The forty surviving manuscript volumes of notes taken by late medieval students in Ulm reveal that grammar truly formed the school's curricular basis (cf. Bodemann and Dabrowski 2000: 34–46). Fifteen volumes contain notes largely or exclusively on this subject. Other volumes deal with Classical Latin authors. In the fifteenth century, instruction in Ancient Greek was also offered in Ulm—decades before the first academic chairs in Germany were founded in Leipzig and Wittenberg for this language in 1515 and 1518 respectively (cf. Rhein 2017: 16–18). Logic, extant in five volumes, is also well represented, whereas the third branch of the trivium, rhetoric—a subject highly esteemed by humanists—can barely be found. To a lesser degree, the school also offered courses in areas related to the quadrivium, such as astronomy, computing, arithmetic, and music, as well as to philosophy, including Aristotelian physics, metaphysics, and ethics. Particularly notes from

1436 to 1449 prove that the fields of theology, liturgy, and canon law did at times constitute another substantial branch of the school's advanced curriculum. A surviving class schedule from the early sixteenth century indicates that such instruction was in part intended for prospective clergy preparing for ordination at the bishop's seat of Constance, 125 km south of Ulm (cf. Bodemann and Dabrowski 2000: 40).

Similarly, Roth's notes reveal that early sixteenth-century Central German Latin schools offered many university-level courses (cf. Fasbender 2016: 74–83). Beyond tracts on logic and some notes on rhetoric, the quadrivial subjects of astronomy, arithmetic, and music are represented in the collection as well as philosophy, metaphysics, and ethics. Roth was also instructed on the sacraments, prayers, the Penitential Psalms, writings of Augustine, and church and secular history. In addition, he started to learn Greek partly on the basis of the Pauline Epistles. Roth's study of Greek, ancient and contemporary poetry, and Cicero's works all attest to the impact of humanism on Renaissance education. Strikingly, the earliest surviving notes documenting a systematical instruction in Latin grammar in Roth's education are from his university years in Leipzig from 1512 to 1517. As a student in Wittenberg from 1523 to 1527, he attended Philip Melanchthon's lectures on rhetoric, the third branch of the trivium, although he had attained a master's degree in Leipzig and was focusing his studies on theology and jurisprudence.[4]

Several crucial insights can be gleaned from the two voluminous collections of notes related to Ulm and Roth. They reveal a remarkably high level of education in prominent Latin schools in Renaissance Germany. Many offered a curriculum that coincided to a significant degree with lectures commonly associated with the faculty of arts. The collections also suggest that it was not unusual for Latin schools to provide students with basic theological instruction. Jurisprudence and medicine, however, played either a marginal role in curricula or were entirely absent from the Latin schools. By surveying student notes, it also becomes clear that the age-old practice of classifying fields of knowledge into the trivium or quadrivium did not dictate the actual curricular framework of educational institutions. Other factors could be more decisive. For instance, since schools provided music for the church liturgy, funerals, and certain secular events,[5] notes related to this quadrivial subject can be found in the Ulm collection and extensively in Roth's collection (cf. Bernhard and Sachs 2019). University lectures on music are, however, quite rare.[6]

Students' notes beyond those connected to Ulm and Roth also offer unique insights into private and extracurricular teaching. Melanchthon, for instance, held on his own initiative exegetical lectures on Sundays specifically for foreign students in Wittenberg.[7] Although no announcements of this highly popular lecture are known to exist (cf. Domtera-Schleichardt 2021), we are well-informed on the contents through surviving notes taken by various students. Also, many novel courses were first offered privately before establishing themselves as ordinary lectures, such as Melanchthon's innovative adaptation of the humanist *loci* or commonplace method to biblical exegesis in 1520 (cf. Gehrt 2022: 97–8). Recent research, moreover, has revealed the various inroads of the *studia humanitatis* into university learning. Maximilian Schuh has proven, for example, that several members of the faculty of arts gradually introduced the humanities into the curriculum of the University of Ingolstadt long before the renowned humanist Conrad Celtis began teaching in the Upper Bavarian town as *professor extraordinarius* for rhetoric and poetry in 1491 (Schuh 2013: 174–203). Jürgen Leonhardt has shown that the humanities permeated the margins of academic learning at the University of Leipzig earlier than previously known through extracurricular courses offered after church services on Sundays and feast days.[8] As a final example of the potential of student notes to illuminate blind spots in our knowledge of academic studies, those taken by Stephan Roth during his years in Wittenberg reveal that church sermons held on various days of the week substantially complemented public theology lectures and private studies.[9]

Student notes are not only invaluable for reconstructing the subjects taught at educational institutions, but they also offer unique insights into various structural features of curricula that transcend information commonly found in individual faculty statutes. How rigid or flexible was the curriculum at a particular institution? In what sequence did students learn certain subjects over their educational development? Which subjects did they learn parallel to one another? Who had access to lectures offered by a specific university faculty? Especially voluminous collections of notes taken over a longer period of time by a single person can help to clarify questions of this nature. Among the most extensive notes known to exist today from a sixteenth-century German student are those taken by Johannes Mattenberg (1550–1631).[10] The collection encompasses five folio volumes (1,743 leaves) and six quarto volumes (1,947 leaves) from studies in Marburg, Wittenberg, Jena, and Padua from 1568 to 1579 and includes notes from more than fifty lectures. In 1579, Mattenberg obtained his doctorate in medicine at the University of Valence and served as physician at several courts and towns until his death in 1631.

From 1574 onwards, the year in which Mattenberg presumably obtained his master's degree, his notes focus solely on medicine. Up until then, Mattenberg had also attended various lectures from the faculties of philosophy, theology, and jurisprudence. Surprisingly, the earliest do not pertain to the trivium or quadrivium but to jurisprudence. In 1568, he attended a general introduction to Roman law in Marburg and in the following year a lecture on feudal law held in Wittenberg. From 1570 to 1572, he participated in two lectures on the *Institutiones* issued by the Roman emperor Justinian. At the same time, he attended courses offered by the Wittenberg Faculties of Philosophy and Theology. These included rhetorical and philosophical lectures on Cicero's *Oratio pro Ligario*, *Laelius de amicitia*, and *Epistolae familiares*, a series of translation and style exercises, lectures on dialectic in 1569 and 1570, and on ethics from 1571 to 1573. In the area of mathematics and natural sciences, Mattenberg attended lectures on Melanchthon's *Liber de anima* and on arithmetic in 1570. In 1573, he participated in lectures on astronomy and geometry. Theology also formed an integral part of Mattenberg's studies in Wittenberg. In 1569 and 1570, he attended a lecture on the Gospel of John and later a lecture on the main articles of Christian faith. Mattenberg deepened his knowledge of theology in a lecture on Melanchthon's *Examen ordinandorum*, begun in 1570. In 1570 and 1571, he studied free will as part of a lecture on Melanchthon's *Loci communes theologici*. A collection with numerous Wittenberg debates and theses on theological questions, partly from his own time and partly from the time of Luther and Melanchthon, also testify to Mattenberg's theological studies. The earliest medical notes are from a lecture held in Wittenberg on Galen in 1572.

Reconstructing the lectures that Mattenberg is known to have attended clearly reveals that the curricula at Protestant universities in Central Germany were broadly diversified and that they could be easily individualized according to one's own academic interests without having to obtain an academic degree. Thus, this example dispels the widespread misconception that students categorically had access to courses offered by the higher faculties only after completing a master's degree. This correlates with the findings discussed above for prominent Latin schools, offering courses in the trivium, quadrivium, *studia humanitatis*, and to some degree also in law and theology. Luther and Melanchthon had considered such flexible cross-faculty studies necessary for transforming the University of Wittenberg in the 1520s into a central institution for educating prospective pastors within a relatively short period of time (cf. Gehrt 2015). In addition, this educational reform was a reaction to demands that the Wittenberg theologians also placed on the laity to study the Bible. Indeed, a great number of Protestant students, regardless of their individual academic interests, expanded on the theological knowledge that they had gained at Latin schools or in other earlier learning contexts at the university.[11] Comparable studies at Catholic institutions of higher learning are still lacking.

3. Training for professional practice: Medical students' notebooks

Medicine had a place in academic teaching since the Middle Ages but north of the Alps it was only from the late fifteenth century onwards that it began to attract a considerable number of students. A growing demand for the services of learned physicians on the part of town councils and among the general population made medicine an attractive career option for young men from the urban middle classes, whose families could afford the cost of years of study. This development called for a medical teaching that was more geared towards professional practice. Reading the works of the ancient authorities and learning medical theory remained essential but the future physicians also had to acquire the practical knowledge and the skills they would need to diagnose and cure patients successfully and hold their own in a highly competitive medical world.[12]

University statutes and similar normative sources reflect these developments very poorly. They commonly only spell out the different chairs or areas of teaching and may at best offer lists of authoritative texts on which the professors were expected to comment.[13] The major developments in sixteenth- and seventeenth-century medical education, however, such as bedside teaching, private anatomy lessons, and lectures on specific topics are only sporadically mentioned in these sources. By contrast, they are amply documented in medical students' notebooks.[14] Such notebooks have come down to us in considerable numbers, especially from students who spent some time at prestigious universities, such as Padua and Bologna in the sixteenth century and Leiden in the seventeenth.[15] Occasionally, even a whole set of notebooks that reflect a medical student's course of studies over several years has survived.[16]

Like those of students in other disciplines, the notes of medical students vary considerably in length and comprehensiveness. Many notebooks offer more or less verbatim transcriptions of a series of lectures, presumably often based on dictation.[17] They may even quote the professor as using phrases such as "ego autem dico" ("but I say") or "scitis ergo" ("know therefore"), addressing his students as "vos iuvenes" or giving them personal advice on how to protect themselves against venereal diseases.[18] Student notes on lectures often resemble a systematic treatise or textbook and were valued as such. Students passed them on to others, who copied them.[19] Some lecture notes were eventually published. The voluminous *Opera omnia* of Gabrielle Falloppia (1585), for example, professor of anatomy, surgery, and *materia medica*, first in Pisa and then in Padua, are even based almost exclusively on student notes on his lectures.[20] On the other end of the spectrum, students resorted to note-taking of the *adversaria*-type, assembling hundreds of often very short entries on all kinds of things they heard, read, or saw during their studies.[21]

In addition to lecture notes, students also made excerpts, transcribing passages verbatim and/or summarizing the most important points of a text they had read.[22] Some professors even gave their students reading assignments at the end of the lesson, asking them to read certain passages or chapters in an authoritative work. After lunch, he would talk about the skin, fat and so forth, Gabrielle Falloppia announced in one of his anatomy lectures, for example, and asked his student to read the fourth book of Galen's *De administrationibus anatomicis* and the relevant passages in Galen's *De usu partium*.[23]

While most surviving notebooks by medical students contain first-order notes they assembled in the course of time, some also rearranged and reorganized their original notes by means of common-placing, the humanist paper-technology par excellence, which many of them would have already been familiar with from their school days (Cowling and Bruun 2011). The classical approach that medical students seem to have preferred was to take an empty notebook and to assign a specific heading or topic to the individual pages, either alphabetically or in a systematic order, like the chapters of a textbook. Whenever they learned something noteworthy on a certain topic in lectures or from books or conversations, they would write a brief note on the respective page. In the course of time, various notes on the same topic, possibly from a wide range of sources, would thus fill the page and offer the student a convenient, quick overview of the notes he had gathered, when he needed it, for example, for a disputation or an exam (cf. Stolberg 2013b, 2016).

As documented by numerous student notes, the teaching of medicine, like that of the liberal arts, continued to rely, throughout the early modern period, to a considerable degree on lectures that expounded and commented on a specific authoritative text, like Galen's *Ars medica* or the Hippocratic *Aphorisms*. Avicenna's *Canon medicinae*, which offered an unparalleled synthesis of the whole of medicine, continued to be taught far into the seventeenth century and we find corresponding student notes on Avicenna's discussion of fevers, for example (Siraisi 1987). Already in the sixteenth century, some important changes took place, however. First, there was a gradual shift in the authors whose writings dominated the canon of authoritative texts. The works of Galen and Hippocrates, which increasingly became accessible in the original Greek as well as in new, humanist Latin translations, to some degree replaced the works of Arabic physicians (Nutton 2022: ch. 4).

Student notes also document a major change in the type of lectures offered. Since the mid-sixteenth century, lectures explaining and discussing a specific authoritative text were increasingly supplemented or indeed supplanted by themed lectures, on topics like women's diseases,[24] the diagnosis and treatment of a certain disease,[25] or generally on "practica."[26] Here the professor drew on the writings of a range of authors to offer his students a synthesis of the state of knowledge in a certain field and sometimes added his personal experience. This kind of systematic overview over an area of medicine was often better adapted to the needs of future medical practitioners than the traditional commentary on an authoritative text. A themed rather than a commentary-based approach to lecturing was virtually inevitable when a professor dealt with topics that ancient authors had either not covered thoroughly, such as thermal springs,[27] or not at all, as in the case of new diseases like the so-called "French disease."[28]

This shift from commentary on authoritative texts towards a more practice-oriented, theme-based approach to lecturing was closely linked to and reinforced by a related development. In medicine, as in natural philosophy, the writings of the ancient authorities and the knowledge of many generations they embodied were increasingly supplemented by the "book of nature," that is, by findings and explanatory models that relied on empirical observation.[29] In medicine, this empirical turn gained particular momentum. It was hoped that the combination of reason and method, on the one hand, and experience and personal observation, on the other, would allow physicians to diagnose and cure diseases more successfully (Stolberg 2022: 24–81). In the process, three areas gained new prominence in medicine and therefore also in surviving student notes: 1) anatomy, 2) botany and pharmaceutics, and 3) practical medicine and bedside teaching.

In anatomy, demonstrations on actual corpses came to take a central place since the early sixteenth century.[30] Physicians hoped that knowing the structure of the human body and its parts would help them not only to treat injuries but also to better understand the disease processes inside the body and thus ultimately enable them to treat their patients more effectively. Historians have focused their attention almost exclusively on the large public anatomical demonstrations and the theaters that eventually were built for this purpose. However, student notes show that anatomical teaching at the dissection table was far from limited to the public anatomies, which often took place only once a year—if at all. In Italy, students also attended so-called private anatomical demonstrations on humans and, at least as important, on animals. Rather than looking down from the upper ranks of a large anatomical theater, a small group of students gathered around the dissection table where they could observe the finer structures, like the eyes and cranial nerves, from a close distance. Notes on what students actually saw in the cadavers are usually quite short: standing around the table and taking notes at the same time was impractical. The students took extensive notes, however, sometimes also with little diagrams or pictures, on the preceding lecture, in which the anatomist explained and discussed in detail the parts and their functions he would subsequently demonstrate in the dissection.[31]

The teaching of botany and more generally of the "simples," that is of vegetable, animal, and mineral substances of medicinal value, initially still relied largely on lectures that commented and expanded on the works of Theophrastus, Dioscorides, and other ancient authorities (Reeds 1991). Neither the spoken word nor visual illustrations could equip students with the skills and experience they would need to identify medicinal plants, however, and to assess the quality of medicinal preparations when they were later asked as town physicians to inspect local pharmacies.

Starting in Pisa and Padua, universities founded botanical gardens where students could go on their own or with their professors and see plants in their different stages of development (Findlen 2006). Sometimes students and professors also made field trips in search of rare plants or visited local pharmacies to see the different kinds of medicinal preparations.[32] Some students documented this type of teaching in their notebooks and exceptionally a student would even draw up a list of all the plants he had seen in the local botanical garden.[33]

Teaching practical medicine was virtually revolutionized in the sixteenth century. Professors complemented their systematic overviews on the nature, causes, diagnosis, prognosis, prevention, and treatment of diseases, based on authoritative textbooks on medical practice such as Rhazes' *Ad Almansorem* or the relevant parts of Avicenna's *Canon medicinae* not only with extracurricular lectures and courses on individual diseases or on fields such as surgery or women's diseases, which called for specialized practical knowledge and skills. They also spiced their lectures with real and fictional cases, referred to their personal experience, and equipped the students with countless recipes for different medicines that they could use on their future patients.[34] Moreover, starting in Ferrara, Padua, and Bologna bedside-teaching gained importance.[35] Professors took their students with them on their visits to patients in local hospitals or in the patients' private homes. This allowed them to witness how an experienced clinician applied a highly methodic approach to understand the nature and causes of the patient's ailments and to arrive at a therapy that would fight the disease at its very roots. Sometimes students also got a chance to examine a patient's urine themselves, feel the pulse, or palpate his or her abdomen for swellings or tumors under the professor's guidance, in short, to develop also the manual and sensory skills they would need for successful medical practice. The statutes are silent on this important part of medical education. It is thus almost exclusively from manuscript and published student notes that we know about the bedside-teaching of Giovanni Battista da Monte, of Antonio Musa Brasavola, of Elideo Padoani, who inaugurated this new method in the 1530s and 1540s,[36] and of Franciscus Sylvius who made Leiden a center of clinical teaching in the seventeenth century.[37]

Another innovative and popular approach to clinical instruction, of which there is not even a hint in the statutes, is documented in student notes from Padua: the so-called *collegia*. In a *collegium*, several professors discussed a specific case in front of a student audience. The first professor, usually the lowest ranking one, presented the case, expressed his opinion on the nature of the disease and its causes, and proposed a suitable treatment. Then, the other professors, one after the other, pronounced themselves on the case, expressed their agreement or disagreement with what those preceding them had said, and added aspects of their own. These *collegia* took place quite frequently and the students clearly appreciated them. Dozens of *collegia* are documented in great detail in manuscript student notes[38] and in printed collections of *consilia* or *consultationes* (for example, Trincavella 1587).

4. Conclusion

In several respects, student notes can provide a more adequate understanding of academic education in past centuries than articulated ideals and institutional documents. They are invaluable for reconstructing curricular and extracurricular teaching and are in many cases the best sources for tracing the introduction of new subject matter and teaching methods into academic studies. Moreover, collections of notebooks from one and the same person document educational careers of individual students and highlight the degree to which they could make personal choices and cross-disciplinary boundaries. They also underscore that a holistic approach to the history of academic studies must also include Latin schools and other institutions of higher learning as well as extracurricular and private forms of appropriating knowledge and skills.[39]

Student notes dispel some widely held misconceptions, such as the impermeability between university faculties or the dilapidated state of education prior to the Renaissance and the Reformation. At the same time, they open new insights. Notes readily attest, for example, to the importance of theology for Protestant university students in general, regardless of their career goals. This has long been overlooked because it is not expressly revealed in normative documents. Similarly, some of the new, innovative approaches to the teaching of medicine, such as bedside teaching, private dissections, and the discussion of clinical cases in the so-called *collegia* are documented almost exclusively in student notes, thus showing that the training of future physicians was, in some places at least, far less theoretical than has widely been assumed.

This brief survey has drawn almost exclusively on the notes taken by students of German origin at universities in the Holy Roman Empire and Italy from the fifteenth century to seventeenth. Similar research on student notes that document the actual practice of teaching in other geographic, cultural, confessional, and institutional contexts would be highly welcome and are indeed indispensable for comparative purposes. There are, for instance, several indications that the curriculum at early Jesuit colleges, organized according to the *modus Parisiensis* (cf. Codina 2000), was structured more rigidly than at Protestant universities and was distinctly stratified, reflecting the hierarchy of the faculties and individual fields of study.[40] To gain a clearer picture, in-depth research incorporating student notes is needed. Tropia (2019) offers one of the few studies of this kind. Turning to medicine, German universities were much slower than those in France and the Netherlands, for example, in introducing the new, more practice-oriented teaching formats the Italian universities had developed. For a more comprehensive and nuanced account of the actual practices of higher learning and teaching that student notes make possible, an online repository of surviving student notes would be of immense value. Maybe this volume can provide the initial spark for such an undertaking.

Notes

1. Some of the most important recent studies are briefly discussed or mentioned in the pages below.
2. Roth's collection of student notes is described in detail in Metzler (2008: 19–269, 572–80, appendices nos. 6.1–2); Metzler (2010: 222–5). His notes on music theory are edited in Bernhard and Sachs (2019).
3. Cf. Bodemann and Dabrowski (2000: 38); Ridder-Symoens (1992: vol. 1, 172–7).
4. Similarly, Anja-Silvia Goeing (2016) has found traces of extracurricular rhetoric training for law students in Padua at the end of the fifteenth century.
5. Cf. Niemöller (1969) and Töpfer (2015).
6. For the University of Wittenberg, for instance, the only student notes from music lectures known to exist from the sixteenth century are those from Georg Donat. They have been edited in Aber 1913–14. Also, of the more than 2,000 individual academic announcements from 1540 to 1569 that were published collectively, none refer to lectures on music. Cf. Domtera-Schleichardt (2021).
7. On Melanchthon's Sunday lectures, see Michel (2011).
8. Leonhardt (2004); Leonhardt and Schindler (2007); Bräuer et al. (2008); Leonhardt (2008).
9. On notes that Roth took on sermons, cf. Metzler (2008: 574–80); Metzler (2010: 224). On the widespread Protestant practice of taking notes on sermons as part of school and university education, cf. Gehrt (2021: 70–6).
10. Mattenberg's manuscripts are preserved in: Forschungsbibliothek Gotha, Chart. A 623; Chart. A 626–7; Chart. A 629–30; Chart. B 491–3; Chart. B 494, fol. 96r–224v and presumably also 85r–95v;

Chart. B 495; and Chart. B 499. Alongside Mattenberg's and Roth's notes, those taken by Georg Handsch (1529–1578) are extraordinarily extensive. On this collection, cf. Stolberg (2022: 24–81).

[11] Cf. esp. Gehrt (2015: 283–7); Gehrt (2022: 94–5, 100–1, 128).

[12] For general overviews of the history of medical education before 1700 see O'Malley (1970); Siraisi (1996); Grendler (2002: 314–52); Stolberg (2022: 24–81); for studies more specifically on Italy, Germany, and the Low Countries, respectively, see Siraisi (2001), Nutton (1997), and Lindeboom (1970).

[13] As Brockliss (1996: 563) underlines, statutes tended to lag behind the reality of teaching even in this respect, however, reflecting changes rather than inaugurating them.

[14] The information the letters provide can be complemented by that from letters medical students sent to friends, families, and benefactors. The database of the Würzburg project on early modern physicians' letters currently lists about 1,500 letters by medical students from 1500 to 1700 and offers a detailed summary of the contents for several hundreds of them (see www.aerztebriefe.de; the summaries are so far in German only but a parallel English-language version is being prepared).

[15] See, for example, Universitätsbibliothek Erlangen, MSS 909, 910, 911, 981 (student notes from Padua and Bologna by Johannes Brünsterer and others); Universitätsbibliothek Eichstätt, Cod. st. 307, Cod. st. 308, and Cod. st. 604 (student notes from Rome); Staats- und Universitätsbibliothek Göttingen, MSS Meibom 84 and 85 (notes by a student of Franciscus Sylvius in Leiden); for lecture notes from German universities see, for example, Universitätsbibliothek Eichstätt Cod. st. 603 Ingolstadt 1595/86. For further references to (mostly sixteenth-century) medical students' notebooks that have survived among others, in the libraries in Berlin, Bologna, Copenhagen, Ferrara, Forlì, Göttingen, Kassel, London, New Haven, Oxford, Urbania, and Vienna, see the references below and Stolberg (2022: esp. 555–8).

[16] See, in particular, Österreichische Nationalbibliothek, Vienna (ÖNV), Cod. 11209, Cod. 11210, Cod. 11224, Cod. 11225, Cod. 11226, Cod. 11231, and Cod. 11238 (student notes by Georg Handsch in 1550s Padua); Forschungsbibliothek Gotha, Chart. A 626, Chart. A 629, Chart. B 492, J. Mattenberg's medical notebooks from Wittenberg and Padua.

[17] For example, ÖNV, Cod. 11224, notes by Georg Handsch on Bassiano Landi's lectures on Galen's *Ars parva* (Padua 1552).

[18] See, for example, Landesbibliothek und Murhardsche Bibliothek, Kassel, 4° MS med. 19, notes on G. Falloppia's lectures on ulcers and the French disease, Padua 1555, fol. 140r: "Solum vos moneo ut scitis [sic] cauti ne incidatis in hunc morbum [i.e., the French disease]. Eligatis ergo vobis puellas iuuenes et non infectas." Further examples—among many others—can be found in Staats- und Universitätsbibliothek Göttingen, MS Meibom 20, lecture notes by an unidentified student on Falloppia's anatomy lectures (Padua, 1550s), fol. 239r; Wellcome Collection London, Western Manuscripts, MS 568, student notes on Giovanni Battista da Monte's lectures on Rhazes, fol. Aii.

[19] See, for example, ÖNV, Cod. 11228, Georg Handsch's copy of student notes on a lecture by Augustinus Schurff on Rhazes' *Ad Almansorem* in Wittenberg in 1537.

[20] Stolberg (2023).

[21] For a detailed account of early modern medical common-placing see Stolberg (2013b, 2016).

[22] For example, Forschungsbibliothek Gotha, Chart. B 492, fol. 200–31, J. Mattenberg's excerpts from the chapters on fevers in Avicenna's *Canon medicinae*.

[23] Staats- und Universitätsbibliothek Göttingen, MS Meibom 20, lecture notes of an unidentified student (Padua, 1550s).

[24] For example, Universitätsbibliothek Erlangen, MS 981, student notes on Massaria's lectures on *De morbis mulierum* (Padua 1591).

[25] For example, Forschungsbibliothek Gotha, Chart. A 626 and Chart. A 629, foll. 75–110, Johann Mattenberg's notes on Girolamo Mercuriale's lectures *De tremore* (Padua, c. 1578) and on Girolamo

Capivaccia's *Methodus generalis curandi* (Padua 1578); University Library Bologna, A. 46, notes on Antonio Fracanzano's lectures on fevers (Padua 1553).

26 For example, Universitätsbibliothek Erlangen, MS 1002, Georg Marius' notes on Guillaume Rondelet's lectures on *Practica* (Montpellier 1552).

27 For example, Bodleian Library Oxford, MS Canon. Misc. 119, student notes on Falloppia's lectures *De aquis thermalibus*.

28 For example, Landesbibliothek und Murhardsche Bibliothek, Kassel, 4 MS med. 19, fol. 1r–140r, Wellcome Collection London, Western manuscripts 269, and Biblioteca comunale Urbania, MS 95, notes by different students on Falloppia's lectures on ulcers and the French disease (Padua 1555, 1560/1, and 1561). The French disease is commonly thought to have been caused by the same agent, *Treponema pallidum*, which causes syphilis today but initially, in the sixteenth century, its symptoms were much more serious and often life-threatening.

29 Grafton and Siraisi (1999: 369–400); for medicine, in particular, see Cook (2010) and Stolberg (2013a).

30 Cunningham (1997); Findlen (2006); Klestinec (2011).

31 For example, Cod. 11210, with student notes by Georg Handsch on what he learned from Gabrielle Falloppia's anatomical demonstrations; Staats- und Universitätsbibliothek Göttingen, MS Meibom 20, notes by an unidentified student on anatomical demonstrations he witnessed in Padua during the 1550s; see Eriksson (1959) and Mache (2019) for modern editions of student notes on anatomical demonstrations in sixteenth-century Bologna and Padua.

32 ÖNV, Cod. 11210, fol. 140r, student notes by Georg Handsch on Antonio Fracanzano's teaching.

33 Ibid., fol. 120v–125r; cf. Stolberg (2022: 67–73).

34 Cf., for example, Sambale (2018) for an edition of student notes on the surgical lectures of Girolamo Fabrizi d'Acquapendente.

35 Ongaro (1994); Stolberg (2014, 2018).

36 For example, ÖNV, Cod. 11238, notes by Georg Handsch on patients he saw with his professors in the 1550s in Padua; Biblioteca Ariostea, Ferrara, Collezione Antonelli, MS 531, Curationes Antonij Musae Brasavoli; Da Monte (1565); Padoani (1607).

37 Cf. Staats- und Universitätsbibliothek Göttingen, MS 85, notes by an unidentified student who accompanied Franciscus Sylvius on patient visits in the 1660s in Leiden; Sylvius (1664).

38 Herzog August Bibliothek Wolfenbüttel, Cod. Guelf. 20. 22. Aug. 4to and Biblioteca communale, Siena, C IX 32 each offer student notes on dozens of *collegia* in mid- and late sixteenth-century Padua; further student notes on *collegia* are, for example, in Wellcome Collection, London, Western Manuscripts, MS 567 and MS 602.

39 On the broad spectrum of academic institutions in early modern Europe, see Frijhoff (2016). The common ground shared by Latin schools and universities, also in cultural and social areas, is impressively demonstrated by Ross (2015) for Zwickau in the sixteenth and seventeenth centuries. See also Gehrt (2017) on the academic centennial commemoration of the Reformation. Gehrt (2022) and Schmidt (2018: 169–78) offer rare insights into personal academic studies and private lectures and seminars at universities respectively.

40 Cf., for example, the early educational conceptions composed by Jerónimo Nadal in 1553 and 1563 in Nadal (1965, 1974).

References

Early modern printed sources

Da Monte, Giovanni Battista. 1565. *Consultationum medicarum opus absolutissimum.* Basel: per Henricum Petri et Petrum Pernam.

Falloppia, Gabrielle. 1585. *Opera omnia.* Frankfurt: Apud haeredes Andreae Wechelii, Claud. Marnium & Io. Aubrium.

Padoani, Elideo. 1607. *Processus, curationes et consilia in curandis in particularibus morbis [...] medicinae candidatis in praxi eum sequentibus communicata, nunc primum edita a Joh. Wittichio.* Leipzig: Nicolaus Nerlichius.

Sylvius, Franciscus. 1664. *Collegium medico-practicum.* Frankfurt am Main: Thomas Matthias Götz.

Trincavella, Vettore. 1587. *Consilia medica post editionem venetam et lugdunensem, accessione CXXVIII consiliorum locupletata, et per locos communes digesta.* Basel: Konrad von Waldkirch.

Secondary literature

Aber, Adolf. 1913–1914. "Das musikalische Studienheft des Wittenberger Studenten Georg Donat (um 1543)." *Sammelbände der internationalen Musikgesellschaft* 15: 68–98.

Bernhard, Michael, and Klaus-Jürgen Sachs. 2019. *Musiklehre zwischen Mittelalter und Humanismus: Das Studienkonvolut des Stephan Roth (Zwickau, Ratsschulbibliothek 24.10.26).* Hildesheim–Zürich–New York: Georg-Olms-Verlag.

Bodemann, Ulrike, and Christoph Darbrowski. 2000. "Handschriften der Ulmer Lateinschule: Überlieferungsbefund und Interpretationsansätze." In *Schulliteratur im späten Mittelalter*, edited by Klaus Grubmüller, 11–47. Munich: Wilhelm Fink Verlag.

Bräuer, Miriam, Jürgen Leonhardt, and Claudia Schindler. 2008. "Zum humanistischen Vorlesungsbetrieb an der Universität Leipzig." *Pirckheimer Jahrbuch für Renaissance- und Humanismusforschung* 23: 201–16.

Brockliss, Laurence W.B. 1996. "Curricula." In *A History of the University In Europe*, edited by Hilde de Ridder-Symoens, vol. 2: *Universities in Early Modern Europe (1500–1800)*, 563–620. Cambridge: Cambridge University Press.

Codina, Gabriel. 2000. "The Modus Parisiensis." In *The Jesuit Ratio Studiorum*, edited by Vincent Duminuco, 28–49. New York: Fordham University Press.

Cook, Harold J. 2010. "Victories for Empiricism, Failures for Theory: Medicine and Science in the Seventeenth-Century." In *The Body as Object and Instrument of Knowledge: Embodied Empiricism and Early Modern Science*, edited by Charles T. Wolfe and Ofer Gal, 9–32. Dordrecht: Springer.

Cowling, David, and Mette B. Bruun, eds. 2011. *Commonplace Culture in Western Europe in the Early Modern Period.* Leuven–Paris–Walpole, MA: Peeters.

Cunningham, Andrew. 1997. *The Anatomical Renaissance. The Resurrection of the Anatomical Projects of the Ancients.* Aldershot: Scolar Press.

Domtera-Schleichardt, Christiane. 2021. *Die Wittenberger Scripta publice proposita (1540–1569): Universitätsbekanntmachungen im Umfeld des späten Melanchthon.* Leipzig: Evangelischer Verlagsanstalt.

Eriksson, Ruben, ed. 1959. *Andreas Vesalius' First Public Anatomy at Bologna 1540: An Eyewitness Report.* Uppsala: Almqvist & Wiksells.

Fasbender, Christoph. 2016. "'Colligi in Kempnicz': Zum Erkenntniswert mitteldeutscher Schulhandschriften des Spätmittelalters für das Curriculum mitteldeutscher Lateinschulen." In *Wissenschaftliche Erziehung seit der Reformation: Vorbild Mitteldeutschland*, edited by Rudolf Bentzinger and Meinolf Vielberg, 63–83. Erfurt: Franz Steiner Verlag.

Findlen, Paula. 2006. "Anatomy Theaters, Botanical Gardens, and Natural History Collections." In *Early Modern Science*, edited by Katharine Park and Daston Lorraine, 272–88. Cambridge: Cambridge University Press.

Frijhoff, Willem. 2016. "University, Academia, Hochschule, College: Early Modern Perceptions and Realities of European Institutions of Higher Education." In *Zwischen Konflikt und Kooperation: Praktiken der europäischen Gelehrtenkultur (12.–17. Jahrhundert)*, edited by Jan-Hendryk de Boer, Marian Füssel, and Jana Madlen Schütte, 67–88. Berlin: Duncker & Humblot.

Goeing, Anja-Silvia. 2016. "Paduan Extracurricular Rhetoric, 1488–1491." In *For the Sake of Learning: Essays in Honor of Anthony Grafton*, edited by Ann Blair and Anja-Silvia Goeing, vol. 2, 543–60. Leiden–Boston: Brill.

Gehrt, Daniel. 2015. "Die Harmonie der Theologie mit den *studia humanitatis*: Zur Rezeption der Wittenberger Bildungskonzeptionen in Jena am Beispiel der Pfarrerausbildung." In *Die Leucorea zur Zeit des späten Melanchthon: Institutionen und Formen gelehrter Bildung um 1550*, edited by Matthias Asche, Heiner Lück, Manfred Rudersdorf, and Markus Wriedt, 263–312. Leipzig: Evangelische Verlagsanstalt.

———. 2017. "Gelehrtenkultur und Reformationsgedenken 1617 am Beispiel der ernestinischen Herzogtümer: Formen, Kontexte und dynamische Prozesse." In *Konfession, Politik und Gelehrsamkeit: Der Jenaer Theologe Johann Gerhard (1582–1637) im Kontext seiner Zeit*, edited by Markus Friedrich, Sascha Salatowsky, and Luise Schorn-Schütte, 177–223. Stuttgart: Franz Steiner.

———. 2021. "Maple Wood Heirlooms and the Re-formation of a Dynastic Identity: Sermon Notes Taken by Elector John of Saxony as Grapho-Relics." *Renaissance and Reformation* 44 (1): 59–85.

———. 2022. "Beyond the Institution: Private Studies in the Theological Education of Lutheran Pastors and Scholars." In *Frühneuzeitliches Luthertum: Interdisziplinäre Studien*, edited by Sascha Salatowsky and Joar Haga, 89–131. Stuttgart: Franz Steiner.

Grafton, Anthony, and Nancy Siraisi, eds. 1999. *Natural Particulars: Nature and the Disciplines in Renaissance Europe*. Cambridge, MA: Harvard University Press.

Grendler, Paul F. 1995. "Schooling in Western Europe." In *Books and Schools in the Italian Renaissance*, edited by Paul F. Grendler, 776–88. Aldershot, Hampshire et al.: Variorum.

———. 2002. *The Universities of the Italian Renaissance*. Baltimore: Johns Hopkins University Press.

Klestinec, Cynthia. 2011. *Theaters of Anatomy: Students, Teachers, and Traditions of Dissection in Renaissance Venice*. Baltimore: Johns Hopkins University Press.

Leonhardt, Jürgen. 2004. "Gedruckte humanistische Kolleghefte als Quelle für Buch und Bildungsgeschichte." *Wolfenbütteler Notizen zur Buchgeschichte* 29: 21–34.

———. 2008. "Classics as Textbooks: A Study of the Humanist Lectures on Cicero at the University of Leipzig, ca. 1515." *Scholarly Knowledge: Textbooks in Early Modern Europe*, edited by Emidio Campi, Simone De Angelis, Anja-Silvia Goeing, and Anthony T. Grafton, 89–112. Geneva: Droz.

Leonhardt, Jürgen, and Schindler, Claudia. 2007. "Neue Quellen zum Alltag im Hörsaal vor 500 Jahren: Ein Tübinger Forschungsprojekt zur Leipziger Universität." *Jahrbuch für historische Bildungsforschung* 13: 31–56.

Lindeboom, Gerrit A. 1970. "Medical Education in the Netherlands 1575–1750." In *The History of Medical Education*, edited by Charles D. O'Malley, 201–34. Berkeley–Los Angeles: University of California Press.

Mache, Ursula. 2019. *Anatomischer Unterricht in Padua im 16. Jahrhundert: Edition, Übersetzung und Kommentierung der Aufzeichnungen eines böhmischen Studenten*. Duisburg: WiKu-Verlag.

Metzler, Regine. 2008. *Stephan Roth 1492–1546: Stadtschreiber in Zwickau und Bildungsbürger der Reformationszeit*. Stuttgart: Verlag der Sächsischen Akademie der Wissenschaften.

———. 2010. "Der Nachlass Stephan Roths (1492–1546) in der Ratsschulbibliothek Zwickau (mit Anhang)." *Neues Archiv für Sächsische Geschichte* 81: 215–34.

Michel, Stefan. 2011. "Die Sonntagsvorlesungen Philipp Melanchthons: Vom akademischen Vortrag zum homiletischen Hilfsmittel." In *Philipp Melanchthon: Lehrer Deutschlands, Reformator Europas*, edited by Irene Dingel and Armin Kohnle, 177–90. Leipzig: Evangelische Verlagsanstalt.

[Nadal, Jerónimo]. 1965. "Regulae de scholis collegiorum, [1553]." In *Monumenta Paedagogica Societatis Jesu*, vol. 1: *1540–1556*, edited by Ladislaus Lukács, 185–210, no. 13. Rome: Institutum Historicum Societatis Iesu.

———. 1974. "Ordo studiorum Germanicus, 1563." In *Monumenta Paedagogica Societatis Jesu*, vol. 2: *1557–1572*, edited by Ladislaus Lukács, 85–133, no. 13. Rome: Institutum Historicum Societatis Iesu.

Niemöller, Klaus Wolfgang. 1969. *Untersuchungen zu Musikpflege und Musikunterricht an den deutschen Lateinschulen vom ausgehenden Mittelalter bis um 1600*. Regensburg: Gustav Bosse Verlag.

Nutton, Vivian. 1997. "Medicine at the German Universities, 1348–1500: A Preliminary Sketch." *Würzburger medizinhistorische Mitteilungen* 16: 173–90.

———. 2022. *Renaissance Medicine: A Short History of European Medicine in the Sixteenth Century*. Abingdon–New York: Routledge.

O'Malley, Charles D. 1970. "Medical Education during the Renaissance." In *History of Medical Education*, edited by Charles D. O'Malley, 89–102. Berkeley: University of California Press.

Ongaro, Giuseppe. 1994. "L'insegnamento clinico di Giovan Battista da Monte (1489–1551): una revisione critica." *Physis* 31: 357–69.

Reeds, Karen Meier. 1991. *Botany in Medieval and Renaissance Universities*. New York–London: Garland Publishing.

Rhein, Stefan. 2017. "Philipp Melanchthon und seine griechischen Dichterschüler." In *Hellenisti! Altgriechisch als Literatursprache im neuzeitlichen Europa*, edited by Stefan Weise, 15–46. Stuttgart: Franz Steiner Verlag.

Ridder-Symoens, Hilde de, ed. 1992. *A History of the University in Europe*. 2 vols. Cambridge: Cambridge University Press.

Ross, Alan S. 2015. *Daum's Boys: Schools and the Republic of Letters in Early Modern Germany*. Manchester: Manchester University Press.

Sambale, Janine. 2018. *Chirurgischer Unterricht in Padua im 16. Jahrhundert: Kommentierte Edition und Übersetzung der studentischen Aufzeichnungen von Konrad Zinn*. Diss. med. Würzburg (open access: https://opus.bibliothek.uni-wuerzburg.de/frontdoor/index/index/docId/17470, last accessed January 21, 2025).

Schmidt, Steffie. 2018. *Professoren im Norden: Lutherische Gelehrsamkeit in der Frühen Neuzeit am Beispiel der theologischen Fakultäten in Kopenhagen und Uppsala*. Göttingen: Vandenhoeck & Ruprecht.

Schuh, Maximilian. 2013. *Aneignungen des Humanismus: Institutionelle und individuelle Praktiken an der Universität Ingolstadt im 15. Jahrhundert*. Leiden–Boston: Brill.

Siraisi, Nancy G. 1987. *Avicenna in Renaissance Italy: The "Canon" and Medical Teaching in Italian Universities after 1500*. Princeton: Princeton University Press.

———. 1996. "Die medizinische Fakultät." In *Geschichte der Universität in Europa*, vol. I: *Von der Reformation zur Französischen Revolution (1500–1800)*, edited by Walter Rüegg, 321–42. München: Beck.

———. 2001. *Medicine and the Italian Universities 1250–1600*. Leiden–Boston: Brill.

Stolberg, Michael. 2013a. "Empiricism in Sixteenth-Century Medical Practice: The Notebooks of Georg Handsch." *Early Science and Medicine* 18: 487–516.

———. 2013b "Medizinische *Loci communes*: Formen und Funktionen einer ärztlichen Aufzeichnungspraxis im 16. und 17. Jahrhundert." *NTM—Zeitschrift für Geschichte der Wissenschaften, Technik und Medizin* 2: 37–60.

———. 2014. "Bedside Teaching and the Acquisition of Practical Skills in Mid-Sixteenth-Century Padua." *Journal of the History of Medicine and Allied Sciences* 69: 633–61.

———. 2016. "Medical Note-Taking in the Sixteenth and Seventeenth Centuries." In *Forgetting Machines: Knowledge Management Evolution in Early Modern Europe*, edited by Alberto Cevolini, 243–64. Leiden–Boston: Brill.

———. 2018. "Teaching Anatomy in Post-Vesalian Padua: An Analysis of Student Notes." *Journal of Medieval and Early Modern Studies* 48: 61–78.

———. 2022. *Learned Physicians and Everyday Medical Practice in the Renaissance*. Berlin–Boston: De Gruyter Oldenbourg.

———. 2023. *Gabrielle Falloppia, 1522/23–1562: The Life and Work of a Renaissance Anatomist*. London: Routledge.

Töpfer, Thomas. 2015. "Schule und musikalische 'Dienstleistungen': Ihre Bedeutung für die Visualisierung und Performanz der 'Guten Ordnung' in der frühen Neuzeit: Konturen eines vernachlässigten interdisziplinären Forschungsfeldes zwischen Musik- und Bildungsgeschichte." In *Choral, Cantor, Cantus firmus. Der Lutherische Choral in der Musik-, Sozial- und Bildungsgeschichte*, edited by Erik Dremel and Ute Poetzsch, 73–92. Halle: Verlag der Franckeschen Stiftungen.

Tropia, Anna. 2019. "From Paris to Gotha: The Circulation of Two Parisian Jesuit Courses between the 16th and the 17th Century." *Mediterranea: International Journal for the Transfer of Knowledge* 4: 75–106.

CHAPTER 7

Intellectual History

Lorenz Demey,* Marc Laureys, Maxime Maleux, and Andy Peetermans

1. Introduction

The importance of higher education in shaping the intellectual life of early modern Europe is widely recognized. Universities were designed to encourage social interaction and the exchange of ideas among current and future intellectuals, which enabled the transmission through time of knowledge and ideas. These transmission processes were crucial for the evolution of intellectual thought, at the same time providing both the necessary preconditions for continuity and a platform for innovations to emerge and grow. Therefore, it is clear that gaining a deeper insight into what happened in and around university lecture halls is bound to benefit our understanding of early modern Europe's intellectual culture(s) at large.

What we seek to argue is the following: student notes enable us to clearly see salient aspects of intellectual life at the university that tend to be rendered invisible by alternative source types, among which official policies, published textbooks, and outward-facing programmatic declarations. As such, they constitute unique sources for practitioners of intellectual history.

To make this point, we present a selection of four case studies. First, we turn to fifteenth-century Bologna, where the annotations to a manuscript copy of the Roman poet Juvenal reveal the persistence of conservative educational approaches, in blatant disregard of the revolutionary rhetoric of the period's humanist scholars. The three remaining case studies bring us to the old university of Leuven. The first two of these concern the field of logic, and they show that student notes from late fifteenth to late seventeenth-century Leuven not only shed new light on a hitherto ill-understood episode in the history of logic, but even provide valuable new input for present-day logic research. Thus, it becomes clear that the Leuven lecture hall was home to considerably higher degrees of non-conformism and creativity than would be suggested by official policies and the contents of published textbooks. A similar point is brought home in a different way in the fourth and final case study, which is concerned with the teaching of Hebrew in sixteenth-century Leuven and Paris.

Before we move to these case studies, however, we present some brief orienting notes on the broader field of inquiry that is intellectual history. That this chapter's title speaks of "intellectual history," as opposed to, for example, "history of ideas" or "history of knowledge," is not to be read in overly programmatic or polemical tones. Indeed, the labels "intellectual history" and "history of ideas" in particular have been used synonymously so often that it hardly seems worthwhile to maintain any kind of strict distinction between the two. The quintessential *Journal of the History of Ideas*, which first appeared in 1940 and continues today, even conspicuously included the phrase "intellectual history" in its subtitle for much of its history. Nonetheless, it is worth noting that since the 1960s recurrent attempts have been made to posit a contrast between an approach termed History of Ideas—generally presented as flawed and to be superseded—and an alternative methodology (or several of them) styled Intellectual History.

In such a dichotomy, History of Ideas is primarily associated with the approach of the American scholar Arthur Lovejoy (1873–1962), who sought to understand the evolution of ideas or concepts primarily in terms of the internal makeup and dynamics of the ideas or concepts themselves, as famously exemplified by his 1936 book *The Great Chain of Being: A Study of the History of an Idea*. The various proponents of Intellectual History—the best-known of whom may be the British historian Quentin Skinner—have criticized this Lovejoyan History of Ideas as being overly abstract and essentially ahistorical, arguing that in reality ideas do not exist in some sovereign realm with laws of its own. Instead, human intellectual thought develops in highly concrete historical contexts and is shaped by those contexts, rather than through some inner logic. This is sometimes put in stronger terms: texts from the past and the ideas expressed in them cannot be adequately interpreted divorced from their original contexts, and any reading that attempts to do so will necessarily be an anachronistic misreading. This broadly shared insistence on the necessity of contextualization—sometimes called "(Skinnerian) contextualism"—does not, however, mean that there exists agreement among intellectual historians on what exactly counts as a relevant context, or on what constitutes a sound methodology: intellectual history as a field is highly heterogeneous.[1]

In the twenty-first century, a new approach that presents itself as a separate field called History of Knowledge has entered the picture. It started to take shape in about 2000, but has enjoyed a marked rise in prominence in more recent years; the first issue of the flagship *Journal for the History of Knowledge* appeared in 2020.[2] In contrast to much of twentieth-century intellectual history, History of Knowledge stresses the necessarily embodied nature of all knowledge. In the eloquent words of Roberts (2012: 51):

> Plato notwithstanding, knowledge cannot exist or travel on its own in our material world. It needs a physical carrier, whether a human, a book, an illustration, a machine or an instrument. That is, it needs to be embodied.

It is only through the mediation of concrete physical carriers—be they individual human brains, individual copies of books, or other—that "circulation of knowledge" (a central concept in this approach) can take place. Moreover, each transfer from one carrier to another (for example, from a human brain to a written page or vice versa, or from one human brain to another) necessarily introduces transformations, which can be more or less substantial. It is inherent to the act of passing on knowledge that the knowledge that is being passed on is somehow changed in the process.[3]

While the case studies brought together in this chapter do not directly engage with this new History of Knowledge, it is clear that the ideas about embodiment underlying the concept "circulation of knowledge" are eminently applicable to student notes. Indeed, the genesis of first-order classroom notes involves several transfers from one knowledge carrier to another: from the brain of the teacher to the highly volatile carrier that is air (that is, speech takes place), and through this medium to the brains of individual students; then from the brain of each student to his sheet of paper. (Needless to say, even this description of events omits several layers of physical, biological, and psychological complexity.) In the case of second- or third-order notes (that is, reworked notes), each subsequent reworking even in the simplest of cases involves transfers from the sheets containing the earlier notes to the brain of the student, and from there to new sheets of paper. Thus, it seems that student notes might be of significant interest for scholars engaging in History of Knowledge.

2. Revolutionary rhetoric versus didactic continuity: Juvenal in Bologna

The manuscript "MS Lat 40" of the Houghton Library in Cambridge, MA, containing the sixteen *Satires* of the ancient Roman poet Juvenal, is an interesting test case for the scope and impact of Renaissance humanism on the teaching of classical authors in Quattrocento Italy.[4] This Houghton Juvenal is densely annotated with interlinear and marginal comments. Several categories can be distinguished within this corpus of notes: some offer definitions and explanations of individual words, others focus on syntax, especially the use of a particular Latin case in a sentence, yet others clarify the meaning of a sentence by means of a paraphrase or additional explanatory text, and, finally, there are also notes that explain historical, mythological, or antiquarian details.[5] All share the same concern, namely to provide a systematic word-by-word, line-by-line explication of the literal sense of Juvenal's text. The colophon (on f. 77r) informs us that the scribe, who unfortunately remains unnamed, finished copying the manuscript on July 23, 1462 in Bologna. This information thus neatly provides a place and time for the production of this book—on the assumption that the colophon was not copied along with the rest from its model.

An annotated classical manuscript from the university town of Bologna in the second half of the fifteenth century immediately suggests a humanist setting. Some details of the physical appearance of the codex corroborate that impression, but the entire picture is not as straightforward as it might seem at first sight. The text is written in a humanist minuscule with some cursive traits. It opens with a four-line gilt initial S, entwined in a white vine scroll on a multi-colored background that extends into a border that runs over fourteen lines of text and into the upper margin. This type of decoration became extremely popular in fifteenth-century humanist manuscripts. Also, the text is written in long lines (one column, not two), with generous margins, and starts above the first line drawn (that is, "above top line"), not below it—in imitation of early medieval manuscripts, on which humanists liked to model their codices.

Other features, however, evince continuity rather than rupture. The further initials, undecorated and only two lines high, reflect a practice from the Gothic era, in that they are alternately copied in red and blue ink and mainly designed to mark the beginning of each satire (rather than for any aesthetic purpose), thus structuring the text in the manuscript. The asymmetrical ruling pattern, furthermore, with a double vertical line on the left, to set off the initial (capital) letter from the rest of the verse, and a single one on the right, is very close to a type of which Derolez (1984: 95) notes that it is attested only in Northern Italy and mostly used for verse—Bologna and Juvenal, therefore, fit perfectly in this respect—but also that it is rather rarely employed for humanist manuscripts.

Whereas the form of this codex reveals at least some traces of Renaissance humanism, its content is starkly medieval. It seems natural to presuppose a teaching context for the annotations in the manuscript, not least because of the continuous popularity of Juvenal as a school author since the tenth century. Given the orderly layout of the notes and the general care invested in the production of this manuscript, the exegetical apparatus seems to be of a second- or even third-order, rather than first-order nature and could be penned either by a student, drawing on a lecture course he visited, or by a teacher, preparing material for a course. This teaching could have taken place in Bologna, but the manuscript need not necessarily have been used in the place where it was written.

In any case, the notes reveal a strikingly conventional and elementary *lectura Iuvenalis*, entirely in the medieval tradition and devoid of any traces of the new philology, advocated by Renaissance humanism since its first exponent, Petrarch. In the course of the fifteenth century, the humanist exegesis of classical authors slowly emancipated itself from the age-old *enarratio poetarum*, which had been part of the grammar curriculum in schools since antiquity. More attention was paid to rhetoric and style, knowledge of the mythological, historical, and antiquarian background of classical texts improved, and the analysis of source texts, allusions and quotations attained higher standards. In the latter half of the Quattrocento, these developments went hand in hand with a growing self-awareness of the commentator, aided by the new medium of print.

This self-awareness also found its expression in polemics and rivalries, not only among humanist commentators, but also against old-style *grammatici*, allegedly ill-prepared or incompetent for the job of teaching the classics. Gaspare Veronese, for instance, one of Juvenal's first humanist exegetes, attacked "stupid and ignorant grammarians," who miserably failed to properly explain the *Satires*. Manuscript evidence from the fifteenth century, however, has shown that the traditional practice of grammar teaching did not disappear. Neither the many high-sounding programmatic statements and treatises, nor the spectacular philological achievements of major humanists from Leonardo Bruni and Poggio Bracciolini through Lorenzo Valla to Angelo Poliziano, were able to impose the often-assumed curricular revolution in grammar teaching.[6] Instead, the traditional practice of grammar teaching evolved only very gradually between the Middle Ages and the Renaissance. Basic explanatory techniques, grounded in glossing individual words and short phrases and privileging grammatical analysis, vocabulary training (including etymology and synonyms) and paraphrase, continued in a fundamentally unaltered form. Even well into the era of Renaissance humanism, at a time when the movement was solidly established in Italian culture and learning, the humanists' engagement with classical literature did not necessarily have a profound impact on school practice.

MS Lat 40 of the Houghton Library evidences this evolution rather than revolution in the fifteenth-century teaching of the classics. Behind the humanist flair of the codex lurks an unassuming, run-of-the-mill elucidation of the *Satires*, consisting of basic instruction in grammar, as well as a modest amount of rhetoric and some elementary information on classical civilization. In 1462, admittedly, the annotator of the Houghton Juvenal could hardly have benefited from any advances in the humanist exegesis of Juvenal, since the first humanist (partial or comprehensive) commentaries of Juvenal had only just started to appear, still in manuscript form. The most important humanist commentators of Juvenal appeared only from the 1470s onward. The Houghton Juvenal usefully reminds us that, while these commentators gradually mastered with ever greater expertise the challenging problems in expounding Juvenal, regarding, for instance, the *Graeca* and the antiquarian lore included in the *Satires* or specific characteristics of his satirical style, a more lowly explication of the text, far removed from the revolutionary work of the luminaries of Quattrocento humanism and reflecting more modest didactic ambitions, remained part and parcel of the teaching of the classics in Quattrocento Italy (and beyond).[7]

3. **Official policies versus didactic non-conformism: The university of Leuven and the *Wegestreit***

The fifteenth and early sixteenth centuries are among the least well-understood periods in the historiography of logic. For Northern and Central Europe, this period is characterized by the *Wegestreit*, that is, the battle between two competing approaches to philosophy and logic: the ancient way (*via antiqua*) and the modern way (*via moderna*). The *antiqui* followed thirteenth-century realist authors such as Albertus Magnus and Thomas Aquinas, whereas the *moderni* took their cue from fourteenth-century nominalists such as William of Ockham and John Buridan. The philosophical nature of the debate is hard to pin down exactly, as it concerns a wide range of metaphysical, logical, and semantic issues. From a more sociological point of view, however, it is clear that the *Wegestreit* came to be thoroughly institutionalized, with many newly founded universities taking a clear side in the debate. For example, the universities of Heidelberg and Vienna belonged to the *via moderna*, while those of Cologne and Cracow sided with the *via antiqua*.[8]

In this context, it is natural to ask where the University of Leuven, founded in 1425, positioned itself in the debate. The canonical answer is that Leuven belonged to the *via antiqua*.[9] This is supported by various historical sources, such as a decree from 1427, which explicitly forbade professors in the Leuven arts faculty to teach the doctrines of Ockham or Buridan, and another decree from 1447, which repeated this prohibition and also recommended the teaching of Albertus Magnus and Thomas Aquinas instead (Geudens 2020: 3–4). This evidence, however, is limited to official statutes and documents, and thus seems to ignore the possibility that the reality of teaching might diverge from the official regulations. To obtain a more accurate and complete picture, we need to take other sources into account as well. Student notes are very promising in this regard, since they reflect much more closely what was *actually* being taught in Leuven logic courses.

In recent years, a number of scholars have therefore started investigating Leuven student notes on various areas of logic, such as topical logic and modal logic. For example, Bartocci (2017: 226) has analyzed two late-fifteenth century Leuven commentaries on Aristotle's *Topica*, and concludes that they "appear to have been permeated with Buridanism."[10] After examining a much broader set of student notes, Geudens (2020: 286) reached a similar conclusion: "There was a modernist undercurrent in Leuven topical logic from the 1450s well into the 1530s."[11] Furthermore, based on a detailed analysis and formal reconstruction of an early sixteenth-century Leuven commentary on Aristotle's *De interpretatione* and *Analytica priora*, Geudens and Demey (2022: 89) have recently argued it to be "an exponent of the approach to modal logic that is typical of the

Paris *via moderna* and is ultimately rooted in the work of John Buridan."[12] Thus, the study of student notes has brought about a major reassessment of Leuven's position in the *Wegestreit*: in spite of the *via antiqua* policies found in official documents, didactic practice contained clear *via moderna* elements.

4. Textbook canonicity versus didactic creativity

4.1. Aristotelian diagrams beyond the square of opposition

Aristotelian diagrams are visual representations of a number of concepts or statements, as well as certain logical relations holding between them. By far the oldest and most well-known Aristotelian diagram is the square of opposition for the categorical statements of syllogistics, an example of which is shown in Figure 7.1.

This square indicates, inter alia, that the statements "every man is just" and "no man is just" are *contrary* to each other: they cannot be true together, but they can be false together: for example, in a situation—real or fictitious—in which some men are just and some are not. Aristotelian diagrams are so named because their theoretical roots can be traced back to the logical works of Aristotle, but the first actual diagrams were drawn only from the second century CE onward (Lemaire 2017). These diagrams enjoy a rich history in philosophy and logic, and today they are also widely used in other disciplines that are concerned with reasoning, such as linguistics, psychology, and artificial intelligence (Demey and Smessaert 2018).

In current logic research, it has become clear that these diagrams can be studied as objects of independent mathematical interest. This realization has given rise to the burgeoning research program of *logical geometry*, a key element of which is a systematic typology of Aristotelian diagrams: there are exactly two "families" of Aristotelian squares (with one of these families comprising the famous squares of opposition), five families of hexagons, eighteen families of octagons, and so on. Furthermore, the vast majority of these Aristotelian families can be further divided into different subfamilies.[13] Apart from its mathematical elegance, this typology also raises an interesting historical question: are all of these Aristotelian families actually exemplified by concrete diagrams found in extant sources?

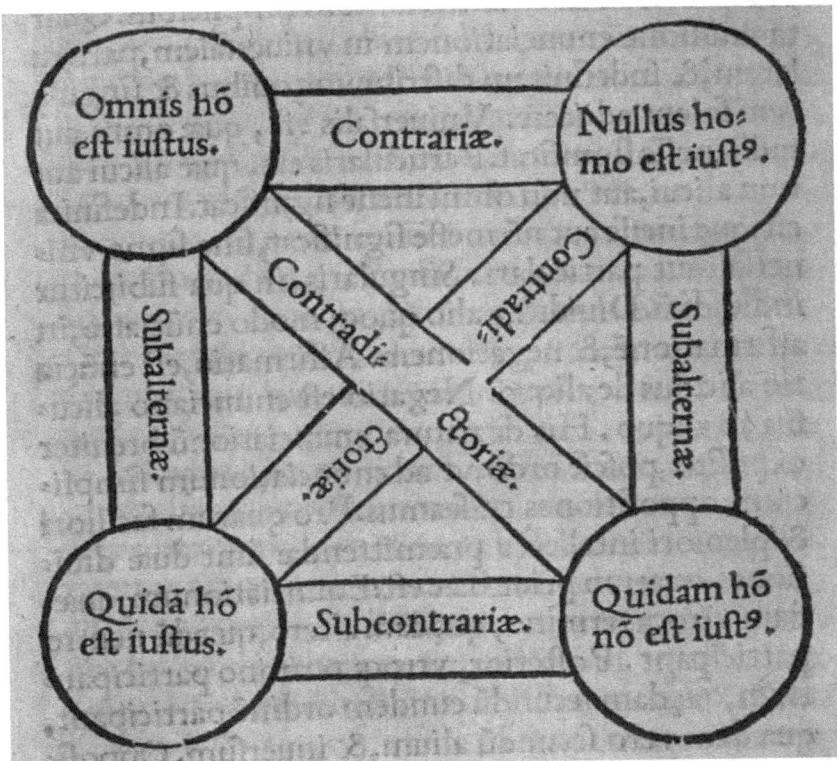

Figure 7.1. Square of opposition. Frans Titelmans, *Compendium dialecticae*. Paris: Simon Colinaeus. 1542. Fol. 8ᵛ.

If we restrict ourselves to printed sources, the overwhelming majority of diagrams turn out to be squares of opposition, and thus to belong to just one single Aristotelian family within the typology. In student notes, by contrast, we do tend to find some more unexpected diagrams from time to time. We can only speculate about the reason for this; perhaps the flexible and informal format of course notes allowed for more intellectual creativity, inviting adventurous logicians to push beyond the boundaries of the canonized square of opposition. For example, one of the early sixteenth-century manuscripts that was already considered in Section 3 contains the diagram shown in Figure 7.2. This belongs to one of the eighteen families of Aristotelian octagons, often called the family of "Buridan octagons," after the first author to construct a diagram belonging to this family.[14]

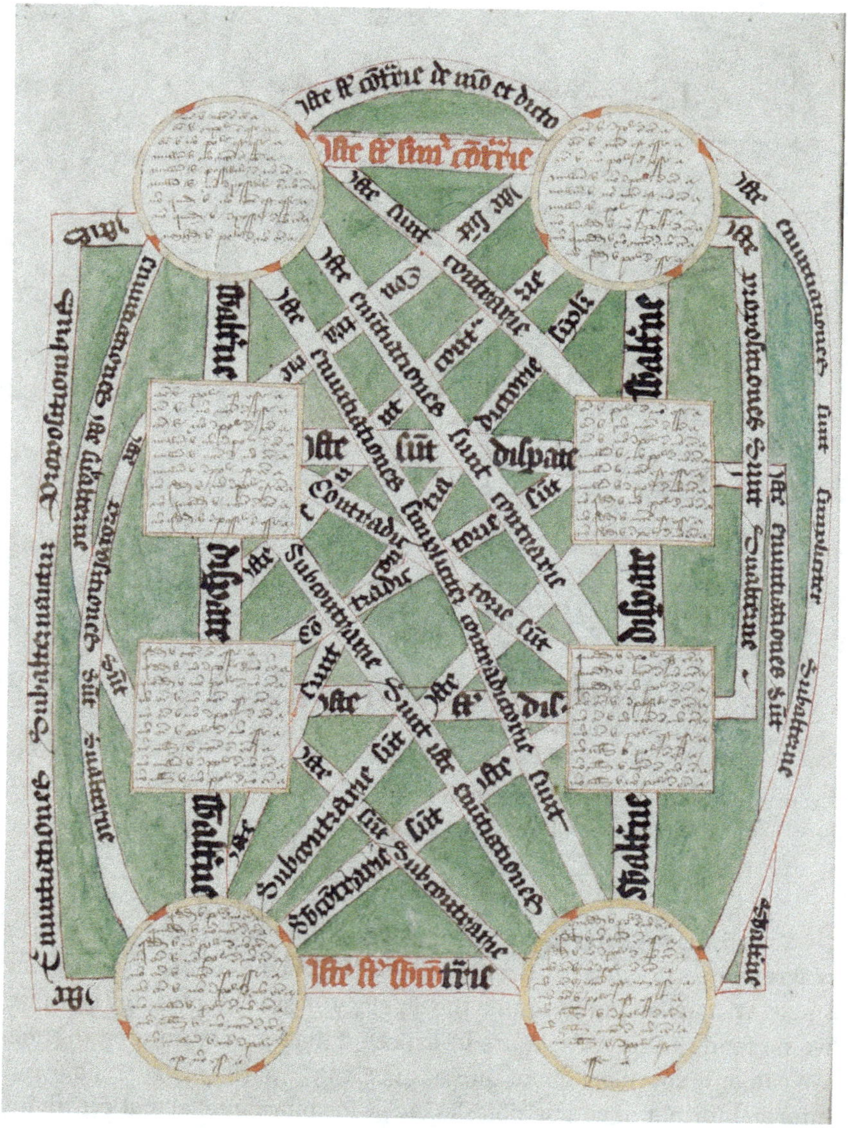

Figure 7.2. Buridan octagon of opposition. Saint-Omer, Bibliothèque d'agglomération, MS 609, c. 1502. Fol. 223ᵛ.

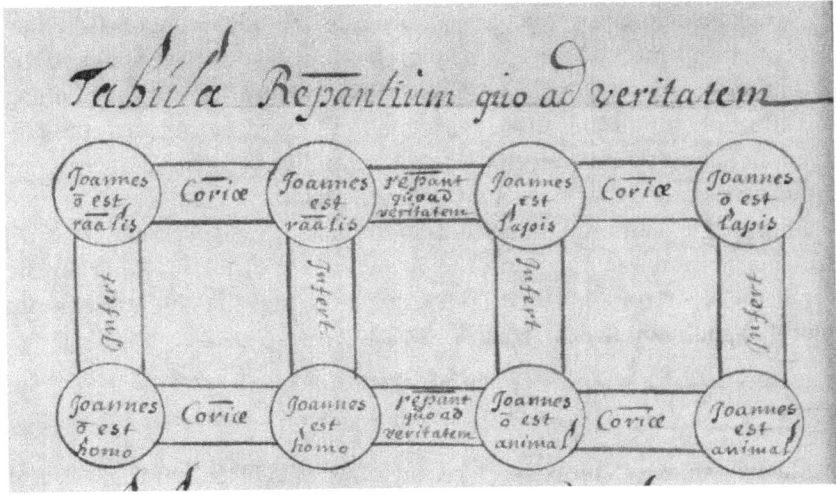

Figure 7.3. Buridan octagon of opposition. Brussels, KBR, Ms. II 4480, 1697. Fol. 92ᵛ.

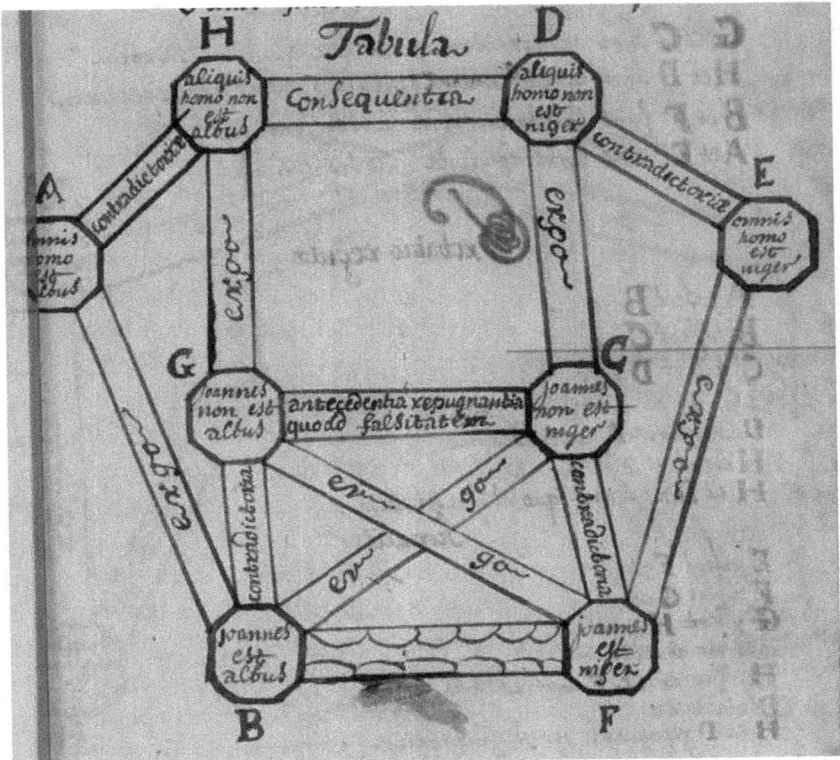

Figure 7.4. Lenzen octagon of opposition. Leuven, KU Leuven Libraries, Special Collections, Ms. 353, 1693. Fol. 517ʳ.

For some more examples, let us consider some student notes from late seventeenth-century Leuven.[15] The diagram in Figure 7.3 belongs to the family of Buridan octagons, just like that in Figure 7.2, but they belong to different subfamilies of this Aristotelian family. By contrast, the diagram in Figure 7.4 belongs to yet another family of Aristotelian octagons (sometimes called the "Lenzen octagons"), and is by far the oldest known example of this family. Student notes thus constitute a veritable treasure trove of Aristotelian diagrams: they provide rich historical input for the typology of Aristotelian diagrams, thus showing that the latter is not merely a mathematical artefact.

4.2. Hebrew in Leuven and Paris

At the beginning of the sixteenth century, the philological study of Biblical Hebrew spread throughout the humanist *respublica litterarum* ("Republic of Letters").[16] The Hebraist Johannes Reuchlin (1455–1522) published his pioneering Hebrew grammar *De rudimentis Hebraicis* in 1506, after several years of intensive study with Jewish teachers. Only twelve years later, in 1518, the first Hebrew lessons started at the Leuven Trilingual College (Collegium Trilingue), where the language was taught alongside Latin and Greek. This college would contribute its share to the development of humanist Hebrew grammaticography, thanks to several of its professors and students.

Johannes Campensis (c. 1490–1538) taught from 1521 until 1531 and published a grammar entitled *Ex variis libellis Eliae* (1528), a grammar based on the grammatical ideas of the Jewish grammarian Elia Levita (1469–1549), whose works were translated into Latin by Sebastian Münster (1488–1552). Campensis' pupil Nicolaus Clenardus (1493/5–1542) wrote a grammar of his own, the highly successful *Tabulae in grammaticen Hebraeam* (1529), which differed in layout from the other grammars of the time. Indeed, Clenardus' *Tabulae* were praised for their pedagogical disposition in clear paradigm tables, printed in a large font and with a minimum of additional explanations.

Campensis' successor as professor of Hebrew at the Collegium Trilingue was Andreas Gennepius Balenus (†1568). This lesser-known Hebraist taught for thirty-six years (from 1532 until 1568), yet without publishing any pedagogical material as his predecessor had done. We do know that Balenus made use of the grammar of Clenardus in his teaching, and probably also in a more limited way of Campensis' work. Without the evidence offered by student notes, one might imagine that Balenus' grammar teaching would have been a fairly straightforward continuation of the framework already present in these two grammars. The various student sources arising from Balenus' professorship with us, however, point toward a somewhat more complicated relationship. For example, if we look at Balenus' use of terminology, we find that he diverged considerably from Campensis' relatively monolingual Latin terminological apparatus. Whereas Campensis strove to describe every category of Hebrew grammar with a Latin term—even when other grammarians would use a Hebrew term from the indigenous Jewish grammatical tradition—Balenus valued a multilingual approach, offering students Latin, Hebrew, and even Greek equivalents for a given concept. A fitting example in this case is the Hebrew *root*. This concept—which denoted the lexical core of a given word, for example *b-r-k* "to bless," whence *barukh* "blessed"—was borrowed from the Jewish Hebrew grammatical tradition in the Latin guise *radix*. It went on to enrich the terminological apparatus of grammarians, alongside Latin (*primitivum*) and Greek (*thema* / θέμα) equivalents. Judging from the student notes, Balenus used these three terms (*radix, thema, primitivum*) indiscriminately throughout his long professorship.

Clenardus' pioneering pedagogical grammar was adopted as a pedagogical handbook not only by Balenus but also by the Parisian *lecteur royal* François Vatable (†1547). It is known from Clenardus' own letters that he went to Paris and sold many hundreds of copies of his Greek and Hebrew grammars. According to this narrative, Clenardus' grammar was enormously popular and influential in the history of Hebrew teaching in France (see Kessler-Mesguich 2013). However, what this narrative glosses over is how Clenardus' grammatical ideas were actually discussed in the classroom. Two sets of student notes stemming from Vatable's grammar classes have survived, one of which is kept at the Bibliothèque Mazarine (in a copy of Clenardus 1529) and one at the Biblioteca Nazionale Centrale di Roma (in a copy of Clenardus 1534; see Maleux 2023: 286–7). Several Latin notes in these two sources point toward a critical reading of Clenardus' grammar, with Vatable apparently favoring the ideas of Jewish grammarians such as David Kimhi (1160–1235) and Elia Levita:

> Master Vatable does not like that Clenardus has reduced the eight or seven conjugations (according to Elia) to four. (Translation cited from Maleux 2023: 288)

Moreover, on several occasions Vatable explicitly claimed that Clenardus was simply wrong. Most of these cases involve instances where Clenardus' paradigms contain verbal forms not found in any Biblical Hebrew texts. As such, Vatable's grammatical ideas seem to be rooted in empirical analysis, whereas Clenardus' *Tabulae*—whose purpose was to provide a practical and straightforward schematic overview of declensions and conjugations—was more prescriptivist in nature:

> Vatable said that he never saw this verb ending in a *tzere* in this passive sense. (Translation cited from Maleux 2023: 288)

Thus, these notes demonstrate (1) that the use of a reference grammar need not imply that the teacher agreed with the grammatical ideas expressed in it or that it was influential (as it might be the case that there are few valuable alternatives), and (2) that, contrary to what printed grammars might suggest, there was room for a more empirical descriptivist approach, at least in Vatable's classroom.

5. Conclusion

We have argued that student notes hold great promise as sources for intellectual history, and that this promise has even to some extent already been fulfilled. Specifically, they enable us to recover aspects of the intellectual life taking place at early modern universities, which more official and outward-facing sources—either inadvertently or by design—tend to hide from view. The notes show us universities where teaching was often less conformist and more creative than we might otherwise have believed. On a secondary note, we have also suggested that student notes might be fruitfully approached from a History of Knowledge perspective, especially from an angle inspired by the concept of embodiment.

Notes

* Lorenz Demey's work on this chapter (Sections 3 and 4.1) was partly funded through a research project (3H220024/G063622N) from the Research Foundation—Flanders (FWO). Thanks to Christophe Geudens and Hans Smessaert for their useful feedback on an earlier version of the parts on the history of logic.
1 Readers who wish to become better acquainted with the field of intellectual history can start by turning to Whatmore (2016), bearing in mind that no single scholar can present a coherent yet inclusive view of such a disparate field. That approaches more akin to the Lovejoyan one have by no means been rendered obsolete, for example, is made clear by Potts (2019).
2 For a first introduction to History of Knowledge, see Burke (2016) or Östling and Larsson Heidenblad (2023).
3 For deeper explorations of the concept "circulation of knowledge," see Östling et al. (2018).
4 The present case study is a shortened version of Laureys (2023); many further details can be found there, including bibliographical indications. The codex under discussion can be consulted in a digitized version: https://iiif.lib.harvard.edu/manifests/view/drs:7861101$7i. Last accessed on April 30, 2024. It is described in Light (1997: 66–9).
5 For specific examples, see Laureys (2023: 9–13).
6 See above all the seminal work of Black (2001), especially pp. 173–274 ("Latin Authors in Medieval and Renaissance Italian Schools: The Story of a Canon") and pp. 275–330 ("Reading Latin Authors in Medieval and Renaissance Italian Schools"). For an alternative view on the Latin curriculum in Italian schools during the Renaissance—highlighting innovation rather than tradition—see Grendler (1989: 111–271).
7 Readers interested in the broader issue of humanist theory and practice in school education may wish to turn to Groenland (2010).
8 For more details about the *Wegestreit*, see Geudens (2020).
9 For a recent example, see Biard (2010: 673).
10 The two manuscripts studied by Bartocci are Cambrai, Bibliothèque municipale, MS 962 (860), written in 1469 (professor Hugo de Dordraco, copied by student Nicolaus Scampion of Brussels) and Cambrai, Bibliothèque municipale, MS 964 (862), written in 1481–2 (professors Henricus de Eyndonia, Petrus de Thenis, and Henricus de Gandavo, copied by student Theodoricus Regis). Cf. Smeyers (1975) and Geudens and Masolini (2016) for more information about these manuscripts.
11 Geudens considered twelve sets of lecture notes in total, including the two already analyzed by Bartocci (2017). See Geudens (2020: 296–326) for detailed information on the manuscripts.
12 The manuscript studied by Geudens and Demey is Saint-Omer, Bibliothèque d'agglomération, MS 609, written in about 1502 (professor John Fabri of Valenciennes, copied by student Allardus Tassart). This manuscript also contains a commentary on the *Topica*, which is among the twelve studied in Geudens (2020).
13 Mathematically speaking, the Aristotelian families and their subfamilies are defined in terms of Aristotelian and Boolean isomorphisms, respectively: see Demey (2018a, 2018b); Demey and Smessaert (2018).
14 This very diagram constitutes one of the main arguments in favor of Geudens and Demey's claim that Leuven occupied a more modernist outlook than has hitherto been assumed. After all, this type of diagram was drawn for the first time by the modernist authority John Buridan, and can subsequently be found exclusively in *via moderna* authors; hence, its occurrence in a Leuven manuscript is a strong indication of its author's position in the *Wegestreit* (Geudens and Demey 2022: 84–6).

[15] See Coesemans (2019) for more historical background.
[16] See Bots and Waquet (1997). The present case study is based on parts of Maleux (2023); many further details can be found there, including bibliographical indications.

References

Bartocci, Barbara. 2017. "Dialectical Reasoning and Topical Argument in the Middle Ages: An Inquiry into the Commentaries on Aristotle's Topics (1250–1500)." Unpublished PhD dissertation, Tours: Université François Rabelais de Tours.

Biard, Joël. 2010. "Nominalism in the later Middle Ages." In *The Cambridge History of Medieval Philosophy*, edited by Robert Pasnau, 2 vols, 2, 661–73. Cambridge: Cambridge University Press.

Black, Roger. 2001. *Humanism and Education in Medieval and Renaissance Italy: Tradition and Innovation in Latin Schools from the Twelfth to the Fifteenth Century*. Cambridge: Cambridge University Press.

Bots, Hans, and Françoise Waquet. 1997. *La République des Lettres*. Paris: Éditions Belin.

Burke, Peter. 2016. *What is the History of Knowledge?* Cambridge: Polity Press.

Clenardus, Nicolaus. 1529. לוּחַ הַדִּקְדּוּק *Tabula in grammaticen Hebraeam*. Leuven: Dirk Martens. Paris, Bibliothèque Mazarine, 10058 Q-1/4 [containing anonymous manuscript notes].

———. 1534. לוּחַ הַדִּקְדּוּק *Tabula in grammaticen Hebraeam*. Paris: Chrétien Wechel. Rome, Biblioteca Nazionale Centrale, 71. 3.A.3 [containing anonymous manuscript notes].

Coesemans, Steven. 2019. "Faculties of the Mind: The Rise of Facultative Logic at the University of Louvain." Unpublished PhD dissertation, Leuven: KU Leuven.

Demey, Lorenz. 2018a. "Boolean Considerations on John Buridan's Octagons of Opposition." *History and Philosophy of Logic* 40: 116–34.

Demey, Lorenz. 2018b. "Computing the Maximal Boolean Complexity of Families of Aristotelian Diagrams." *Journal of Logic and Computation* 28: 1323–39.

Demey, Lorenz, and Hans Smessaert. 2018. "Combinatorial Bitstring Semantics for Arbitrary Logical Fragments." *Journal of Philosophical Logic* 47: 325–63.

Derolez, Albert. 1984. *Codicologie des manuscrits en écriture humanistique sur parchemin*, vol. 1: Textes. Turnhout: Brepols.

Geudens, Christophe. 2020. "Louvain Theories of Topical Logic (c. 1450–1533): A Reassessment of the Traditionalist Thesis." Unpublished PhD dissertation, Leuven: KU Leuven.

Geudens, Christophe, and Lorenz Demey. 2022. *The Modal Logic of John Fabri of Valenciennes (c. 1500): A Study in Token-Based Semantics*. Cham: Springer.

Geudens, Christophe, and Serena Masolini. 2016. "Teaching Aristotle at the Louvain Faculty of Arts, 1425–1500: General Regulations and Handwritten Testimonies." *Rivista di Filosofia Neo-Scolastica* 4: 813–44.

Grendler, Paul. 1989. *Schooling in Renaissance Italy: Literacy and Learning, 1300–1600*. Baltimore–London: John Hopkins University Press.

Groenland, Juliette. 2010. "Humanism in the Classroom, a Reassessment." In *The Making of the Humanities*, edited by Rens Bod, Jaap Maat, and Thijs Weststeijn, volume I: *Early Modern Europe*, 199–229. Amsterdam: Amsterdam University Press.

Kessler-Mesguich, Sophie. 2013. *Les études hébraïques en France de François Tissard à Richard Simon (1508–1680)*. Geneva: Droz.

Laureys, Marc. 2023. "Juvenal in Bologna (1462)." *Humanistica Lovaniensia* 72: 3–20.

Lemaire, Juliette. 2017. "Is Aristotle the Father of the Square of Opposition?" In *New Dimensions of the Square of Opposition*, edited by Jean-Yves Béziau and Stamatios Gerogiorgakis, 33–69. Munich: Philosophia.

Light, Laura. 1997. *Catalogue of Medieval and Renaissance Manuscripts in the Houghton Library, Harvard University*, volume 1: *MSS Lat 3-179*. Tempe, Arizona: Medieval & Renaissance Texts & Studies.

Maleux, Maxime. 2023. "The Teaching of the Old Testament Revolutionized? The Sixteenth-Century Low Countries and the First Institutionalized Hebrew Curriculum." Unpublished PhD dissertation, Leuven: KU Leuven.

Östling, Johan, and David Larsson Heidenblad. 2023. *The History of Knowledge*. Cambridge: Cambridge University Press.

Östling, Johan, Erling Sandmo, David Larsson Heidenblad, Anna Nilsson Hammar, and Kari H. Nordberg, eds. 2018. *Circulation of Knowledge: Explorations in the History of Knowledge*. Lund: Nordic Academic Press.

Potts, John. 2019. *Ideas in Time: The Longue Durée in Intellectual History*. Aix-en-Provence: Presses universitaires de Provence.

Roberts, Lissa. 2012. "The Circulation of Knowledge in Early Modern Europe: Embodiment, Mobility, Learning and Knowing." *History of Technology* 31: 47–68.

Smeyers, Maurice. 1975. "Een collegeschrift van de Oude Leuvense Universiteit (1481–1482), een codicologisch en iconografisch onderzoek: Bijdrage tot de studie van het universitair onderricht tijdens de Middeleeuwen." *Arca Lovaniensis* 4: 243–303.

Whatmore, Richard. 2016. *What is Intellectual History?* Cambridge: Polity Press.

CHAPTER 8

Book History

Xander Feys and Raf Van Rooy

1. **Introduction**

The student notes researcher does not only need to have a decent grasp of book history (see Chapters 3–4), but can also substantially contribute to book-historical research itself. This chapter will present a four-part case study on the Leuven Trilingue, revealing what student notes can bring to the book-historical table. The view we offer will be fragmentary though kaleidoscopic. In particular, the analysis of student notes not only helps the researcher map book circulation (Section 2), but also sheds light on interleaving practices (Section 3), student interactions (Section 4), and *Sammelband* set-ups (Section 5). Here, too, the basis of our analysis will be DaLeT, the Database of the Leuven Trilingue, and a recent PhD dissertation.[1]

2. **Book circulation**

Until recently, scholars of the Trilingue focused on provenance marks like ex libris notes and other historical sources like correspondence, auction catalogs, and a bookshop inventory to reconstruct the Trilingue's library and book landscape (for example, Delsaerdt 2001; Verweij 2002; Tournoy 2018, 2020; Feys 2020, 2024), in addition to the print output of major Trilingue printers Thierry Martens, Rutgerus Rescius (at the same time Greek professor), and Servaes van Sassen (see, for example, de Vocht 1951–5; Adam and Vanautgaerden 2009; Feys 2024). Recent research teaches us that student notes, too, can substantially contribute to reconstruct if not the Trilingue library, then at least the book circulation at this institution among professors, students, and visitors. Indeed, student notes reveal what source texts were used in explaining Latin, Greek, and Hebrew authors, in many cases even offering indications as to which text editions were used. Even if it will turn out to be impossible to determine whether all of these books formally belonged to the Trilingue library, the information nonetheless enriches our view of the Trilingue as an institute of higher learning on the international market for intellectual consumption. Indeed, despite the flourishing trade in humanist textbooks in the city of Leuven with printers like Martens, Rescius, and van Sassen, many books were imported from centers outside the city and even the Low Countries, most notably from humanist hotspots in the Italian lands (for example, Venice), the kingdom of France (for example, Paris and Strasbourg), and the Holy Roman Empire (especially Basel and Cologne).

One illuminating case study concerns the use at the Trilingue of a body of commentaries (scholia) on the text of Homer's *Odyssey* that puzzled us at first. The notes student Johannes Aegidius took during Rutgerus Rescius' courses on this text contain repeated references to an *interpres*, "interpreter," an ambiguous Latin word that can refer to a translator as well as a commentator. So initially we looked for a Latin translator of the *Odyssey*, as the glosses accompanied by *interpres* were frequently in Latin, as in Annotation ID 240, accompanying the Greek word ἀντίθεον (*antítheon*):

> Diis contrarium dicit interpres
> The interpreter says "opposite to the gods."

However, we also encountered several bilingual and Greek glosses accompanied by the rubric *interpres* (for example, DaLeT Annotation IDs 164, 209, 486), and noticed that two similar instances were also marked by *Didymus* toward the end of the corpus of notes (DaLeT Annotation IDs 1122 and 1325):

> Didimus legit χείρας
> Didymus reads χείρας [instead of κῆρας]

> Antiq[ua] exe[m]plaria habe[n]t κύθε & ita Didimus legit a κεύθω ·/· vbi occultat, hoc e[st] vbi sepultus
> Old copies have κύθε and Didymus reads it like this, from κεύθω, that is, where [the earth] hides [him], this is where he is buried.

It is at this point that we realized that Aegidius in his notes was referring to a body of Homer scholia that humanists initially attributed to Didymus

Chalcenterus, an Alexandrian philologer from the first century BCE, but correctly identified as an anonymous work not long after their discovery of the text.[2] With Eusthathius of Thessalonica's commentaries not yet (fully) available in print (appearing for the first time in the mid-1540s in Rome), the scholia initially attributed to Didymus proved the best alternative for humanist readers of Homer, also because they had the virtue of being concise and thus being better suited for a pedagogical context. This collection of glosses is now generally referred to as the D scholia.

The repeated references to an *interpres* help the researcher identify which edition was used in the Trilingue, since only one publication featured this term prominently on the titlepage, an edition that appeared in 1539 in Strasbourg with Windelin Rihel I.[3] This edition attributed the scholia not to Didymus but to an anonymous *Homeri interpres*, "interpreter" or "commentator of Homer."[4] We, moreover, happen to have come across a copy of this edition that once belonged to several, mostly Frisian, students in Leuven, including some who can be related to the Trilingue milieu: most notably Stephanus Mommius from Zwolle, whom a later scholar praised for his knowledge of the three languages, and who composed a Latin–Greek poem in honor of Johannes Isaac Levita's Hebrew grammar (Feys and Van Rooy 2023: 8; see Figure 8.1). This find confirms the identification of the edition used by professor Rescius in the Trilingue classroom, adding a new element to the college's book circuit that was previously unknown. Although the edition featured in the stock of Trilingue bookseller Hieronymus Cloet from 1543, the title was misidentified as a translation rather than as a commentary (Delsaerdt 2001: 474, n. 384), like we had initially done ourselves when we started studying the notes.[5]

Now that the Didymus question had been solved, we still had to find out which Latin translation of the *Odyssey* (if any) Rescius relied on while teaching his course. In the student notes of Aegidius we found numerous verbatim similarities to the word-for-word rendering by the scholar Andreas Divus (fl. 16th century), originally from Justinopolis or Koper in present-day Slovenia. Even though Divus is not mentioned by name in Aegidius' notes, the similarities between the student notes and the printed Latin translation are simply too plentiful to be coincidental, indicating that this popular translation was indeed used at the Trilingue. The fact that Divus was available in Leuven is not only apparent from Aegidius' notes, but also from the fact that at least one preserved copy of the 1538 Parisian reprint is bound in a so-called Spes binding, a typical Leuven phenomenon.[6]

Figure 8.1. Titlepage of the KU Leuven-owned *Homeri interpres* of 1539.
KU Leuven Libraries, Special Collections, CaaA2747.

3. Interleaving for intermezzi

While researching annotated books, one will sooner or later come across copies that contain additional interleaved pieces of paper or even full pages meant for note-taking. Generally, these interleaved pages feature notes that were too extensive to add interlinearly or marginally to the printed text. More space to take notes also entails a greater chance for more detailed references to sources the professor or student might have consulted or cited, making them great starting points for book-historical analysis. This is the case for the student notes of Nicolaus Episcopius the Younger (Bischoff; c. 1531–December 1565/January 1566). As a member of the influential publishing family Froben-Episcopius, which most notably issued many works by Erasmus of Rotterdam, it comes as no surprise that Nicolaus enjoyed an excellent education. At the age of fifteen, he embarked on a *peregrinatio academica*, a study trip across Europe.[7] After studying in Paris for some years, he arrived in Leuven by the fall of 1549. Two sets of notes taken during his time in Leuven have survived and are now held by the Basel University Library. Both bodies of notes reflect the Latin literature courses taught at the Trilingue by Petrus Nannius, professor since early 1539. First, from September 24 until December 9, 1549, Nicolaus attended a course on *Aeneid* 12 (shelfmark Ba Va 28:1). Second, starting on January 8, 1550, he took part in Nannius' lectures on Cicero's *Pro Caelio* (shelfmark Ba Va 28:4). While the notes on *Aeneid* 12 cover the entire 952 verses of that book, those on *Pro Caelio* end abruptly halfway through the oration and record no end date, indicating that he stopped attending Nannius' classes or perhaps had left Leuven altogether sometime during the early months of 1550. Be that as it may, on both occasions, Nicolaus relied on text editions published by the local printer Servatius Sassenus (van Sassen; *fl.* 1530–1557).

The booklets, clearly targeted at a student audience, feature ample space in between the lines of the printed texts, as well as wide margins. The student Episcopius also interleaved both textbooks with additional pieces of paper meant for note-taking. They are striking examples of the editorial genre called *feuille classique* (cf. Chapters 1 and 4). Now, let us consider the following example of an interleaved annotation (ID 2759) taken from Nicolaus' notes.[8] The longest note in the entire corpus (consisting of 579 words) contains an extensive discussion of the word *dictamnus* or *dictamnum* ("dittany"), a type of plant, occurring at verse 12.412.[9] In the story, the goddess Venus had plucked the herb, infused it with her divine healing and other medicinal ingredients, and gave it to the healer Iapyx as a cure for Aeneas, who had been struck by the arrow of an unknown adversary (12.318–23). Episcopius' annotation collects several excerpts on the medical qualities of dittany, taken from the works of classical and contemporary authors. Like the other interleaved glosses, it is drawn up in a relaxed hand and contains several rubricated elements, once again suggesting that it is the result of a redaction that took place after class (so-called *Reinschriften*).

The mini-essay starts with an excerpt taken from the widely read botanical work *De natura stirpium libri tres* by the French scholar Johannes Ruellius (Jean Ruel; 1474–1537). Exceptionally, Episcopius has added a source reference, detailing the chapter number and page number of the edition he used, namely the one published in 1543 by his father (Nicolaus Episcopius the Elder) and uncle (Hieronymus Froben; USTC 605096). Most likely, he copied directly from this source, a fact suggested by the preservation of some diacritics and punctuation marks also occurring in the printed text. Still, he did not copy slavishly. For example, Episcopius inserted, in two instances, words in Greek rather than their printed Latinized counterparts, a reflex he might have adopted from Nannius, who was a noted scholar of Greek (USTC 601711). The second work the student excerpted was *De materia medica* by the first-century Greek pharmacologist Pedanius Dioscorides, citing tacitly from the Latin translation made by Ruellius. Possibly, he relied on the edition issued by Michael Isengrin in Basel in 1542.[10] Episcopius only mentioned that the relevant section on *dictamnum* is found in chapter 3.31. In the 1516 *editio princeps* (USTC 144550) and some later editions of Ruellius' translation (for example, USTC 681876), the section on *dictamnum* features in chapter 3.35, but in Isengrin's edition it occurs in chapter 3.31, which is not a typographical mistake. Additionally, the first sentence of the earlier editions contains a multitude of synonyms for dittany, which are all missing from Isengrin's edition as well as from Episcopius' note.

Following the Dioscorides excerpt, Episcopius added four shorter quotations, taken from Pliny the Elder's *Naturalis historia* (25.92–4, 26.142, and 26.153) and Cicero's *De natura deorum* (2.126). In these cases, it is difficult to conjecture which editions Episcopius used. The lengthy annotation concludes as follows (see Figure 8.2):

> Hæc omnia doctissimorum optimorumq[ue] authorum testimonia hic adijcere placuit, quo herbæ nobilissimæ præstantissima[m] uim et uulneru[m]

præsentissimu[m] remedium, optime ac facilime cognosceres, neq[ue] ~~tot~~ libror[um] inuestigatione fastidiosa ac tædiosa op[us] iam esset. Tantę molis erat ~~ut~~ unica[m] dictione[m] explicare.

At this point, it seemed a good thing to add all these testimonies of very learned and capable authors, by which you could very well and easily learn of the superior power of this most noble herb and its excellent medicinal qualities, and by which there would now be no need for an awful and tedious inquiry into books. So vast was the effort to explain this one word.

It seems reasonable to assume that this meta-comment should be understood from the perspective of Nannius addressing the classroom. Most likely, he had read out loud the relevant excerpts on dittany during class at a normal rate speech, at the end of which he humorously highlighted the effort it had taken to research the rare word, quipping on Vergil's famous line *Tantae molis erat Romanam condere gentem*, "So vast was the effort to found the Roman race" (*Aen.* 1.33). After class, Episcopius took care to piece back together the professor's explanation by copying the excerpts directly from the printed sources. In the process, he also retained Nannius' concluding remark, presumably on the basis of now lost first-order notes that also contained the references to Ruellius and the ancient authors. It seems unlikely that Episcopius personally owned copies of all the specialized literature he quoted from. Possibly, he relied on the books present in the library of the Trilingue or in any case circulating near the college. For, in about 1543, copies of Ruellius' *De natura stirpium libri tres*, his translation of Dioscorides, as well as multiple editions of Cicero and Pliny the Elder were available in the humanist bookshop of Hieronymus Cloet.[11] Strikingly, Episcopius the Younger only added a detailed reference

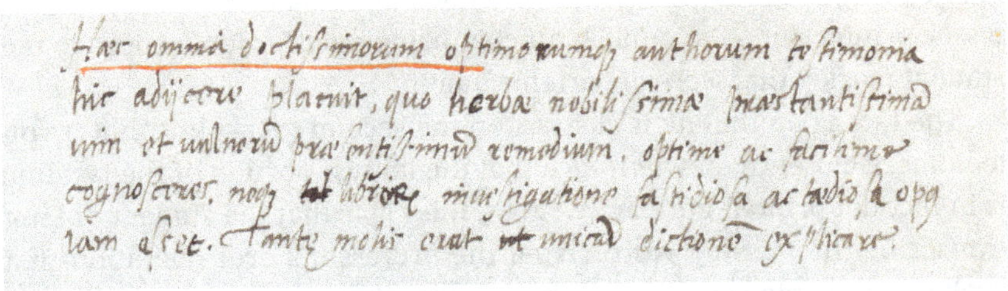

Figure 8.2. Concluding section of Nicolaus' note on dittany (fol. 15ᵛ). Basel, University Library, Ba Va 28:1.

to a printed book published by the family-run *Officina Frobeniana*, perhaps out of a sense of pride.

In conclusion, this elaborate note on dittany, which reminds one of an entry in a commonplace book, provides much information about both the use and the circulation of books in the Trilingue classroom. The professor helped the students with excerpting, and at least some students took the pains to consult the original sources cited by the professor. The way in which these excerpts were copied can help us identify which editions were used. During class, the student had probably noted a draft version down, which he integrated as an interleaved page in the clean version of his notes. Interleaving served to accommodate a laborious intermezzo, consisting of a mini-essay with various excerpts from other printed books.

4. Student practices in handling books and their flaws

The commercialization of the printing press made the classroom experience less tedious. Students were able to simply buy textbooks to which they could add notes directly. The need to copy the reference text that was the subject of a lecture was now largely a thing of the past. However, the mechanical process of printing was not foolproof. Things could still go awry. Let us focus once more on Rescius' classes on Homer to which end he had published editions of the *Iliad, Odyssey, Batrachomyomachia*, and *Homeric Hymns* in 1535. The publication was initially delayed because of a lack of paper supply, and it seems that the printing process was not perfect either.[12] Johannes Aegidius' copy (DaLeT Copy ID 1), for example, has some imperfections in certain spots, where not enough ink was used in the printing process, resulting in a hardly legible text, as on the bottom of folium B iv^r (see Figure 8.3). This infelicity perhaps indicates that the employees at Rescius' printshop were not always that careful, as the professor-printer aimed to publish quickly, bringing affordable books to the student market that were of variable quality.

The fading on the ink is clearest on the second-to-last line, but if you look more closely, you will notice that the largest portion of the last line is in fact not printed but handwritten. It is clear that the student did not transcribe the missing words from the professor's oral recitation that probably took place and would have given rise to various orthographic errors (Van Rooy 2022: 192). Instead, the student Johannes Aegidius tried

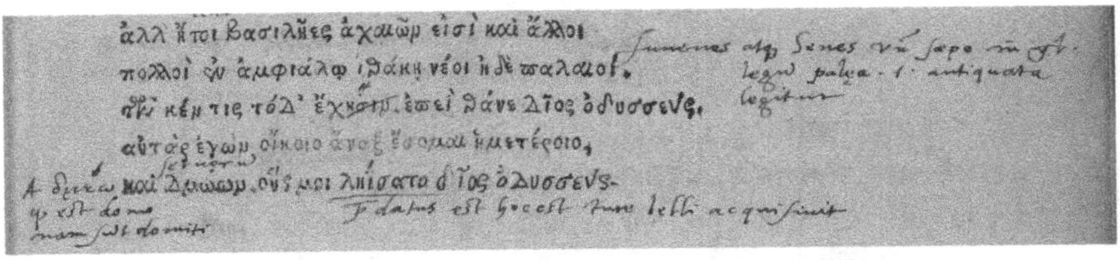

Figure 8.3. Aegidius' copy of the 1535 Homer edition (Leuven: Rescius), fol. B iv^r. Ghent, University Library, BIB.CL.00451.

Figure 8.4. Gerardus Aemilius' copy of the 1535 Homer edition (Leuven: Rescius), fol. B iv^r. Eton, Eton College Library, Fa.4.13.

to meticulously copy and imitate the form of the printed letters, probably looking at the copy of a fellow student sitting next to him, for instance Gerardus Aemilius Roterodamus, whose notes from the same course survive (see Figure 8.4).[13] Aegidius was in any case explicit about the fact that he was among a crowd of students. While adding a Latin translation ("co[n]ueniebamus" ["we were coming together"]) to the Greek word ἐμισγόμεθ' (*emisgómet*^h'), he added something that must have been a reference to the being together of the students in the classroom: "vt nos nu[n]c" ("like us now"; DaLeT Annotation ID 459).

The imperfection in Aegidius' copy, in sum, tells us something about student interactions in the classroom; most students would have owned a copy of their own and helped their neighbors out when their own copies of the textbook contained flaws. The student would take pains to imitate the printed letters of the text, perhaps to keep a clear distinction between printed text and handwritten notes, or to keep the reference text esthetically uniform.

5. Pedagogic pragmatism

In the sixteenth century, confessional tensions between Catholics and Protestants emerged and increasingly sharpened over time. This tension led the Catholic Church to closely monitor the print output in its territories. As a consequence, Catholic officials led by the Pope compiled a list of prohibited books, the so-called *Index librorum prohibitorum*, first published in 1557. Before that, local lists were issued in the Low Countries, the Italian lands, and France. For instance, in 1550, emperor Charles V commissioned a "catalogue or inventory of bad prohibited books and other good ones that one may teach the young students, following the advice of the University of Leuven."[14] In that book, the following grammarians for Greek were allowed: the local scholars Adrien Amerot, Nicolaus Clenardus, and Johannes Varennius—presumably all Catholic—as well as Jacobus Ceporinus, a protégé of Huldrich Zwingli and thus moving in reformed circles. This catalog thus proves that pedagogical purposes could supersede confessional concerns. A Protestant manual could be used if it did not contain anything suspect.

Sammelbände (collected volumes consisting of various works) further corroborate the pedagogic pragmatism evidenced in the 1550 Leuven book index.[15] A *Sammelband* recently acquired by KU Leuven Libraries and containing five Greek and Latin manuals printed between 1522 and 1534 carries countless handwritten annotations of Rodolphus Vuren, most likely a student at the Breda Latin school before it became reformed in 1591.[16] The volume contains, among other things, a rare manual of rhetoric of reformer Philip Melanchthon, right hand of Protestant pioneer Martin Luther (printed in Hagenau by Thomas Anshelm in 1522—USTC 666745), next to an utterly rare edition of Jacobus Ceporinus' Greek grammar (Antwerp: Johannes Steels, 1534—USTC 407376) and a copy of a Greek edition of the gospel of Mark (Leuven: Rutgerus Rescius & Bartholomaeus Gravius, 1534—USTC 410771). While the presence of a local edition of Ceporinus' Greek grammar may not be surprising in light of the index mentioned in the previous paragraph, the presence of Melanchthon's rhetoric in the volume of a Catholic student in Breda is unexpected, as the entire oeuvre of this prominent Protestant theologian was on the *Index librorum prohibitorum*. Judging by the notes by student Rodolphus Vuren, it seems that classroom praxis allowed greater lenience than the *Index*. Even though Melanchthon's name has been obscured by ink (Figure 8.5)

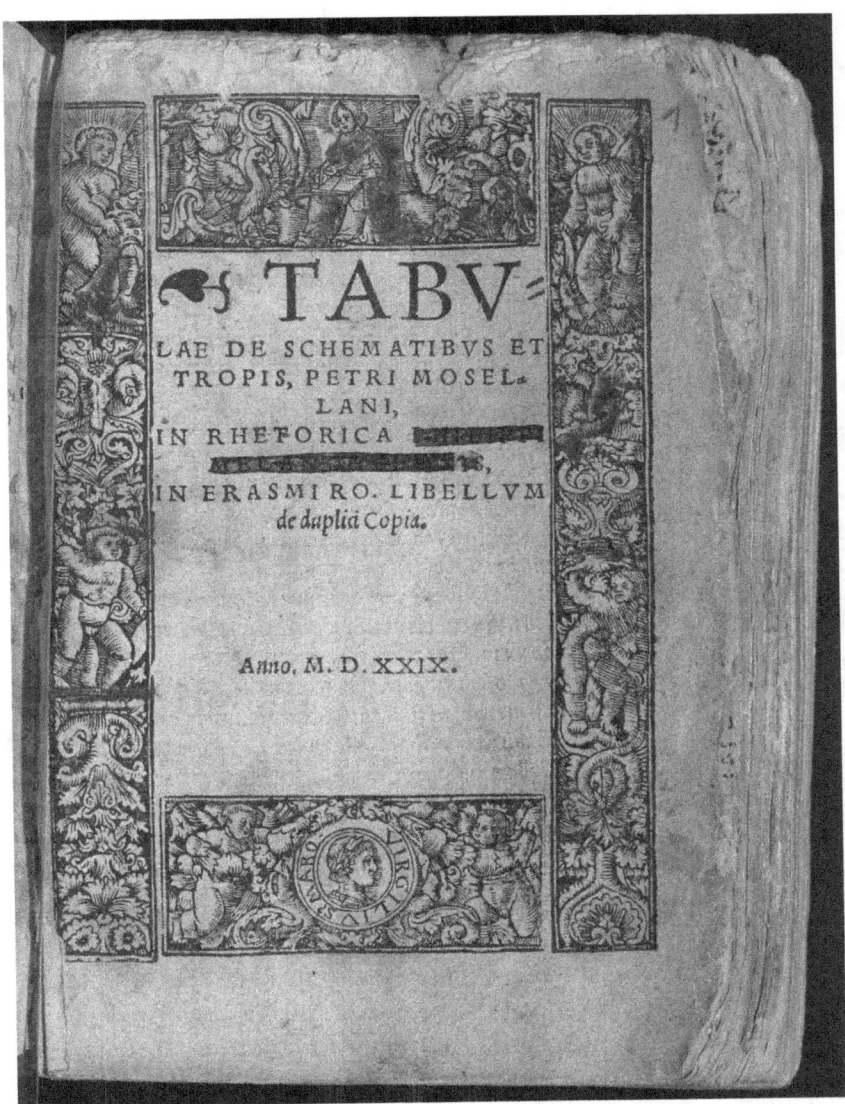

Figure 8.5. *Tabulae de schematibus et tropis, Petri Mosellani, In rhetorica, Philippi Melanchtonis, In Erasmi Ro. Libellum de duplici copia* (Antwerp: Michael Hillenius Hoochstratanus, 1529). Leuven, KU Leuven Libraries, Special Collections, CaaA2724.

in the *Tabulae de schematibus et tropis, Petri Mosellani, In rhetorica, Philippi Melanchtonis, In Erasmi Ro. Libellum de duplici copia* (Antwerp: Michael Hillenius Hoochstratanus, 1529—USTC 437459) and the titlepage of his abovementioned rhetoric manual *Institutiones rhetoricae* (Hagenau: Anshelm, 1522) is lacking altogether, the student did annotate these two copies extensively. This seeming cognitive dissonance reveals a certain pragmatism at schools, where teachers resorted to confessionally suspect handbooks when it suited their didactic purposes, and they saw no danger for accusations of heresy.[17]

In sum, student notes in a *Sammelband* can point to certain book use practices where confessional differences are concealed for didactic reasons. Catholic teachers appreciated the virtues of Protestant handbooks and used them extensively in their classes, although they seem to have had a policy of anonymizing the Protestants' works in some form or other. For instance, teachers could simply avoid mentioning Protestant authors in class or encourage their students to rip out the titlepage or to blacken the name of suspect authors. Including the works in a *Sammelband* may also have facilitated the circulation of Protestant works in Catholic teaching institutions.

6. Conclusion

In typical student notes research, the focus is on the contents of student notes, and of course understandably so. The case studies above have tried to show that the contents and material properties of the notes, if taken together, can also shed new light on diverse book-historical practices, including book circulation and sharing, interleaving practices, censorship, and *Sammelband* uses. This chapter has no doubt touched only on a fraction of what student notes may offer to book history. It is our hope that our modest example may inspire aspiring student notes researchers to in-depth investigations that surpass by far the limited scope of this exhibitory chapter.

Notes

1. See www.dalet.be (last accessed April 30, 2024) and Feys (2024).
2. Cf. Weaver (2022: 124, 152). Poliziano had also already used the term *interpres* to refer to the Homeric scholiast(s) in his 1488/9 lectures (Poliziano 2019: XCVII–XCIX, *passim*). We owe this information to Luigi Silvano.
3. USTC 708625, mistakenly identified as an edition in Latin. For more context on Cloet's bookshop and the inventory that was made of it, see the Introduction to this research companion.
4. Based on the title in Cloet's book inventory, Delsaerdt (2001: 474, n. 384) assumed that it concerned a translation, like we initially did when studying the notes.
5. A later entry in the inventory of Cloet's bookshop reads "Didinus in Odeceam Homeri Grece." This can only refer to the *editio princeps* of the D scholia on the *Odyssey* (Venice, 1528; USTC 826729) or its reprint (Paris, 1530; USTC 181212). See Delsaerdt (2001: 527, n. 933).
6. This copy is held in Brussels, KBR, shelfmark II 43.143 A (LP). The *editio princeps* of Divus' translation appeared in Venice in 1537 (USTC 835807). On the Leuven Spes binding, see Fogelmark (1990).
7. On Nicolaus' *peregrinatio academica*, see the more detailed account in Feys (2024: ch. 1.2.9).
8. This section is largely based on Feys (2024: ch. 4.3.4).
9. This note features on the recto and verso side of fol. 15. Images can be found here: https://www.dalet.be/bookpage/71. Last accessed April 26, 2024.
10. USTC 601711.
11. Cf. Delsaerdt (2001: 433 [n. 9], 445 [n. 117], 498 [n. 624], 499 [n. 628], 511 [n. 750], 523 [n. 888]).
12. In 1533-4, Rescius planned to issue all of Homer in separate fascicles. However, this plan did not come to fruition due to a lack of paper. In 1535, Rescius published the *Iliad*, *Odyssey*, *Batrachomyomachia*, and *Homeric Hymns* in two volumes. See de Vocht (1951–5, vol. 3: 113-115); Feys (2024: ch. 2.4.3).
13. DaLeT Person ID 64. Aemilius' notes survive in Eton, Eton College Library, Fa.4.13 (DaLeT Copy ID 59).
14. Van Rooy (2017: 63): "Die catalogen oft inuentarisen vanden quaden verboden boucken: ende van andere goede / diemen den iongen scholieren leeren mach / na aduys der Uniuersiteyt uan Loeuen." See De Bujanda (1986) for detailed information on the Leuven índices from 1546, 1550, and 1558.
15. The following paragraphs draw on Feys and Van Rooy (2021).
16. Leuven, KU Leuven Libraries, Special Collections, CaaA2724.
17. A similar conclusion can be reached for Nicolaus Episcopius the Younger's notes on *Aeneid* 12 discussed above. In at least six instances, the student—perhaps through Petrus Nannius' mediation—tacitly referred to Melanchthon's scholia on Vergil. See DaLeT Annotation IDs 1738, 1746, 1760, 1811, 1821, and 1859.

References

Adam, Renaud, and Alexandre Vanautgaerden. 2009. *Thierry Martens et la figure de l'imprimeur humaniste (une nouvelle biographie): Avec une liste de ses éditions et les adresses aux lecteurs signées par l'imprimeur. Ouvrage publié à l'occasion de l'exposition conçue et réalisée par la Maison d'Érasme 23 avril – 28 juin 2009*. Vol. 1. Turnhout: Brepols–Bibliothèque Sainte-Geneviève–Musée de la Maison d'Érasme.

DaLeT: Van Rooy, Raf, Xander Feys, Maxime Maleux, and Andy Peetermans. S.d. DaLeT: Database of the Leuven Trilingue. www.dalet.be. Last accessed April 30, 2024.

De Bujanda, J. M. 1986. *Index de l'Université de Louvain: 1546, 1550, 1558*. Sherbrooke–Genève: Centre d'Études de la Renaissance–Éditions de l'Université de Sherbrooke–Droz.

Delsaerdt, Pierre. 2001. *Suam quisque bibliothecam: Boekhandel en particulier boekenbezit aan de Oude Leuvense Universiteit, 16de–18de eeuw*. Leuven: Universitaire Pers Leuven.

Feys, Xander. 2020. "A Hippocrates for Eight Stuivers: On Petrus Nannius' Library and the Earliest Known Leuven Book Auction (1557)." *De Gulden Passer: Tijdschrift voor boekwetenschap* 98 (1): 239–57.

Feys, Xander. 2024. "Language and Literature Teaching in the Sixteenth Century: Vergil and Homer at the Louvain Collegium Trilingue." Unpublished PhD dissertation, Leuven: KU Leuven.

Feys, Xander, and Raf Van Rooy. 2021. "Marcus in Breda: Op het spoor van een Leuvens tekstboek (Rescius, 1534)." *Ex Officina: Nieuwsbrief van de Vrienden van de Universiteitsbibliotheek* 34 (1): 2–4.

Feys, Xander, and Raf Van Rooy. 2023. "Poetic Pen Trials in a Homeric Textbook: A Pseudo-Didymus from 1539 Returns to Leuven." *Ex Officina: Stories from the Stacks of KU Leuven Libraries*: 7–8.

Fogelmark, Staffan. 1990. *Flemish and Related Panel-Stamped Bindings: Evidence and Principles*. New York: Bibliographical Society of America.

Poliziano, Angelo. 2019. *Appunti per un corso sull'Odissea*. Edited by Luigi Silvano. 2nd edn. Alessandria: Edizioni dell'Orso.

Tournoy, Gilbert. 2018. "De boekenschenking van Joris van Oostenrijk aan het Leuvense Collegium Trilingue." *De Gulden Passer: Tijdschrift voor boekwetenschap* 96 (2): 283–95.

Tournoy, Gilbert. 2020. "Nouvelles recherches sur les livres de Jérôme de Busleyden et de la bibliothèque du Collège des Trois Langues à Louvain." *Annales de l'Institut archéologique du Luxembourg – Arlon* 149–50: 93–134.

Van Rooy, Raf. 2017. "Taalhandboeken en censuur." In *Erasmus' droom: Het Leuvense Collegium Trilingue 1517–1797. Catalogus bij de tentoonstelling in de Leuvense Universiteitsbibliotheek, 18 oktober 2017 – 18 januari 2018*, edited by Jan Papy, 63–5. Leuven–Paris–Bristol, CT: Peeters.

Van Rooy, Raf. 2022. "In Rutger Rescius' Classroom at the Leuven Collegium Trilingue (1543–1544): His Study Program and Didactic Method." In *Trilingual Learning: The Study of Greek and Hebrew in a Latin World (1000–1700)*, edited by Raf Van Rooy, Pierre Van Hecke, Toon Van Hal, 179–205. Turnhout: Brepols.

Verweij, Michiel. 2002. "Een onbekend handschrift van het Collegium Trilingue in Londen." *Ex Officina: Nieuwsbrief van de Vrienden van de Universiteitsbibliotheek* 15(3): 4–5.

de Vocht, Henry. 1951–5. *History of the Foundation and the Rise of the Collegium Trilingue Lovaniense 1517–1550*. 4 vols. Louvain: Librairie Universitaire Ch. Uystpruyst.

Weaver, William P. 2022. *Homer in Wittenberg: Rhetoric, Scholarship, Prayer*. Oxford: Oxford University Press.

CHAPTER 9

Visual History

Alicja Bielak and Gwendoline de Mûelenaere

1. Introduction

"Pictures [...] are very apt to mislead."[1] Although Pliny the Elder's reservation about pictures applied to botanical sketches, it can be linked to a broader objection of the ancients toward images. First, it was believed that art is never fully mimetic and therefore unable to reflect nature. Second, art is deceptive—a sketch is created from immediate experience, and as such is hardly trustworthy. Pliny's skeptical approach to images is reflected in the attitude of scholars toward the role of visual representations in science, which for a long time remained in the margins of interest of both science and art historians. In fact, it is only in the last thirty years that research on the dialog between the pictorial arts and the creation and diffusion of knowledge has gained strength, based on the legacies of Erwin Panofsky, Alexander Koyré, and more recently of Michael Baxandall, Svetlana Alpers, and Samuel Y. Edgerton. In the mid-1990s, seminal publications—for instance, by Horst Bredekamp, Lorraine Daston and Katherine Park, Paula Findlen, Martin Kemp, and Eileen Reeves— gave a new dimension to the relationship between the history of art and the history of science. The interest in objects that had previously been overlooked was pointed out: natural-historical drawings and specimens, geometrical diagrams, scientific instruments, and mechanical marvels were placed in dialog with paintings and sculptures (Marr 2016: 1,000).

Among these new orientations, the *Bildwissenschaft* ("science of the image"), a German variety of visual studies, proposed different approaches to images, their interpretation, and their social significance.[2] Other trends highlighted the complementarity of art and science, and the necessary collaboration between scientists, artists, engravers, and printers to make the empirical turn possible—marked by such richly and artfully illustrated publications as *De humani corporis fabrica* (1543) by Andreas Vesalius.[3] Research on early modern art and science, and in particular on images related to the acquisition, production and presentation of knowledge, has gained further momentum since the early 2000s.[4]

In recent studies, art historians tend to avoid the term "science" (which does not have the same meaning as *scientia* in early modern times) in favor of "knowledge" and "technique," broader and less anachronistic terms. The expression "epistemic images," which was not used by the early moderners, is more and more present in the studies on early modernity. Given its relative youth and the wide range of definitions available today, there is still no consensus as to the precise meaning of an "epistemic image" (Marr 2016: 1,005). One of the definitions states that it is "an image made with the intent not only of depicting the object of scientific inquiry but also of replacing it" (Daston 2015: 17–18). A broader definition considers that an epistemic image refers to "any image that was made with the intention of expressing, demonstrating or illustrating a theory" (Lüthy and Smets 2009: 399n2).

In this chapter devoted to illustrated student notebooks, we want to highlight the various roles of this heterogeneous imagery: next to epistemic images there are also, among other types, ornamental and humorous images. Such visual material can give us information about the authors of the manuscripts and their curriculum, but also about topical religious or political concerns, extracurricular activities, and social networks developed during the study years, as do the *libri amicorum* that flourished in parallel from the sixteenth century onward. Our analysis will be based on the collected corpus from the old university of Leuven and the colleges and universities in the Polish–Lithuanian Commonwealth written from the mid-sixteenth century to the eighteenth. About 658 student notebooks produced at Leuven have been preserved, 490 of which contain at least one image, and 206 notebooks contain ten images or more. Most of these notebooks can be consulted in the Magister Dixit database.[5] The visual elements in student notebooks are presented in Section 2. Then, we propose a classification of the most common images inserted in this corpus, by function and subject matter (Section 3). Finally, we discuss in particular the role of emblems as didactic and mnemonic devices through several examples (Section 4).

2. Visual elements in notebooks

Student notebooks bear witness to the teaching methods and contents of the courses given in medieval and early modern European universities. At arts faculties in particular, students took note of lectures on logic, physics, metaphysics, or ethics dictated by the professor. Analyzing such documents eventually leads the researcher to come across visual elements—from *probationes pennae* and *nota bene* markings (*manicula*) through organized visualizations of information (tables, diagrams, charts) to hand-drawn pictures or pasted engravings. Graphic materials accompanied students in the classroom, in the library, and at home thanks to the invention of printing. Teachers started using blackboards, hung decorative syllabuses on classroom doors and large thesis broadsides, and even applied paintings directly on the school walls.[6] This specific practice can be exemplified by the geometric diagrams placed in the mid-1600s on the walls of the *Lectorium of Pythagoras* and serving as teaching aids at the university of Cracow in Poland (Figure 9.1).

Figure 9.1. Partly reconstructed geometrical figures painted on the wall of the *Lectorium of Pythagoras* in the Collegium Maius in Cracow, Poland, *c.* 1650. Museum of the Jagiellonian University.

2.1. Heterogeneous visual languages

The drawn or engraved images inserted in the notebooks use very heterogeneous visual languages, and do not all seem, a priori, to be directly related to the subject being taught. At the very beginning of the notebook, the reader can often find a decorative drawing imitating a title page or a purchased engraving with blanks to be filled in with information about the student, professor, academic year, and subject (Figures 9.2–3).

In the Leuven notebooks, the name of the pedagogy, or college, was often mentioned.[7] Other ornamental elements include floral decorations,

Figure 9.2. Pen drawing in Ioannes Perowic, *Tractatus in primam D. Thomae partem Theologiae scholasticae de Trino Deo et Uno*, 1627–9. BN, MS 3321 II, title page.

banderols, or initials. Students also portrayed university buildings, the students' everyday life—involving drinking, smoking tobacco, and spending time in taverns (Figure 9.4)—as well as humorous and comical scenes (Van Vaeck and Verberckmoes 2012). Religious scenes were the first representations included in notebooks in Leuven, in the fifteenth and sixteenth centuries.[8]

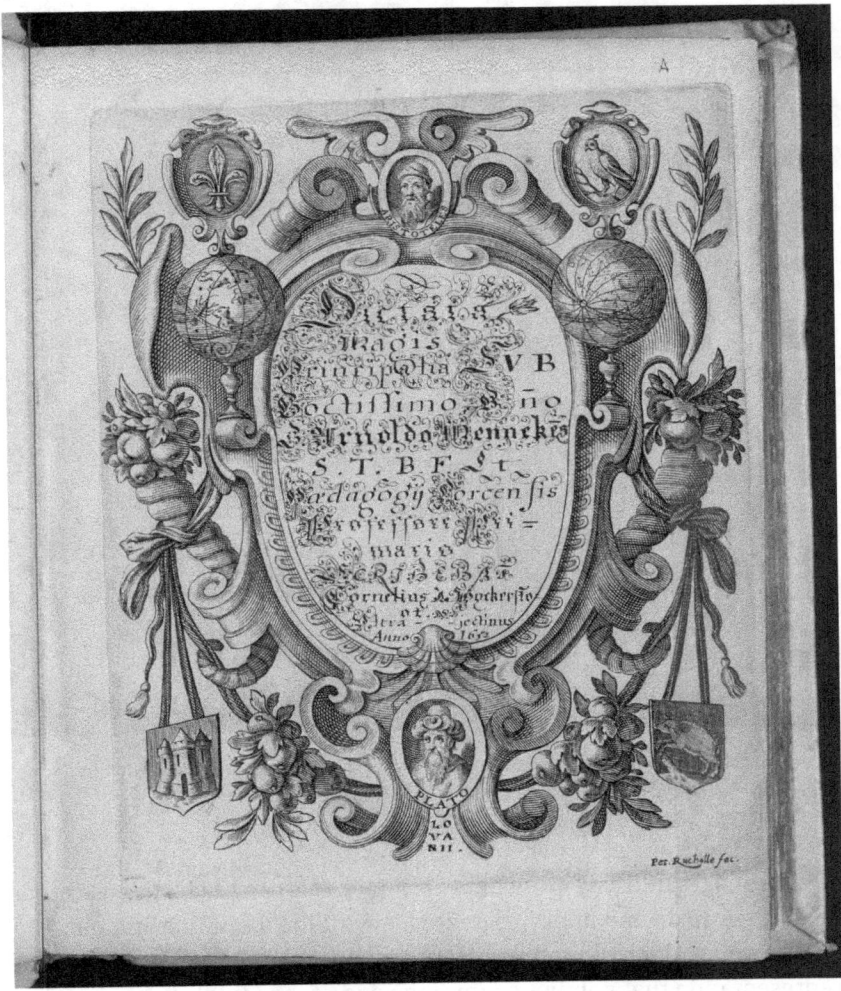

Figure 9.3. Peter Rucholle, engraved titlepage with signs of the four pedagogies in Cornelius Van Wijckersloot, *Logica*, 1652–3. UCLouvain, MS C2, fol. A^r.

Figure 9.4. *Tractatus de differentia*, colored pen drawing with humorous inscription in Ludovicus van Colen, *Logica*, 1663–4. KBR, MS II 1249, f. 36ʳ.

The images fulfilling an evident epistemic role can be classified according to their form and appropriateness toward the discipline at hand. The forms can be divided into two categories: one diagrammatic—a mode of representation that dominated until the end of the Middle Ages—and the other naturalistic. The choice depended on the visualization needs for

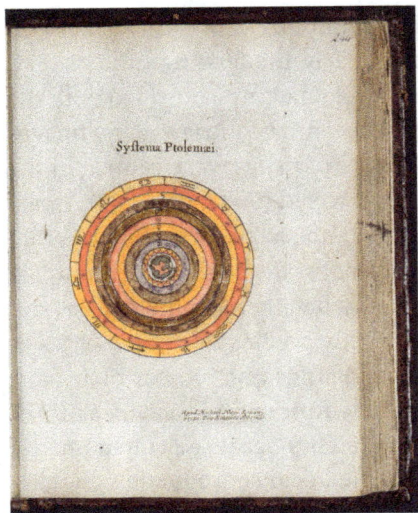 

Figure 9.5a–b. Michael Hayé, *Systema Ptolemaei* and *Systema Copernici*, colored engravings in Leo Josephus Daco, *Physica. Metaphysica*, 1678. KBR, MS II 106, fol. 244^r and 250^r.

each field of study. For instance, notes on astronomy, which mobilized knowledge in mathematics and physics to study celestial objects and phenomena, included several systems of representation: descriptive images (for example, of scientific instruments such as armillary spheres and astrolabes), purely mathematical diagrams, and visual depictions of mechanisms that cannot actually be seen by the naked eye (Figure 9.5a–b).[9]

To support the teaching of the various branches of physics, a set of fifty-five engravings produced by the printers Michael Hayé and Lambert Blendeff started to appear in about 1670 in Leuven notebooks. Many of these engravings show mathematical deconstructions of physiological, mechanical, or astronomical topics (Vanpaemel 2011: 249). According to Geert Vanpaemel, "the Louvain [set of] engravings should be considered as a vehicle for the introduction of Cartesianism in the Faculty." In fact, the obvious Cartesian orientation of the images was not in line with the more prudent position of the faculty, as they did not correspond entirely to the doctrine taught.[10]

The requirement for naturalistic representation has been present in natural philosophy since antiquity.[11] Conrad Gessner (1516–1565), important for modern natural history as the author of the first zoological encyclopedia, sketched the observed animals himself "so that students may more easily recognize objects that cannot be very easily described in words" (Hall 1996: 17). The outset of early modern natural history, including the twin disciplines of botany and anatomy, coincided with the rise of printing. In the sixteenth and seventeenth centuries, many images produced in these fields, replicable by way of print, were central in the diffusion of knowledge about the natural world (Swan 2011: 186). In art history, an argument first made by Erwin Panofsky (1962: 140) entails that "the rise of those particular branches of natural science which may be called observational or descriptive—zoology, botany, paleontology, several aspects of physics and anatomy—was directly predicated upon the rise of the representational techniques." Ivins and Millis (1953: 3), for their part, argue that the print practice encouraged scientific progress not because of the naturalism of the images it disseminated but because printed images are multiple and identical, so the stable means of reproduction enabled the unification and development of modern sciences. This view gives an epistemologically and socio-historically grounded model of the manner in which pictures helped to shape science (Swan 2011: 187–8). In student notebooks, loose prints displaying a naturalistic way of visualization proved to be a very useful didactic aid (Figure 9.6).

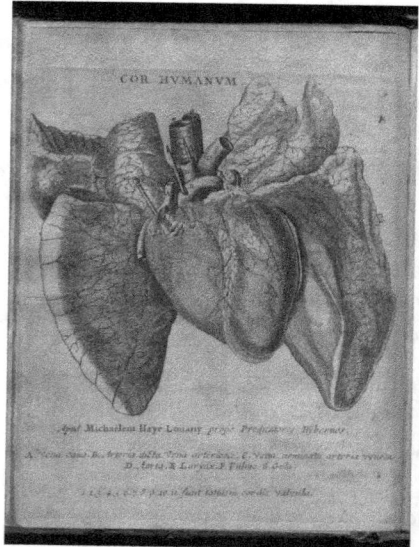 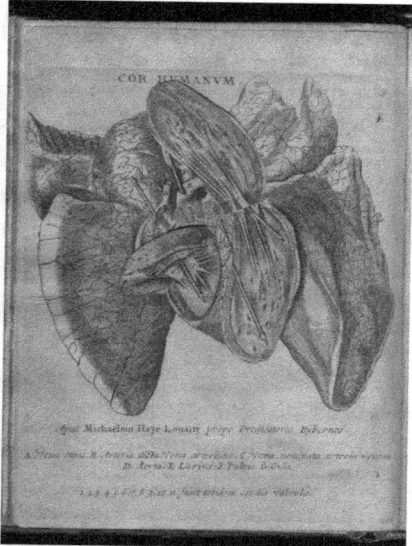

Figure 9.6a–b. Michael Hayé, *Cor humanum*, engraving in Albertus Boone, *Physica. Metaphysica*, 1680–1. Interactive anatomical charts (on the right: two movable elements are lifted). UCLouvain, MS C165, f. 48^v.

2.2. Diagrams

Among the most frequent illustrations in the notebooks are those accompanying topics on the *trivium*, a division of the liberal arts including grammar, logic, and rhetoric and taught in Europe from the Middle Ages to the eighteenth century. These images include diagrams on logic and dialectic, three of which are discussed in detail below: the Porphyrian tree, Aristotelian diagrams (for example, the square of opposition), and the *pons asinorum*.[12]

Firstly, the *arbor* ("tree") model constituted a fundamental pillar of the materiality of reasoning in Western history. The tree figure was used commonly as a mnemonic device from the twelfth century. The first formal tradition that presided over the medieval culture of the distributing tree gave rise to the so-called Porphyrian tree (*arbor porphyriana*), which presents Aristotle's classification of categories (Figure 9.7). The tree consists of three columns of words: the middle column (assimilated to the trunk of a tree) contains alternatingly the series of *genus* and *species*, while the left and right columns (assimilated to the branches of the tree) contain

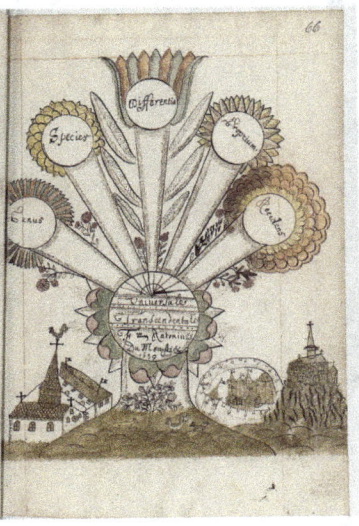

Figure 9.7. Pen drawing in Paweł Szczebietowicz, rhetoric and dialectic notebook written during the lectures of Mikołaj Sulikowski, 1634–5. Warsaw, BN, MS 6743 I, fol. 55ᵛ.

Figure 9.8. *Universale Transcendentale*, drawing in a philosophy notebook of Antoine du Moustier, 1639. Paris, BnF, Département des Manuscrits, Fonds latin 18441, fol. 66ʳ.

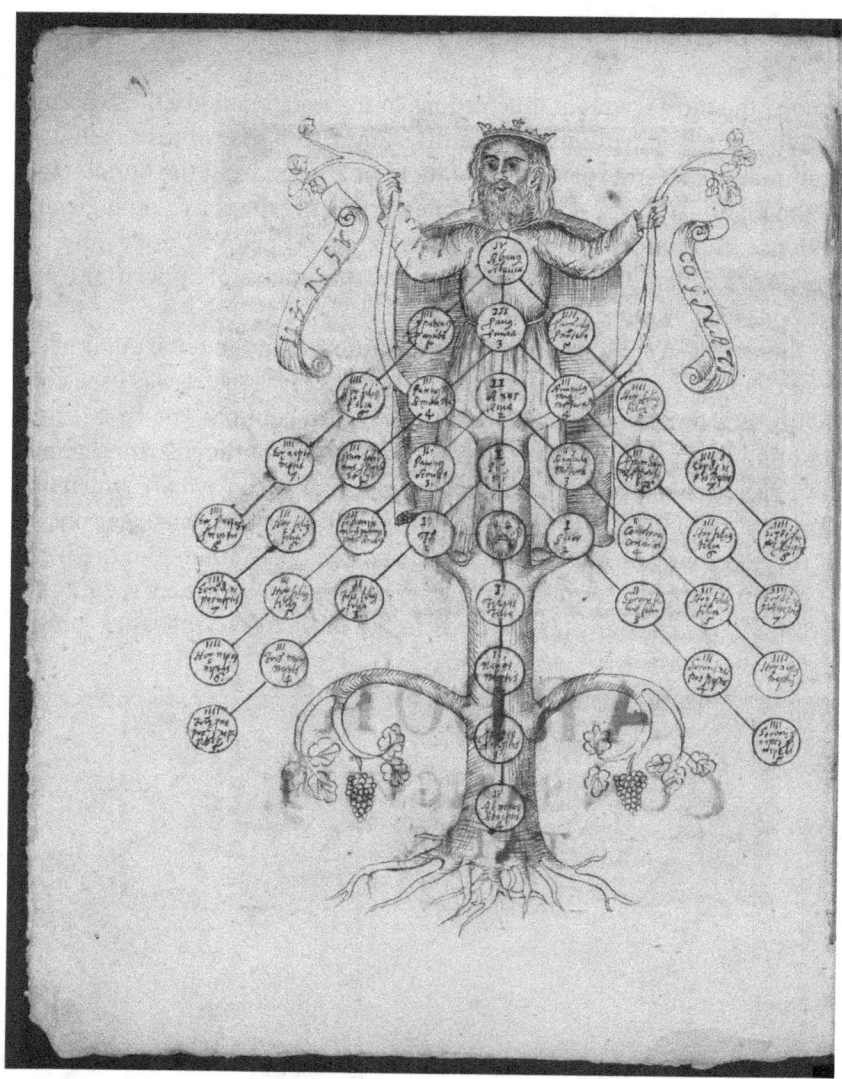

Figure 9.9. Pen drawing in Tomasz Drezner, *Explanatio Institutionum Imperatoris Iustiniani nec non Institutionum Iuris Polonici ab anno 1612*, 1610–12. BN, MS BOZ 1526, fol. 10ᵛ.

the *differentiae*. A variation of this widespread model can be found in a Paris notebook (Figure 9.8). The drawing offers a visualization of the *Isagoge*, Porphyry's introduction to Aristotle's *Categories*. The five predicables (*praedicabilia*) indicated here—*genus, species, differentia, proprium,*

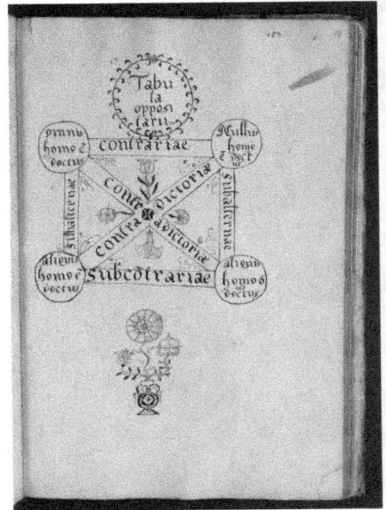 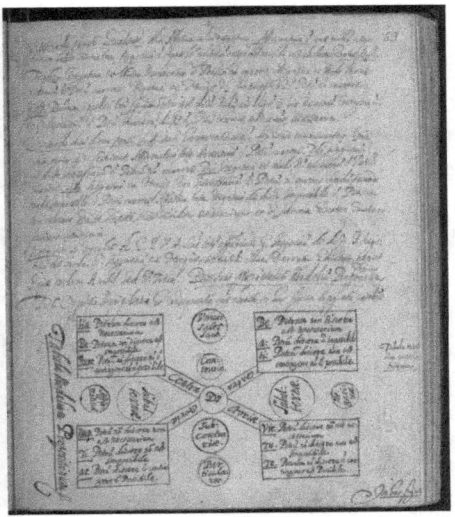

Figure 9.10. *Tabula oppositarum*, pen drawing in Petrus Michon and Johannes de Bundele, *Logica*, 1621–6. KBR, MS 3487-3490, fol. 158ʳ.

Figure 9.11. Expanded *tabula oppositorum* drawing in Paweł Szczerbietowic, rhetoric notebook written during the lectures of Mikołaj Sulikowski, 1634–5. BN, MS 6743 I, fol. 69ʳ.

accidens—are known from Aristotle's *Topica*. This layout differs from the deductive model present in Porphyry's tree, which emphasizes primarily the first three predicables (*genus, species, differentia*).

Another tradition nourishes the medieval culture of the distributive tree: that of genealogy. Tree diagrams such as *arbores juris* (*consanguinitatis* and *affinitatis*), showing family connections in order to regulate inheritance issues, can be found in notebooks on civil law (Figure 9.9; Virenque 2022: 7).

A second kind of diagram widely represented in notebooks on dialectic is the square of opposition or *tabula oppositarum* (Figures 9.10–9.11). This diagram was based on Aristotle's classification of propositions (singular, particular, universal) and their reciprocal logical relations (for example, opposition, contradiction).[13] The classification, outlined in *De interpretatione*, was widely commented on in the Latin world from Boethius onward.

Third, the *pons asinorum* ("donkeys' bridge") was a device facilitating the search (*inventio*) of possible "middle-terms" connecting the major and minor terms of valid syllogistic figures (Figure 9.12). This basic skill in dialectic was presented to students at the start of their curriculum and

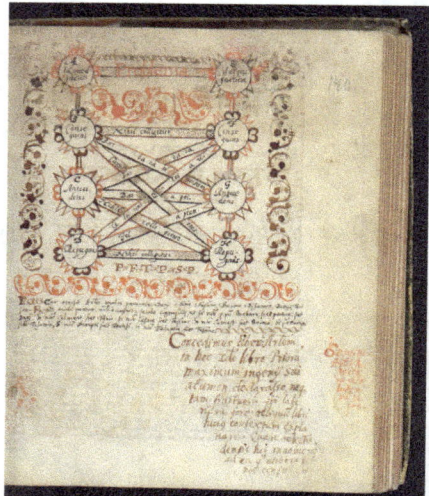 

Figure 9.12. *Pons asinorum*, pen drawing in *Prolegomena in universam Aristotelis logicam tradita in Collegio Posnaniensi a Rdo P. Matthaeo Bembo*, 1598–9. BN, MS 6963 I, fol. 140ʳ.

Figure 9.13. *Pons asinorum*, engraving in Georgius Jodoigne, *Logica*, 1677–8. KU Leuven Libraries, Special Collections, MS 250, fol. 132ʳ.

allowed them to overcome the traps of logic.[14] The hexagonal diagram, prepared for the first time by the Byzantine grammarian and philologist John Philoponus (c. 490–c. 570), embodied Aristotle's rules of middle-term finding described in the *Prior Analytics* (43a–45b). Many Leuven notebooks include an engraving specially prepared for the course and printed by Michael Hayé. It depicts the diagram with humorous surroundings referring to the student's difficulties in learning logic (Figure 9.13).[15] The boy who wants to go from F to B, without following the path of valid syllogisms, falls into the donkey pond where he joins lazy, gambling, and silly students. These are accompanied by things that distract them from their studies: cards, dice, pot and pipe, hunting rifle, tennis racket, musical instruments, and fashionable clothes (Papy 2012: 117).

Figures like trees and diagrams were starting points for mastering the basic rules of logical inference (Carruthers 2008: 250–3). Recently, Ayelet Even-Ezra (2021), by analyzing medieval diagrams from a historical, linguistic, and cognitive perspective, has shown that the way people represented their inner thoughts in images not only resembled but also changed their manner of thinking.

2.3. The materiality of the image

The study of images in manuscript notes in the age of print also requires an examination of their material dimension and, consequently, of their distribution. A variety of techniques and practices can be found in the notebooks, such as original ink drawings, small doodles, drawings after engravings; coloring; collages; association of visual material with new titles or with other drawings and engravings; and insertion of printed material (thesis broadsides, illustrated broadsheets, printed lists of students folded and pasted to fit the book format).

The first type of illustrations is sketched or painted images. They may have originated in the student's imagination, but they often had their inspiration in book illustrations or prints. A drawing can tell us what the student had in mind when he sketched it, even if he did not admit it in the text of the notes. An example would be the sketches in a notebook written down at some point between 1676 and 1732 by the Polish student P. Kisielewicz who took notes of lectures based on *Descriptio universae naturae ex Aristotele* by the French author Jacques Charpentier (1524–1574). The notes on the internal senses were accompanied by a drawing showing a cross-section of the human head and locating the *sensus communis* and four other parts of the brain: imaginative, phantastic, estimative, and cogitative (Figure 9.15). The illustration is absent from the Cracow edition of Charpentier's book (1579), as well as from other editions. In fact, the engraving draws on Gregor Reisch's (c. 1470–1525) *Margarita philosophica*, a popular sixteenth-century summary of the late medieval curriculum in philosophy (thirteen editions, *princeps* in 1503; Figure 9.14; Cunningham and Kusukawa 2010: xxviii–xxx). Being familiar with the graphic pattern, one can notice differences, including an additional explanation made by the student on the illustration (absent in the printed edition): "sunt sensus quinque quorum peccata relinque" ("there are five senses, whose sins you must abandon!"). The formula was already present in some versions of the *Carmen de Misteriis Ecclesiae* by the thirteenth-century French professor Johannes de Garlandia (c. 1270–1320), who created a rhymed didactic text to improve students' mastery of the material. Thanks to the illustration, we learn some new facts about the teaching process of which the notebook was the fruit. It is likely that the teacher dictated the rhyme about sinfulness for both mnemonic and moralizing purposes.

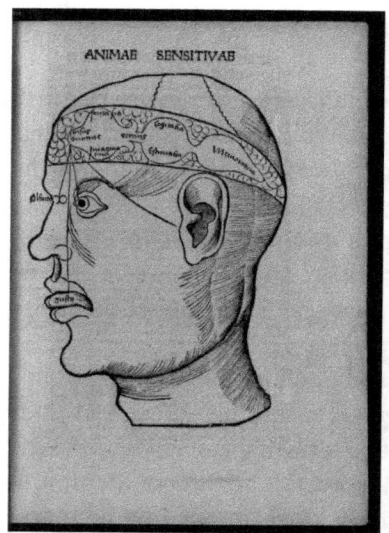 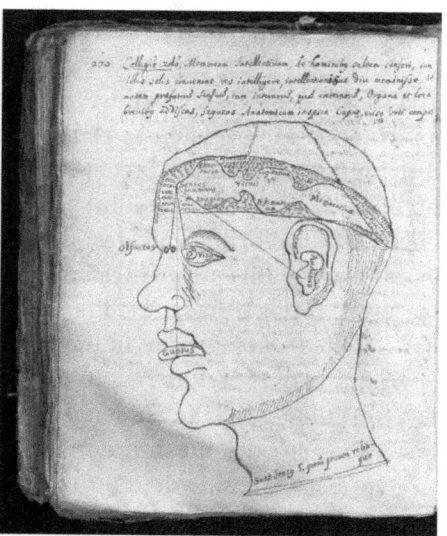

Figure 9.14. Woodcut in Gregor Reisch, *Margarita philosophica*, Friburgi 1503, sig. H2^r: diagrammatic representation of human senses.

Figure 9.15. Pen drawing in anonymous lecture notes, c. 1676–96. BN, MS 12349 II, fol. 186^v.

Moreover, a familiar sketch copying the same engraving is also found in a Leuven notebook dated 1680–1 (Figure 9.16). The drawing accompanies different topics taught by Léger Charles De Decker (1645–1723): Aristotle's local movement (*motus localis*) and the formation of sensations in the brain through vision. This way, the engraving first designed by the Swiss artist Urs Graf (1485–1529) continued to serve students well into the early eighteenth century and was still valued for its stimulation of cognitive powers, yet it did not necessarily relate to the text dictated in class.

Alongside drawings, print played a significant role in the dissemination of knowledge and unification of certain representations, due to its potential to produce multiple impressions: hundreds or thousands of identical copies of the same image. This great power of communication was especially important in such fields as botany, zoology, anatomy, medicine, geography, and astronomy (Dackerman 2011: 20, 26). Prints inserted by Leuven students in their course notes from the early seventeenth century were mainly scientific images (for example, anatomical plates, physical instruments, natural objects), but also allegorical series, personifications, and emblems, that is, an image–text composition consisting of

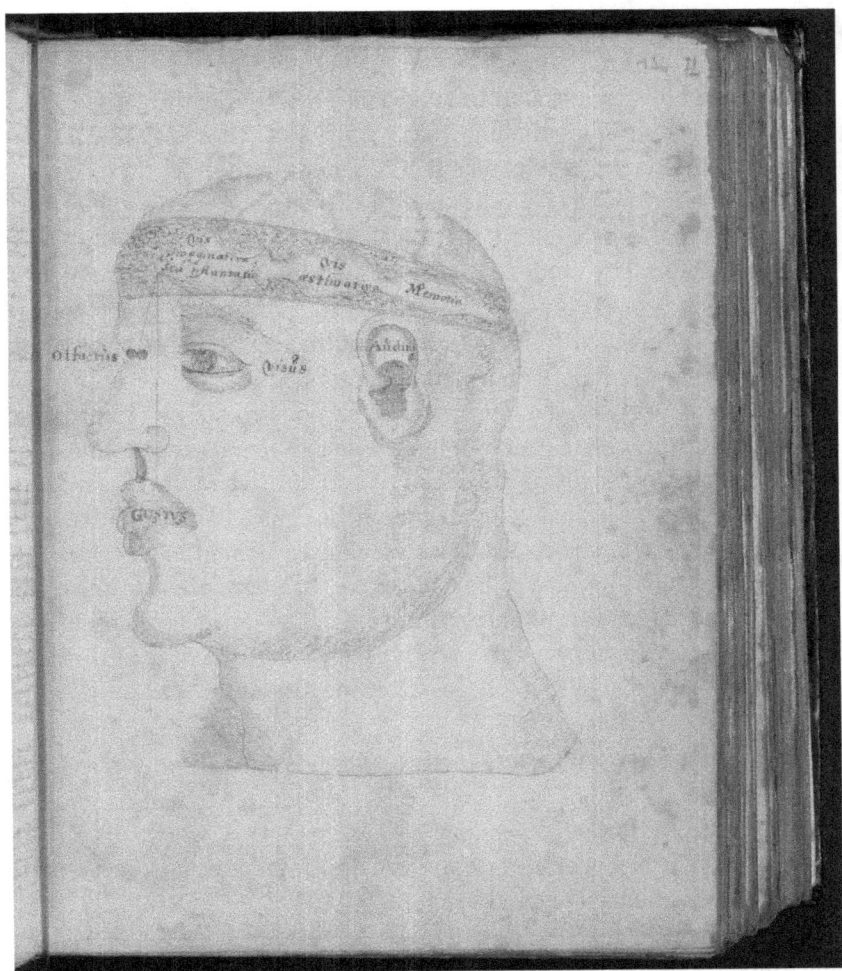

Figure 9.16. *De sensu*, pen drawing in Petrus Boonen, *Physica. Metaphysica*, 1680–1. UCLouvain, MS C165, f. 72ʳ.

a picture, motto, and subscription, as we will see below (Section 4.1). In such cases, engravings, either borrowed from cycles or books, or printed as separate prints, gained a new context and were subjected to activities such as bricolage, reuse, recycling, appropriation of images, and adaptation according to the content.

3. Classification of images in student notebooks

Taking the above into account, we propose a classification of the most frequent images in student notebooks. It is primarily based on the Leuven corpus of notebooks. Our choice is motivated by the fact that Leuven, thanks to the activity of printers (such as Michael Hayé, Lambert Blendeff, Petrus Denique, and Charles-Henri Becker), stimulated a trend of including visual materials in student notebooks, thus increasing their frequency. However, the types of images present in them are not peculiar to this university alone, so the following classification can be treated as a point of departure and comparison for other centers.

A first category, for which Opsomer (2000: 157) suggested a name, pertains to the university tradition in Leuven. A second category includes images providing a direct visual aid for learning. A third category includes representations using a symbolic language, such as allegories and emblems, mainly recycled from previously printed books. This categorization is not intended to be exhaustive. Its main aim is to show the diversity and eclecticism of images inserted in Leuven lecture notebooks, as well as the consistency in certain representations (title pages, diagrams, references to pedagogies or colleges) over the decades.

3.1. Traditional university iconography

Calligraphic lettering
Ornaments: floral decoration, banderols, ornamental cartouches surrounding titles, text shaped in objects[16]
Coats of arms
Religious scenes
Title pages mentioning the names of students and professors, academic year, and pedagogy
Landscapes, townscapes: views of Leuven, of university buildings
representations of the four pedagogies (symbols of the Falcon, the Lily, the Pig, and the Castle), teaching scenes
Popular topics, humor, and comical scenes, often with reference to everyday life of students (drinking, tobacco),[17] *memento mori*, grotesque figures, caricatures

Portraits of saints, the Virgin Mary, philosophers (Plato, Aristotle, Descartes), rulers, artists. Portraits often face titles in order to induce rhythm in the reading and therefore fulfill a mnemonic function.

3.2. Scientific drawings and engravings

Geometrical figures;
Diagrams: *pons asinorum*, Porphyrian tree, logical square;
Representations of Cartesian orientation:[18]
- Anatomical plates: human heart, stomach, respiration, human eye, vision
- Astronomical representations: Ptolemaic, Tychonic, and Copernican systems (Figure 5); stars, phases of the moon, eclipse, comets, winds, rainbows;

Experimental philosophy: two series by Becker in the eighteenth century.[19]

3.3. Symbolic language

Emblems (usually reused from non-academic publications);
Allegories and personifications often in series and sometimes related to chapters in physics (the five senses, the four continents, the twelve months); or personifications of disciplines (for example, *dialectica, geometria, arithmetica, rhetorica*);
Engravings of moral or allegorical nature reused by printers to match the teaching of logic.[20]

4. Emblems as didactic and mnemonic devices

4.1. Scientific emblemata

Emblematics is the name given to a manuscript or printed book composed according to the following principle: the page, or facing pages, contain a title, also called *inscriptio* or motto, with an engraving or a drawing, a *pictura*—whose visual elements are arranged in such a way as to narrate a scene (narrative composition) or to surprise (enigmatic composition). Under this image is added an epigram in verse, also called a *subscriptio*, sometimes followed by a commentary in prose, an *argumentum*

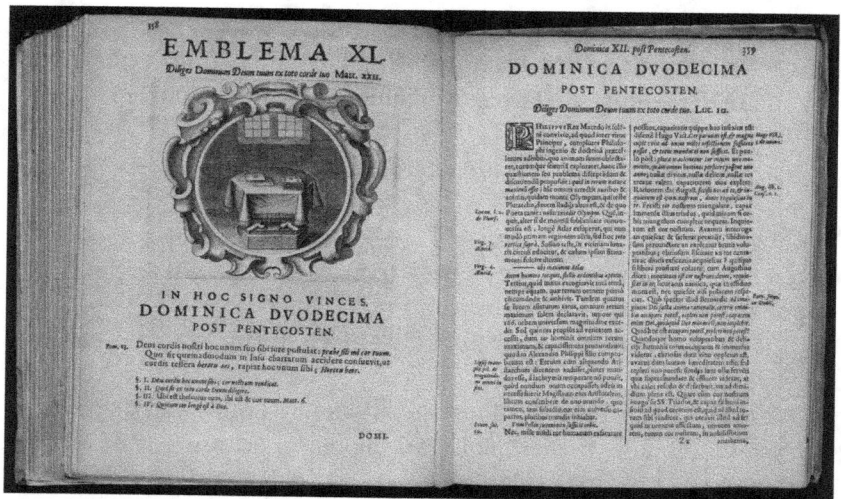

Figure 9.17. *Emblema XL*, in Hendrik Engelgrave, *Lux evangelica sub velum sacrorum emblematum recondita*, Antwerp, 1648, pp. 358–9. Williamstown, Massachusetts, Clarck Institute Library.

(Figure 9.17). This form of books is thus based on an association of two kinds of signs, verbal and visual, in order to create a metaphorical or allegorical composition. The image does not refer to the object it denotes, but to the notion that it connotes. If the combination is double (a title and an image), we speak of a motto; if it is triple (inscription, image, and subscription), we have an emblem. These collections, which have been rediscovered by scholars over the last thirty years, enjoyed considerable success in Europe from 1531 to the first half of the eighteenth century.[21] It is not easy to estimate the number of such books, but the art historian Peter Daly (2008: 2) has suggested that more than 6,500 handwritten and printed emblematic books were produced in early modern Europe, including new editions and translations.[22]

A characteristic of the *emblemata* practice is the recuperation and adaptation of existing visual formulas in various fields: profane love stories, moral and didactic lessons, or religious and meditative narratives. In the sixteenth and seventeenth centuries, the emblematic tradition, with its specific bimedial form, also played a role in early modern science. It is evidenced, for example, by its generous use by Conrad Gessner in his famous compendium of natural history, *Historia animalium* (1551–8, 4 vols.). As the historian of science William B. Ashworth (1996: 17–37) puts it, the "book [of nature] was written in the language of emblems, and if you do not read that language there is little that will make any sense." Emblems and symbols were sometimes included in rhetoric as part of the so-called *eruditionis species* ("display of erudition") and constituted sources of invention and argument (Górska 2009: 99–102). From the end of the sixteenth century, the use of emblematics as aids to memorization in the teaching sphere grew in popularity. Recuperated from previous publications, emblems were by consequence vested with new meaning, as is the case for several engravings reused in handwritten *dictata*.

4.2. Recuperation of emblematic devices

Emblems added in notebooks from Leuven were mainly taken from two series offered for sale by Michael Hayé, which circulated during the period 1660–1764 (Smets 2014: 205–7). The engravings were originally designed for meditative publications, *Lux Evangelica* by Hendrik Engelgrave (1610–1670) and *Firmamentum Symbolicum* by Sebastian a Matre Dei (= Stanisław Szulc, d. 1681). The copperplates were sold to Hayé in the late 1660s.[23] In a second state, a caption was added to each engraving to coincide with the content of the course, either in logic or in physics.[24] The engravings then became part of a long academic tradition as they were frequently used until 1764, and then occasionally until the suppression of the university of Leuven in 1797.

An emblem from the 1648 edition of the *Lux Evangelica* depicts a deck of cards placed on a hexagonal table (Figure 9.17). The two visible cards are the ace of hearts and the five of hearts. The *pictura* is accompanied by a quote from Matthew (22:37): *Diliges Dominum Deum tuum ex toto corde tuo* ("You shall love the Lord your God with all your heart"), and the motto *In hoc signo vinces* ("In this sign you will conquer").[25] Other biblical quotes are offered in the text. They are taken from Proverbs (23:26), "My son, give me your heart" (*praebe fili mi cor tuum*), and Matthew (6:21), "Where your treasure is, there your heart will be also" (*ubi est thesaurus tuus ibi est et cor tuum*). The emblem therefore focuses on love for God, through the daily representation of the heart in the card game.

When the same vignette is used in a student notebook of *Logica* dated 1693–4 (Figure 9.18), it is accompanied by the printed caption *De signo* ("On the sign"). On the facing page, handwritten titles indicate

Figure 9.18. *De signo*, engraving in Norbertus Josephus Ligiers, *Logica*, 1693–4. KU Leuven Libraries, Special Collections, MS 353, fol. 386ᵛ.

Tractatus secundus De signis et vocibus ("Second treaty: Concerning signs and sounds") and *Pars prima De signis* ("First part: On signs"). Here, the symbol of the card suit refers to signs as conventional elements of language, the topic of this chapter in the philosophy course. The engraved composition, originally created to convey a moral message through the combination of words and images, is here adapted to match the logical content of the notebook. The card game denotes signs understood as an entity consisting of a signifier and a signified (heart/love). Therefore, the image in the notebook works on a more basic level than it did in the emblem book. No religious or moral interpretations are involved in this imagery. Rather, it serves as a concrete visual reminder of the academic text (Berger 2017: 141).

Figure 9.19. *De signo et voce*, engraving in red ink in Cornelius van Bommel, *Logica*, 1698–9. KBR, MS II 3595, fol. 267ʳ.

Figure 9.20. *Dialecticae dictatorum pars seconda*, pen drawing in Johannes Peeters, *Dialectica*, 1701–3. Houghton Library, Harvard University, MS Lat 481, seq. 45.

Another composition, taken from a later edition of the *Lux Evangelica* (1652, *emblema* VI, p. 64), was reused to illustrate the same subject. In *Logica* (1698–9), a notebook belonging to Cornelius van Bommel, the caption *De signo et voce* ("On the sign and the sound") was added in handwriting by the student under the engraving in red ink (Figure 9.19). The two engravings served as models for a drawing inserted in a manuscript of *Dialectica* dated approximately 1701–1703 (Figure 9.20).[26] The student, Johannes Peeters, created an original composition on the basis of two images taken from Hendrik Engelgrave's publication, and combined two visual devices already used in previous university notebooks to denote a logical content. The circular drawing includes, written on the wall, the title "Dictations of dialectic, second part on signs and sounds by which is expressed the first operation of the mind."[27] On the tablecloth is written the first question (*Quaestio prima*) addressed in the chapter: "What is a sign and how manifold is it?" (*Quid et quotuplex sit signum*). This original composition shows the personal way in which students could experience the use of symbolic images.

In Peeters' manuscript, eight other large drawings are combinations copied after engraved models, including Hercules as Atlas with a representation of parallax, probably inspired by a scientific engraving (p. 6),[28] and Baucis and Philemon with a depiction of the Leuven Trinity College, after an engraving by Lambert Blendeff (p. 50).[29] In addition, an original composition serving as a title page displays a painter at easel (fol. A). It constitutes a mise en abyme of the student writing the course title on a canvas. According to this visual device, the work's producer, here the student, stages himself creating the representations in his own notebook.[30] The set of colored drawings in this manuscript therefore testifies to the creativity developed by the student who skillfully combined several images from different sources (mythology, classical literature, scientific writings, preaching books, descriptive views of university buildings) to produce meaning. While most emblematic engravings, taken from the *Lux Evangelica* and the *Firmamentum Symbolicum* and enriched with a motto connected with the dictated text, were meant to be inserted in a specific place in the manuscript, students could also, as is the case here, make use of them at their own discretion by playing with the emblematic structure and the rhetorical value attached to it.[31]

Adding such visual material constituted an inventive and amusing pastime for students, but also allowed a personalization of the manuscript, which is reminiscent of the early modern *libri amicorum* tradition. A *liber amicorum* ("friendship book"), also called *album amicorum* ("list of friends"), is a personal notebook where one collects images (painted coats of arms, drawings, engravings) and texts (names, dedications, classical or biblical maxims or quotes, poems) from friends.[32] The practice of keeping an *album amicorum* started in the 1540s in the environment of the Protestant University of Wittenberg. There, Reformers such as Martin Luther and Philip Melanchthon would often encounter students requesting an autograph as a keepsake. The Protestant leaders would then write their entries in the margins of a book the student already owned, like a Bible or a scholarly text. The practice of asking people for an inscription quickly extended to other academic lecturers as well as fellow students. It gained popularity as many students did not restrict themselves to one university but made an academic tour throughout Europe. They used *alba amicorum* to build and maintain cultural, social, and professional networks during their formative years, as well as to remember people (professors, tutors, fellow students, compatriots, travel companions, relatives, and friends) and to document past events (Reinders and Vandommele 2022: 3). Similarly, the ornate student notebook, becoming more than a pedagogical tool, was a tangible witness, gleaming with color and humor, of the time spent at university. Afterward, it was destined to be exhibited among friends and relatives (D'Haenens 1994: 408–9).

4.3. Emblems as memory aids

Examples of this use of emblematics can also be found in Jesuit colleges in the Polish–Lithuanian Commonwealth. Such is the case with the manuscript of lectures on Greek and Roman mythology given by the Jesuit Mikołaj Kazimierz Sarbiewski (1595–1640), poet laureate (*poeta laureatus*) and lecturer on poetry and rhetoric at the Jesuit college in Połock. The didactic method of Sarbiewski was to provide the repository of ancient *loci* and show the possibility for Christian writers and rhetoricians to use them—in accordance with the Jesuit accommodation rule. Ancient mythology was for him a deformed echo of the events described in the Bible. The aforementioned manuscript probably represents a copy of Sarbiewski's lectures written after 1627 (Figure 9.21). The anonymous scribe reproduced, among other things, Claude Paradin's (1512–1578) emblems from the collection *Devises héroïques* (1557) (Figure 9.22). Thus, during a lecture on the symbolism associated with Apollo, Sarbiewski, citing the opinion of the Stoic Chaeremon and Porphyry, mentioned a rooster as one of the god's symbols. This is because the bird supposedly

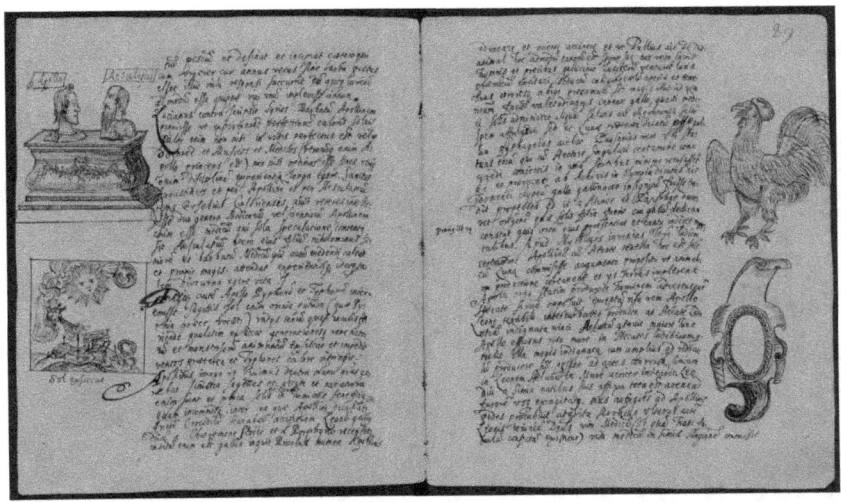

Figure 9.21. Notes from the lectures dictated by Maciej Kazimierz Sarbiewski (1595–1640) in Jesuit College in Polock (*post* 1627). BN MS I 3210, fol. 88ᵛ–89ʳ.

summons the dawn, while Apollo is the sun. In the Paradin collection, an emblem showing an identically depicted bird is described by the motto *Pacis et armorum vigiles* ("Watchmen of peace and war"). Here, the cock stands on a trumpet and symbolizes the summoning of both war and peace. One may wonder whether such an element served a mnemonic function and at the same time indicates (like a *manicula* or *nota bene*) that this paragraph discusses the symbol of the cock as Apollo or whether it supplements its meaning with that proposed by Paradin.

Another example, seen on the adjacent page, features the student's own emblematic composition—a human-faced sun with arrow-tipped rays is depicted in a square frame floating in the clouds in the sky above a dragon pierced by six arrows. Between them on the left is the image of a wind also with a human face and arrows stuck in it, blowing on the reptile. The student added a motto that reads "Sol exsiccat" ("The sun dries up"). The drawing accompanies the following description:

> It is further told that Apollo killed Python and Typhon with arrows. This is because the sun dries up all decay (which in Greek is called πύθω), striking the earth with its rays as if with arrows, and prevents the creation of venomous and monstrous creatures. It also eliminates winds and whirlwinds with its warmth.[33]

Figure 9.22. Claude Paradin, *Devises heroïques*, Lyon 1557, fol. 209.

The student in this example encapsulated the complex story of Gaia's child Pytho in a single symbolic image by choosing to depict him as a dragon, and not as a human as some commentators wanted. The association of rot with the dragon has its source in the Homeric *Hymn to Apollo* (v. 372–4) where Greek *púthein* (πύθειν) stands for "to cause to rot" (Sarbiewski 1972: 261, 724). Under the pen of the student, the taught material transferred into an active image (*imago agens*), a mental image that according to contemporary mnemotechnic treatises could be easily recollected in the memory's repository. The choice of the mental image should be dictated by its capacity of astonishing and moving the recipient, and thus, consequently, become better imprinted in the student's memory (Bolzoni 2004: 19; Yates 2011: 61–5). The sun aiming arrows at a large reptile fulfills such a requirement for amazement and emotional stirring. This practice indicates that a student of the Jesuit college, having studied according to the *ratio studiorum*,[34] used emblems also as part of his own preparation of notes and probably for better memorization of the material.

The insertion of emblems served in this way a mnemonic function. Their page-setting and iconic presence increased the visibility of textual subsets and activated the assimilation of the subject matter—as Francis Bacon (1561–1626) testified in his *De augmentis scientiarum* (1624): "The emblems bring together intellectual things and perceptible things, because what is perceptible is always more striking to the memory and is more quickly imprinted on it than what is intellectual."[35] Emblems were widely used in academic circles all over Europe. Creating and memorizing emblematic structures was particularly encouraged by the Jesuits, as testified by other teaching materials such as *affixiones* and thesis prints.[36] The examples of Johannes Josephus Peeters' manuscript and of Maciej Kazimierz Sarbiewski's script also show the importance of drawing and copying after prints in university notebooks. Copying an image was a method of learning the basic concepts of philosophy and mythology just as the act of copying down the lecturer's words.[37]

5. Conclusion

In the light of this analysis of the graphic elements in early modern student notebooks, we have underlined the fact that many actors were at work in the creation of the images, whether at the level of their invention or their execution. The collection from the university of Leuven provides an exceptional example of such a relationship, in which printers (Hayé, Blendeff, Denique, Becker) shaped, as it were, the contents of notebooks by preparing a series of engravings devoted to specific objects. They often used engravings designed for other publications, which they stripped of their original context. This is the case of the meditative emblems by Hendrik Engelgrave and Sebastian a Matre Dei that had been added to the printers' usual stock by chance (Van Vaeck 2002: 300). Students then used the purchased engravings in their notebooks for different purposes and in different ways. Thus, printmakers and students changed the context and perspective of the images by taking them out of a religious context and giving them a new purpose—a didactic one.

The visual material in the notebooks was the result of the students' creativity and served various functions, mainly of a decorative, mnemonic, and ordering nature. An order was induced throughout the volume by engravings, which were often inserted in series. Multiple copies of the same title page, sets of portraits, sequences of personifications, or allegories were placed to accompany titles or subtitles and make the structure of the text more visible. Drawn or printed images also provided the students with a manual activity to prevent boredom during class or study and to allow them to focus on the content. Furthermore, they could express changes or evolutions in teaching, as was the case with the set of engravings related to the philosophy curriculum at the Leuven faculty of arts (see Vanpaemel 2011). The frequency of illustrations also depended on the study field. The most common illustrations include diagrams associated with the teaching of dialectic and logic, as well as technical sketches characteristic of subjects such as natural philosophy, mathematics, and astronomy.

Additionally, the role of the Jesuits in promoting visual material as teaching devices must be emphasized. The Jesuits were quick to recognize the power of graphic design and began cooperating with leading printing houses in Europe because they knew that beautiful images had a stronger effect on the recipient (Freedberg 1989: 181–3). In addition to the special role of imagery emphasized in the *Ratio studiorum* (for instance, teaching how to create emblems), the script of Sarbiewski's lectures supplemented with emblems demonstrates the concern for aesthetics and the belief in the persuasive and epistemic (mnemonic) role of images for both teachers and students at Jesuit colleges.

Notes

1 "It was their [the Greek writers'] plan to delineate the various plants in colors, and then to add in writing a description of the properties which they possessed. Pictures, however, are very apt to mislead, and more particularly where such a number of tints is required, for the imitation of nature with any success; in addition to which, the diversity of copyists from the original paintings, and their comparative degrees of skill, add very considerably to the chances of losing the necessary degree of resemblance to the originals. And then, besides, it is not sufficient to delineate a plant as it appears at one period only, as it presents a different appearance at each of the four seasons of the year." Pliny the Elder, *Natural History*, 25.4. See Ivins and Millis (1953: 14); Hall (1996: 5). This essay was prepared as part of the ERC Consolidator Grant 2020–864542 project, "From East to West, and Back Again: Student Travel and Transcultural Knowledge Production in Renaissance Europe (c. 1470–c. 1620)," led by Valentina Lepri, and as part of the FWO postdoctoral project "Celebrating Knowledge. Iconological Analysis of the Representations in Handwritten Lecture Notebooks of the Southern Low Countries, 17th–18th Centuries." We wish to thank Danilo Facca for his useful comments.

2 The discipline was established at the beginning of the twentieth century, but gained more importance in the 1990s and later became known to English-speaking scholars, notably with the translation of Bredekamp, Dünkel, and Schneider, *Das Technische Bild*, into English: *The Technical Image* in 2015.

3 Eisenstein (1980); Edgerton (1985: 168–97); Baldasso (2006).

4 See, for example, Galison and Jones (1998); Daston (2004); Smith (2004); Kusukawa (2012).

5 See https://www.kuleuven.be/lectio/magisterdixit/solr-search (last accessed on December 3, 2024), where 576 manuscripts can be consulted. These manuscripts are mainly held at the archives of KBR (Brussels), KU Leuven Libraries (Leuven), and UCLouvain (Louvain-la-Neuve). To this corpus can be added about 82 other manuscripts that have not been systematically digitized. These are held at the Bibliothèque municipale de Cambrai, Edinburgh University Library, Ghent University Library, Société archéologique de Namur, archives of Liège University, Leiden University Library, Historisch Centrum Limburg in Maastricht, University of Pennsylvania Rare Book and Manuscript Library, and in private collections. As yet, no database exists for sources from Poland and Lithuania; the information offered here is based on the work of Alicja Bielak, conducted within the ERC Consolidator Grant no. 2020–864542 (KnowStudents).

6 It is not excluded that, since antiquity, certain courses took place in rooms decorated with posters containing pedagogical images such as diagrams: see Virenque (2022: 7); Klapisch-Zuber (2000: 29).

7 At Leuven, the faculty of arts was organized in four colleges called pedagogies: the Lily, the Pig, the Falcon, and the Castle, where students lived and studied.

8 For religious scenes depicted in fifteenth-century manuscripts from Leuven, see notebooks kept in Edinburgh (University Library, MS 205, 1477) and Cambrai (Bibliothèque municipale, MS 964, 1482). For this last document, we refer to Smeyers (1975).

9 One can often find such depictions in notes on the *Tractatus de sphaera* (c. 1230) by Sacrobosco, an astronomical compendium mandatory across all of Europe up to the second part of the seventeenth century.

10 Vanpaemel (2011: 242, 251). Cf. Chapter 7 on student notes and the relationship between prescription and practice.

11 We saw in the introduction (and the first note of this chapter) that Pliny the Elder pointed out the necessity of appropriate color selection in botanical drawings.

12 Recent monographs on medieval diagrammatology include Schmitt (2019), Hamburger (2020), and Even-Ezra (2021).
13 On the square of opposition, see also Chapter 7.
14 The *pons asinorum* indicates a supposed danger that frightens donkeys, or silly students, causing them to stop at an apparent difficulty. Today, the phrase "donkeys' bridge" still refers to a simple tool to solve a problem or a reminder to easily remember something complex.
15 Papy (2012: 115–19). The engraving by Hayé was pasted in a notebook currently held in the BWMS, MS C.2.1.9 (engraving between ff. 568–9). This testifies to the circulation of the engraving beyond the Low Countries.
16 See, for example, MS 201, fols. 82^v–86^v (acrostic DELAUNOIS in red and black ink): https://lib.is/IE4923148/representation?fl_pid=FL4923720. Last accessed April 30, 2024.
17 For instance, the engravings of *pons asinorum* and *De sillogismo in barocco* by Hayé but also numerous drawings and doodles.
18 See Vanpaemel (2011).
19 The Leuven-based engraver and printer Charles-Henri Becker produced two series of plates depicting the equipment from the cabinet of experimental physics. The plates were used from 1767 until 1797. They deal, on the one hand, with the sphere, the movement, and the light and, on the other, with mechanics, electricity, gravity, perspective, air, hydrostatics, and astronomy. See Opsomer (2000: 176–8).
20 *De forma, et, svbiecto; De argumentatione; De vniuersali Iudicio Excedentes, Entia per accidens, partes phisicae, De equivocis* (see Berger 2017).
21 The year 1531 was the one that the first such collection was printed: the *Emblematum liber* by Andrea Alciato (1492–1550).
22 On the emblem books trade in Europe, see Milazzo (2017).
23 At least 85 of the 104 emblems from Engelgrave's *Lux Evangelica* and 40 *picturae* from Matre Dei's *Firmamentum Symbolicum* circulated as *dictata* engravings. On the recuperation process of these series, see Van Vaeck (2002: 292–6); Van Vaeck and Verberckmoes (2012: 154–63).
24 In printmaking, "state" is a synonym of "proof." For a terminology of printed images, see Stijnman (2021).
25 The Latin phrase "In this sign you will conquer" translates the Greek words ἐν τούτῳ νίκα, which are said to have appeared to Constantine the Great in battle in 312.
26 Antwerp student Johannes Josephus Peeters followed a course taught by Johannes Corbion at the Gymnasium Sanctissimae Trinitatis ("Drievuldigheidscollege") of Leuven university, a college where only the arts were taught. The notebook is currently held at the Houghton Library, Harvard University (MS Lat 481). It is documented in Aubert et al. (1976: figs. 73, 171–2).
27 *Dialecticae dictatorum pars seconda* [sic] *tractatus de signis et vocibus quibus exprimitur prima mentis operatio*.
28 A parallax is the effect of the position change of the observer on what he perceives. Schematic compositions showing this effect were issued by Michael Hayé and Lambert Blendeff in the seventeenth century. See Vanpaemel (2011: 254).
29 Other drawn compositions include a tree of logic, Bacchus, caterpillars and butterflies, dancing farmers, a crocodile, and a savage ("Wildeman").
30 On staging the production process in painting, see Georgel and Lecoq (1987); Stoichita (2015: 229–90).
31 Van Vaeck (2002: 299). See also de Mûelenaere (2023).
32 On the *libri amicorum* tradition, see, for example, Wilson (2012); Reinders and Vandommele (2022).
33 BN, MS 3045 II, fol. 88^v: "Fingitur autem Apollo Pythonem et Typhonem interemisse sagittis. Sol enim omnia putrida (quae πύθω Graece vocantur) radiis terram quasi iaculis feriendo paulatim

exsiccat generationesque venenatorum et monstrosorum animantium impedit. Ventos praeterea et typhones calore infringit."

34 Farrell (1970: 77): "The class contest or exercise should include [...] interpreting hieroglyphics and Pythagorean symbols, maxims, proverbs, emblems, riddles, delivering declamations, and other similar exercises at the teacher's pleasure." Cf. also p. 110 (rule 3): "They may compose symbols or mottoes or again epigrams or brief descriptions."

35 Bacon (1624: 293): "Emblema verò deducit Intellectuale ad Sensibile: Sensibile autem semper fortiùs percutit Memoriam, atque in eâ faciliùs imprimitur, quam Intellectuale." Translation by Opsomer (2000: 165–6).

36 For the Southern Low Countries, see Porteman (1996); Ems (2016); de Mûelenaere (2022).

37 Berger (2017: 127). See also Fransen and Reinhart (2019).

References

Abbreviations

BN: Biblioteka Narodowa w Warszawie (National Library of Poland)
BnF: Bibliothèque nationale de France
BWMS: Biblioteka Wyższego Metropolitalnego Seminarium Duchownego św. Jana Chrzciciela w Warszawie (Poland)
KBR: Koninklijke Bibliothèque Royale (the national scientific library of Belgium)
UCLouvain: Archives de l'Université catholique de Louvain (Belgium)

Useful databases

All databases were last consulted on April 10, 2024.
Magister Dixit: kuleuven.be/lectio/magisterdixit/solr-search
Emblematica: emblematica.grainger.illinois.edu
Medieval Diagrams: repository.edition-topoi.org/collection/MAPD
The Art of Reasoning in Medieval Manuscripts: art-of-reasoning.huygens.knaw.nl/theme3.html
Corpus academicum Cracoviense: cac.historia.uj.edu.pl
The Sphere: sphaera.mpiwg-berlin.mpg.de/database
The Leuven Ontology for Aristotelian Diagrams Database: https://logicalgeometry.org/leonardi/

Secondary literature

Ashworth, William B. 1996. "Emblematic Natural History of the Renaissance." In *Cultures of Natural History*, edited by Nicholas Jardine, J.A. Secord, and E.C. Spary, 17–37. Cambridge: Cambridge University Press.

Aubert, Roger et al. 1976. *L'université de Louvain 1425–1975*. Louvain-la-Neuve: Presses universitaires de Louvain.

Bacon, Francis. 1624. *De dignitate et augmentis scientiarum. Libri IX. Ad regem suum.* Parisiis: Typis Petri Mettayer.
Baigrie, Brian S., ed. 1996. *Picturing Knowledge: Historical and Philosophical Problems Concerning the Use of Art in Science.* Toronto: University of Toronto Press.
Baldasso, Renzo. 2006. "The Role of Visual Representation in the Scientific Revolution." *Centaurus* 48: 69–88.
Berger, Susanna. 2017. *The Art of Philosophy: Visual Thinking in Europe from the Late Renaissance to the Early Enlightenment.* Princeton: Princeton University Press.
Bolzoni, Lina. 2004. "Emblemi e arte della memoria: Alcune note su invenzione e ricezione." In *Florilegio de estudios de Emblemática: A Florilegium of Studies on Emblematics*, edited by Sagrario López Poza, 15–31. Coruña: Sociedad de Cultura Valle Inclán.
Bredekamp, Horst, Vera Dünkel, and Birgit Schneider, eds. 2015. *The Technical Image: A History of Styles in Scientific Imagery.* Chicago: University of Chicago Press.
Carruthers, Mary. 2008. *The Book of Memory: A Study of Memory in Medieval Culture.* Cambridge: Cambridge University Press.
Cunningham, Andrew, and Sachiko Kusukawa. 2010. *Natural Philosophy Epitomised: A Translation of Books 8–11 of Gregor Reisch's* Philosophical Pearl *(1503).* Farnham: Ashgate.
D'Haenens, Albert. 1994. "Que faisaient les étudiants, à partir du XVe siècle, des textes qu'on leur imposait à l'université? Le non-textuel dans les manuels des étudiants de l'université de Louvain." In *Manuels, programmes de cours et techniques d'enseignement dans les universités médiévales*, edited by Jacqueline Hamesse, 401–41. Louvain-la-Neuve: Fédération Internationale des Instituts d'Études Médiévales.
Dackerman, Susan, ed. 2011. *Prints and the Pursuit of Knowledge in Early Modern Europe.* Cambridge, MA: Harvard Art Museum.
Daly, Peter M. 2008. *Companion to Emblem Studies.* New York: AMS Press.
Daston, Lorraine, ed. 2004. *Things That Talk: Object Lessons from Art and Science.* New York: Zone Books.
Daston, Lorraine. 2015. "Epistemic Images." In *Vision and Its Instruments: Art, Science, and Technology in Early Modern Europe*, edited by Alina Alexandra Payne, 13–35. University Park: The Pennsylvania State University Press.
de Mûelenaere, Gwendoline. 2022. *Early Modern Thesis Prints in the Southern Netherlands: An Iconological Analysis of the Relationships between Art, Science and Power.* Leiden–Boston: Brill.
———. 2023. "Academic Print Practices in the Southern Netherlands: Allegory and Emblematics as Epistemic Tools." In *Reassessing Epistemic Images in the Early Modern World*, edited by Ruth Noyes, 131–52. Amsterdam: Amsterdam University Press.
Edgerton, Samuel Y., Jr. 1985. "The Renaissance Development of the Scientific Illustration." In *Science and the Arts in the Renaissance*, edited by John W. Shirley and F. David Hoenger, 168–97. London–Toronto: Associated University Presses.
Eisenstein, Elizabeth. 1980. *The Printing Press as an Agent of Change: Communications and Cultural Transformations in Early-Modern Europe.* Cambridge: Cambridge University Press.
Ems, Grégory. 2016. *L'emblématique au service du pouvoir: La symbolique du prince chrétien dans les expositions emblématiques du collège des jésuites de Bruxelles sous le gouvernorat de Léopold-Guillaume (1647–1656).* 2 vols. Louvain-la-Neuve: Presses universitaires de Louvain.
Even-Ezra, Ayelet. 2021. *Lines of Thought: Branching Diagrams and the Medieval Mind.* Chicago: University of Chicago Press.
Farrell, Allan P. 1970. *The Jesuit* Ratio Studiorum *of 1599: Translated into English, with an Introduction and Explanatory Notes.* Washington: Conference of Major Superiors of Jesuits.

Fransen, Sietske, and Katherine M. Reinhart. 2019. "The Practice of Copying in Making Knowledge in Early Modern Europe: An Introduction." *Word & Image* 35 (3): 211–22.

Freedberg, David. 1989. *The Power of Images: Studies in the History and Theory of Response*. Chicago–London: The University of Chicago Press.

Galison, Peter, and Caroline A. Jones, eds. 1998. *Picturing Science, Producing Art*. London: Routledge.

Georgel, Pierre, and Anne-Marie Lecoq. 1987. *La peinture dans la peinture*. Paris: Adam Biro.

Górska, Magdalena. 2009. "Emblematyka jako źródło staropolskiej erudycji: Geneza i funkcja materiału symbolicznego w polskich kompendiach." In *Staropolskie kompendia wiedzy*, edited by I.M. Dacka-Górzyńska and J. Partyka, 99–132. Warsaw: DiG.

Hall, Bert S. 1996. "The Didactic and the Elegant: Some Thoughts on Scientific and Technological Illustrations in the Middle Ages and Renaissance." In Baigrie (1996: 3–39).

Hamburger, Jeffrey. 2020. *Diagramming Devotion: Berthold of Nuremberg's Transformation of Hrabanus Maurus's Poems in Praise of the Cross*. Chicago: University of Chicago Press.

Ivins William M., Jr., and William Millis. 1953. *Prints and Visual Communication*. Cambridge, MA: Harvard University Press.

Klapisch-Zuber, Christiane. 2000. *L'ombre des ancêtres: Essai sur l'imaginaire médiéval de la parenté*. Paris: Fayard.

Kusukawa, Sachiko. 2012. *Picturing the Book of Nature: Image, Text, and Argument in Sixteenth-Century Human Anatomy and Medical Botany*. Chicago: University of Chicago Press.

Lüthy, Christoph, and Alexis Smets. 2009. "Words, Lines, Diagrams, Images: Towards a History of Scientific Imagery." *Early Science and Medicine* 14: 398–439.

Marr, Alexander. 2016. "Knowing Images." *Renaissance Quarterly* 69: 1,000–13.

Milazzo, Renaud. 2017. "Le marché des livres d'emblèmes en Europe. 1531–1750." Unpublished PhD dissertation, Paris: Université Paris Saclay (COmUE).

Opsomer, Carmelia. 2000. "Illustrated Courses of Natural Philosophy in the Southern Low Countries (1670–1797)." In *Science and the Visual Image in the Enlightenment*, edited by William Shea, 155–84. Canton: Science History Publications.

Panofsky, Erwin. 1962. "Artist, Scientist, Genius: Notes on the 'Renaissance-Dämmerung.'" In *The Renaissance*, edited by Wallace K. Ferguson, 121–82. New York: Harper and Row.

Papy, Jan. 2012. "Logicacursussen aan de Oude Leuvense Universiteit: Scholastieke traditie en innovatie?" In Vanpaemel et al. (2012: 107–24).

Porteman, Karel. 1996. *Emblematic Exhibitions (affixiones) at the Brussels Jesuit College (1630–1685): A Study of the Commemorative Manuscripts (Royal Library, Brussels)*. Turnhout: Brepols.

Reinders, Sophie, and Jeroen Vandommele. 2022. "A Renaissance for Alba Amicorum Research." *Early Modern Low Countries* 6 (1): 1–13.

Sarbiewski, Maciej Kazimierz. 1972. *Dii genrium, Bogowie pogan*. Edited by Krystyna Stawecka. Wrocław: Zakład Narodowy im. Ossslińskich.

Schmitt, Jean-Claude. 2019. *Penser par figure: Du compas divin aux diagrammes magiques*. Paris: Arkhe.

Smets, An. 2014. "'De Leuvense hebben altijd wat': 17de-eeuwse Leuvense collegedictaten bewaard in Leiden en Den Haag." *De Gulden Passer: Journal for Book History* 92 (2): 195–214.

Smeyers, Maurits. 1975. "Een collegeschrift van de oude Leuvense universiteit (1481–1482): Een codicologisch en iconografisch onderzoek. Bijdrage tot de studie van het universitaire onderricht tijdens de middeleeuwen." *Arca Lovaniensis* 4: 243–303.

Smith, Pamela H. 2004. *The Body of the Artisan: Art and Experience in the Scientific Revolution*. Chicago: University of Chicago Press.

Stijnman, Ad. 2021. *Terms in Print Addresses: Abbreviations and Phrases on Printed Images 1500–1900*. 9ea6427a-9293-483f-80d4-9523d4ed999b.filesusr.com/ugd/6b3a67_fad3e94c404a425f8fd-b0e16343985eb.pdf.

Stoichita, Victor I. 2015. *The Self-Aware Image: An Insight into Early Modern Metapainting*. London: Harvey Miller.

Swan, Claudia. 2011. "Illustrated Natural History." In Dackerman (2011: 186–91).

Van Vaeck, Marc. 2002. "Printed Emblem *Picturae* in 17th- and 18th-Century Leuven University College Notes." *Emblematica* 12: 285–326.

Van Vaeck, Marc, and Johan Verberckmoes. 2012. "Humor in de collegedictaten." In Vanpaemel et al. (2012: 187–212).

Vanpaemel, Geert. 2011. "The Louvain Printers and the Establishment of the Cartesian Curriculum." *Studium* 4 (4): 241–54.

Vanpaemel, Geert et al. 2012. *Ex Cathedra: Leuvense collegedictaten van de 16de tot de 18de eeuw*. Leuven: Universiteitsbibliotheek KU Leuven.

Virenque, Naïs. 2022. "De l'arbre à l'arborescence: Mémoire et matérialité des raisonnements du Moyen Âge à l'époque moderne." In *Matières à raisonner*, edited by Françoise Briegel, available online on *Savoirs: Le fil des idées*. https://savoirs.app/en/articles/de-l-arbre-a-l-arborescence-memoire-et-materialite-des-raisonnements-du-moyen-age-a-l-epoque-moderne. Last accessed January 21, 2025.

Wilson, Bronwen. 2012. "Social Networking: The Album Amicorum and Early Modern Public-Making." In *Beyond the Public Sphere: Opinions, Publics, Spaces in Early Modern Europe*, edited by Massimo Rospocher, 205–23. Bologna: Il Mulino.

Yates, Frances. 2011 [1966]. *The Art of Memory*. London: Routledge.

Further reading

Kupfer, Marcia, Adam S. Cohen, and J.H. Chajes, eds. 2020. *The Visualization of Knowledge in Medieval and Early Modern Europe*. Turnhout: Brepols.

Marr, Alexander, and Christopher P. Heue. 2020. "Introduction: The Uncertainty of Epistemic Images." *21: Inquiries into Art, History, and the Visual. Beiträge zur Kunstgeschichte und visuellen Kultur* 1 (2): 251–5.

Topper, David. 1996. "Towards an Epistemology of Scientific Illustration." In Baigrie (1996: 215–50).

CHAPTER 10

History of Orality

Tomás Antonio Valle and Raf Van Rooy

1. Introduction

Words spoken prior to the advent of audio recording technology are, in and of themselves, inaccessible to the modern researcher; yet that very elusiveness lends them a certain fascination. The pioneering work of Milman Parry and his student Albert Bates Lord brought the oral traces in literature to the center of scholarly interest (Parry 1971; Lord 2019). Drawing inspiration from Parry's work on Homer and building upon his own study of Petrus Ramus, Walter Ong presented "orality" and "literacy" as an epistemological, anthropological binary, arguing for a fundamental shift from the former to the latter during the early modern period (Ong 1958, 1967, 2002). In the last few decades, spurred on by the work of Peter Burke, historians have increasingly taken orality as a lens for investigating early modern social and cultural history (Burke 1993; Horodowich 2012; Cohen and Twomey 2015; Roth 2022).

Student notes offer a largely unexplored avenue towards the study of orality, particularly within academic culture. Historians of education occasionally point out or comment on its oral character in passing, but have rarely elaborated on it (for example, Blair 1989: 126n31; Leonhardt and Schindler 2007: 43–4; Brinkmann et al. 2021: *passim*; somewhat more extensively, Ellis 2020: 119–124). Historians of orality, meanwhile, have largely neglected early modern academic life. Yet, the university and the classroom were dense nodes of interpenetration between the oral and the textual, as information about texts was conveyed orally within an at least basically literate public, was written down, memorized, and repeated. Since scholars have increasingly emphasized that oral and literate cultures coexisted and intertwined throughout the Middle Ages and early modernity (McKenzie 1990; Fox 2000; Clanchy 2013), student notes provide a key source for understanding this phenomenon.[1]

Incorporating orality into the study of student notes also expands the horizons of other disciplinary approaches. How did the oral character of early modern education shape the process of teaching and learning? How did orality condition early modern intellectual life and transform ideas as they were discussed and debated? How did students use their notes as paper technologies to cope with and capture the ephemeral, and how does the materiality of notebooks bear witness to oral instruction? How did illustrations interact with the word not only as written but as spoken and heard? And, lastly, what do the traces of orality in student notes reveal about the lives and everyday experiences of the ordinary students who wrote them?

Before answering these questions, the researcher must face a major methodological challenge: demonstrating that a particular student's notes reflect oral communication, or discerning what aspects of the written text bear salient traces of orality. After all, even if the early modern classroom presents an automatically oral context, spoken instruction did not produce annotations in a uniform or predictable way. Here identifying notes as first-order or second-order plays an important role (see Chapter 1), and the character of the handwriting, including the presence or absence of abbreviations or embellishments, can help pick out direct transfers from the student's ear to the page. At the same time, even secondary notes can contain traces of original orality. Students occasionally ascribe words directly to the teacher; usually, though, discerning the oral substratum of student notes requires a close attention to detail and some sense of what the teacher might originally have said.[2] Tell-tale misspellings or similar errors may point to mis-hearings and thus reveal aspects of how knowledge was communicated (and experienced) orally. Other kinds of changes, such as the rearrangement or distortion of a quotation, can also point to transfer via memory and speech.

The two case studies that follow attempt to exemplify both how historians can recover the oral phenomena behind student notes and how recognizing this orality illuminates the sources themselves.

2. Conversational culture at Wittenberg university *c.* 1550

The Herzog August Bibliothek in Wolfenbüttel, Germany, holds an unusual manuscript of notes by one Werner Rolefinck. The otherwise-unknown Rolefinck was a student at Wittenberg from about 1551 to late 1555 or 1556.

During this time, he copied down what the manuscript's opening describes as "remarkable *exempla* from the sayings and deeds of both princes and private persons, gathered from the lectures [*lectionibus*] of the teacher Philip Melanchthon and others."[3] This text, which has received almost no scholarly attention outside of manuscript catalogs (most recently, Thüringer 1982), shines a distinctive light on academic life and culture at mid-sixteenth-century Wittenberg, the educational hub of the burgeoning evangelical movement.

Rolefinck seems to have been a fairly ordinary student. His Latin is competent but without polish, nor does he appear to have had much facility with Greek, judging by its almost entire absence from the text. Even though he clearly wrote the manuscript with care, as a keepsake—there are almost no revisions to the text, and many of the headings are rubricated—the character of the handwriting and the omission of much punctuation suggest that he was not an experienced scribe. The entries themselves reflect the same lack of erudite pretensions. Despite the academic context, the contents are not for the most part scholarly fare: they range quite widely, including maxims, historical anecdotes, similes, short excerpts from lectures, tall tales, and jokes. Rolefinck's principle of selection seems to have been a preference for the memorable and the striking above all else. While the collection is labeled as containing *exempla* and the majority of the entries have a moral point, this edifying value is often overshadowed by the fantastical, funny, or hyperbolic character of the contents. For example, a short "shocking example of lust" tells of a noble Viennese woman who committed bestiality with "an English dog" and was therefore burned at the stake, but the story obviously merits inclusion in Rolefinck's notes because of the monstrous offspring: "seven whelps" with a dog's body and a human head.[4]

The oral origins of this collection surface already in the title's mention of *lectionibus*, which here means "lectures" rather than simply the act of reading. Moreover, this should probably be taken as encompassing both formal and informal instruction, rather than as strictly denoting a classroom context, considering that Melanchthon's students frequently lived with him or received instruction in his home (Sonntag 2019). A few excerpts also claim explicitly to be quoting Melanchthon.[5] Yet the notes themselves are almost certainly second-order, copied down after the fact on the basis of memory or first-order notes made at the time: the extant manuscript contains almost no corrections and few abbreviations, suggesting that it was not written at speed.

Analyzing one excerpt in detail, however, reveals the closeness between Rolefinck's notes and what he heard from his teacher. In an entry entitled, "that old laws should not be done away with or rashly altered," the student quotes what "Demosthenes says against Timocrates."[6] The quotation, corresponding to *In Timocratem* 139–41, in fact appears in Melanchthon's *Philosophiae moralis epitome* (1546), where it justifies the same point. Comparing the two Latin renderings of Demosthenes' Greek shows clear similarities in word-choice, though the two versions are not exactly the same.[7] This strongly suggests three points. First, the differences between the two indicate that Rolefinck copied down this quotation not from the published *Epitome* but from Melanchthon's oral instruction. Second, Melanchthon was likely paraphrasing directly from the Greek text in the classroom (perhaps from memory), rather than quoting his translation in *Epitome*, since the version in Rolefinck's notes omits some portions of the passage included in Melanchthon's textbook and includes others. Most tellingly, Rolefinck includes in full detail the second half of Demosthenes' story, about a one-eyed man, which is only briefly summarized in the *Epitome*, and this portion of his text likewise relies directly on the Greek text.[8] Lastly, the resonance between the manuscript note and Melanchthon's published translation suggests that Rolefinck wrote down the things he had heard with a fair degree of accuracy, despite the process of transmission from oral instruction (possibly through first-order notes) to the second-order notes in this manuscript.

Recognizing that Rolefinck's manuscript conveys oral material, we can perceive in it various aspects of academic orality. For example, his notes indicate the frequent use of the vernacular (in this case, German) as part of university life and conversation. Fittingly enough, German was often used when relating direct speech by Germans, even when the matrix language—the language in which the quotation was embedded—remained Latin.[9] One entry even includes a code-switch within a quotation, to a humorous end. In a story about the Duchess of Württemberg, Barbara Gonzaga of Mantua, she gives a pious injunction to her maid in Latin, before switching to German and complaining about her own unhappy marriage: "*Fear God and live uprightly.* If I had done that, I wouldn't have turned out so wretchedly!"[10]

Rolefinck's notes reveal not only practices of code-switching between Latin and German but also the presence of Greek in academic oral culture. There are no Greek quotations included in the manuscript, implying a limited facility with the language, but there are at least two instances in which single Greek words appear: φιλοστοργία (a philosophical term for affection) and σφραγίς (a signet ring). The specialized character of these terms, along with Rolefinck's apparent uncertainty in accenting the latter, reinforces the idea that he did not learn them from his own reading.[11] Nor does he seem to have learned them in the course of Greek instruction. Both are simply used in the course of stories, in neither case with a clear connection to the word's use in an ancient text. σφραγίς is used metaphorically for the seal of absolution in a story set in contemporary, sixteenth-century Europe; φιλοστοργία appears as part of the moral drawn from a story in Herodotus, but the term itself does not appear in the Herodotean source text. The inclusion of these terms suggests that they formed part of the conversational vocabulary of academic life, which further examination of texts by Melanchthon and his students confirms.[12]

The oral circulation of Greek technical terms among students points to another insight provided by Rolefinck's text: how academic orality transformed humanist erudition. In an excerpt from a public lecture, Melanchthon relates a moralizing quotation from Herodotus, the typical tool for humanist ethical formation: "A woman, having set aside her clothes, [also] sets aside her sense of shame." Yet, rather than launching into a discussion of sexual ethics, Melanchthon uses the line as a springboard for a humorous finger-wag at the lax mores of the Italians: "In Italy it is the custom that men and women go to the baths without any clothes. If I were consul there, I would make sure they were beaten with rods so that they put something on."[13] One might suspect that Rolefinck's love for (in this case literally) the striking has distracted him from a more profound point being made by Melanchthon, but the latter quotes this line elsewhere without any deep moral significance, simply as a maxim expressing the importance of clothes (*CR* 25, 312). Similarly, an anecdote about a Stoic—Stoicism being a constant *bête noire* for Melanchthon—distorts its original source in Diogenes Laertius' *Lives* to ignore the philosophical issues at play, to increase the story's comedic value, and to present its target as a buffoon.[14]

The variety of entries included in Rolefinck's manuscript highlights the broad interests of students attending Wittenberg and the goals of their education, which went well beyond the curriculum of the *artes liberales*. The material displays a clear interest in rulers and current (or recent) events, including stories and anecdotes, mottos and sayings from dukes and princes throughout the Holy Roman Empire as well as from more distant lands such as Denmark, Spain, and Naples.[15] Similarly, a few entries relay sayings carved into public buildings in other parts of the Empire.[16] An education at Wittenberg provided access to the wider world, not through what was printed in textbooks but through the free, oral flow of information. Rolefinck's notebook allowed him to fix in writing the experience and exposure with which his time at university provided him.

In this sense, these notes not only emerged from a conversational culture; they were also intended for redeployment in it. In genre, the notes seem a commonplace book for recording snatches of academic talk, rather than for digesting one's reading. Rolefinck gathered from his education a rhetorical *copia* of striking statements, fascinating stories, and good jokes that he could then use himself later in life. Hence, his manuscript served as a textual bridge between two conversations, one in the past that he heard as a student and one in the future that he himself would take an active role in. Uncovering the oral elements of these student notes points out the intertwinement of orality and literacy at the sixteenth century's largest German university. What is more, it reveals that this relationship was not balanced, but was weighted heavily towards the former: for the average student, writing was ancillary to speech.

3. The oral/aural challenges of teaching and learning

A fine-grained look at the spelling errors in student notes reveals a great deal about historical pronunciation practices, as well as the challenges to learning posed by the reliance on orality in the classroom. In Chapter 2, it has already been shown how a Dutch professor's pronunciation of the word *vagabundos* as *fagabundos* may help locate a set of student notes in place. In fact, Latin pronunciation varied considerably across time and especially across space, without occasioning communicative chaos; the pronunciation of Greek, however, was much more problematic, especially for language learners (Sacré 2014). The wealth of publications devoted to this topic by Erasmus of Rotterdam and others like Adolphus Mekerchus (1528–1591), a former student of the Leuven Trilingue, testifies to the acute nature of the matter (see, for example, also Drerup 1930–2; Barnard 2017; Van Rooy 2020). Briefly put, humanist schools and universities adopted by default the pronunciation of the Byzantine Greek scholars working in Italy and other parts of Europe, which closely resembled the pronunciation of Modern Greek and became associated with the German humanist Johann Reuchlin. This involved pronouncing the letter *beta* (β) like *vita* and many other idiosyncrasies, resulting in a mismatch between spelling and pronunciation. Erasmus, and people working before and after him, reconstructed the way in which Ancient Greek must have been pronounced (Bywater 1908).

The picture becomes blurrier still as certain professors of Greek devised their own mixed systems, taking elements from both the vernacular (Byzantine, Reuchlinian) and the reconstructed ancient pronunciation. An example is Trilingue professor Theodoricus Langius, who adopted the vernacular pronunciation (*vita*) overall, except for the diphthong οι, which he pronounced in some cases not as [i] but as [oi]. This is documented through two testimonies of people who attended his classes: Mekerchus, who would write a pronunciation treatise based on his student experience in Leuven (Van Rooy and Van Hal 2018: 143–4), and Roger Ascham, who described his visit to the Leuven Trilingue in a travel report (Ascham 1865: 249). The cause of this mixture may be that scholars started to use both pronunciations alongside each other, a practice documented in a lecture by the Frisian humanist Suffridus Petri (1527–1597), who taught Greek literature in Leuven in the 1550s–1570s and made the following comment on his teaching method:

> First, I briefly explain and put forward the meaning of each section of text. After that, I recite the same section once in both pronunciations, namely the Erasmian and the vernacular one, although I will use the vernacular one in teaching. (Cited from Van Rooy and Van Hal 2018: 145)

Student notes can bring a fresh perspective on the subject of early modern pronunciations of Ancient Greek, as this type of source is much more detailed than the all too brief testimonies of Mekerchus, Ascham, and Petri. Only a few scholars have put student notes to use to this end, including Ellis (2020), who offers some general remarks on the oral aspects of a body of student notes on Herodotus, compiled by fourteen-year-old Jacques Bongars in Johannes Rosa's classes (Jena, 1568). "To the modern mind," Ellis (2020: 119) observes, "one striking feature is the degree to which the process of reading and interpreting the Greek text in Rosa's classroom was oral rather than visual." Indeed, with no blackboard available, taking notes in Greek classes required a certain amount of mental gymnastics.

The student notes edited in the Database of the Leuven Trilingue demonstrate that in 1540s Leuven the vernacular pronunciation was the default and caused problems for the students listening to the professor, especially if he used Greek as a kind of second metalanguage next to Latin.[17] For instance, in his commentaries on Homer's *Odyssey* 2.196 (οἱ δὲ γάμον τεύξουσι καὶ ἀρτυνέουσιν ἔεδνα, "they will prepare a wedding and make the gifts ready"), professor Rutgerus Rescius offered his students both Latin translations and Greek synonyms of various words on this line, presented in Table 10.1.

Table 10.1. Student annotations on Homer, *Odyssey* 2.196[18]

Annotated word	Student note	Type	Intended form
τεύξουσι	parabunt	Latin translation	
ἀρτυνέουσιν	τετημασουσι	Greek synonym	ἑτοιμάσουσι
ἔεδνα	munera	Latin translation	

Very probably, Rescius commented on the passage as follows: "parabunt et ἑτοιμάσουσι munera," in which case the student would have parsed the final [t] of "et" as the first sound of the Greek verb he had heard being pronounced as [etimasusi]. Alternatively, Rescius may have stated: "ἀρτυνέουσιν est ἑτοιμάσουσι," resulting in a similar process of incorrect word segmentation. In any case, this example shows the problems Greek pronunciation posed for students trying to write down the correct form: the student Johannes Aegidius wrote the incorrect τετημασουσι <tetêmasousi> instead of the expected ἑτοιμάσουσι <hetoimásousi>. We also see confusion between <οι> and <η>, both pronounced as [i] by Rescius. These problems of pronunciation and registration in writing are all the trickier as there is code- and alphabet-switching involved, in this case between Latin and Greek.

Similar problems arise in a note on *Odyssey* 2.326, where Rescius must have offered a Greek synonym and then a Latin translation for the form ἀμύντορας ("helpers"). The word is annotated as follows: "βοητους αυξιλιatores" (DaLeT Annotation ID 1136), where professor Rescius no doubt intended "βοηθοὺς auxiliatores." The Greek synonym, by the way, illustrates that the letter theta <θ> was pronounced [t], without any aspiration (either as [θ] or as [th]). Such examples could be easily multiplied for these student notes, confirming Ellis' (2020) observation that the classroom reading of a text was in the first place an oral experience for the professor-speaker, an aural one for the student-listener.

The large number of errors, left uncorrected in these first-order notes, not only indicates that the professor did not care to monitor the student's progress but also reveals the problematic primacy of orality in the early modern classroom. Overwhelmingly oral instruction had limitations and even generated its own kind of difficulties for the transfer of knowledge. A professor might offer an easier alternative to a word in the text, but if the student failed to recognize his teacher's utterance on the basis of prior knowledge, he could end up learning an incorrect form, as in the case of the non-existent τετημασουσι <tetêmasousi> versus the correct ἑτοιμάσουσι <hetoimásousi>. Relying on listening comprehension and with little direct oversight from the teacher, written notes served as an imperfect means for students to cope with oral/aural learning.

Finally, the case further confirms, together with sources like Suffridus Petri, that Erasmus did not overturn pronunciation practices overnight. Although this is recognized in some secondary literature (for example, Sacré 2014), the specifics of this evolution are unknown. The systematic analysis of student notes and the mistakes they contain can potentially uncover intermediate variants (like that of Theodoricus Langius) and provide a more differentiated understanding of how Greek was orally and aurally experienced across the early modern period.

4. Conclusion

This chapter has illustrated not only that researchers can use student notes to reconstruct the orality of academic culture, but also that this work of reconstruction both illuminates the history of orality and reveals an oral dimension to other historiographical topics. In the first place, both case studies have uncovered the vital role of orality even in universities and schools, the strongholds of literate erudition in the Renaissance. Rolefinck and Aegidius used their notes, notwithstanding their differences of format and content, to capture and store information for which they had primarily oral access. The history of education itself, surprisingly, may provide a rich vein for understanding the long-term intertwinement of orality and literacy.

Beyond this, both case studies demonstrate that examining student notes with orality in mind can unlock their value for a wide range of research questions. This value extends from explicitly oral topics, such as the historical development of pronunciation or practices of code-switching, to broader issues regarding academic culture, the transmission of knowledge, and the lived experience of classroom education. An oral approach to student notes could be further applied to other source genres, such as diaries of professors (see Calis 2019) or even academic printed works (see Valle forthcoming). Bringing oral evidence and perspectives into conversation with more traditional and better studied sources, such as university statutes or published treatises, promises new insights into many areas of historical research.

Notes

[1] For a student-notes-adjacent example of the intertwinement of orality and literacy, see Calis (2019).

[2] Direct ascriptions are not necessarily "more" oral than other notes, nor do they automatically count as unquestionable markers of oral transfer. For the caution that some genres of student notes include such ascriptions as tropes, see Ogorodnikova (2021).

[3] HAB Cod. Guelf. 1169 Helmst., fol. 1: "Exempla insignia factorum dictorumque memorabilium et principum et privatorum collecta ex lectionibus D. praeceptoris Philippi Melanthonis et aliorum." I have kept my transcriptions from this manuscript diplomatic, maintaining the frequent absence of punctuation and incorporating only the modern u/v distinction.

[4] HAB Cod. Guelf. 1169 Helmst., fol. 90^v: "Horrendum exemplum libidinis. Viennae virgo nobilis congressa cum Anglico cane procreavit septem catulos corpore canibus capite vero homini similes et una cum eis est combusta." Interestingly, this anecdote appears verbatim (though without Rolefinck's title) in a manuscript of Luther's *Colloquia* dated 1560, apparently a transcription of earlier material: see Bindseil (1863–6: vol. 3, 8–9). For discussion of sources, see Bindseil (1863–6: vol. 1, xviii–cvi).

[5] For example, the heading at HAB Cod. Guelf. 1169 Helmst., fol. 181: "Philippus Melanthon in lectione Dialectices."

[6] HAB Cod. Guelf. 1169 Helmst., fol. 239^v: "Leges veteres non sunt abolendae aut temere mutandae [...] Demosthenes contra Timocratem dicit [...] ."

[7] Compare Demosthenes, *In Timocratem* 139: ὥστ' ἄν τις βούληται νόμον καινὸν τιθέναι, ἐν βρόχῳ τὸν τράχηλον ἔχων νομοθετεῖ, καὶ ἐὰν μὲν δόξῃ καλὸς καὶ χρήσιμος εἶναι ὁ νόμος [...]; Philip Melanchthon, *Philosophiae moralis epitomes libri duo emendati et aucti* (Strasbourg: Mylius, 1546), 429: "ut, si quis velit novam legem ferre, suadens eam, cogatur dicere collo in laqueum inserto, quod si placet lex, et iudicatur utilis esse [...]"; and HAB Cod. Guelf. 1169 Helmst., fol. 239^v: "ut si quis suasurus esset novam legem proponere suam sententiam universae civitati collo in laqueum inserto ut si res displicuisset, statim strangularetur sin autem placuisset nova lex dimittebatur author incolumis exempto ex collo laqueo."

[8] Compare Demosthenes, *In Timocratem* 141: ἐάν τις ἕνα ἔχοντος ὀφθαλμὸν ἐκκόψῃ, ἄμφω ἀντεκκόψαι παρασχεῖν, ἵνα τῇ ἴσῃ συμφορᾷ ἀμφότεροι χρῶνται; and HAB Cod. Guelf. 1169 Helmst., fol. 240^v: "ut si quis habens geminos oculos effoderet unicum monoculum puniretur effosso utroque oculo ut aequalis esset utrius calamitas."

9   See, for example, HAB Cod. Guelf. 1169 Helmst., fols 24–5, 27^v (Melanchthon), 31^v (Reuchlin), 61^v–63 (several bishops); see also the list of (mostly) German proverbs, fols 68^v–71, and the abundant quotations from Luther: fols 41–3, 58–61^v, and *passim*.
10 HAB Cod. Guelf. 1169 Helmst., fols 25^v–26: "Ducissa Wirtenbergensis. Ducissa Wirtenbergensis cum dimitteret a se ancillam suam dixit Timas [*sic*] Deum et vivas honeste hedde ich das gedan sho wer ich in solch elend nicht geraden." In my translation I render the Latin in italics. See also the mixture in a "common saying" (*dictum usitatum*), HAB Cod. Guelf. 1169 Helmst., fol. 23: "Wen ein Canonicus stirbt tunc triplex gaudium est Primo Diaboli gaudent ad quos defertur anima Ess freuwen sich die erben die das guth bekhomen unde ffreuwet sich der successor der de prebende bekumpt." [When a Canon dies, *there is a three-fold joy: first, the devils rejoice, since the soul is borne down to them*; the heirs rejoice, since they get his property; and the successor rejoices, since he gets his income.]
11 HAB Cod. Guelf. 1169 Helmst., fols 102^v, 142.
12 For a detailed examination of φιλοστοργία as the term was developed and deployed in Wittenberg academic culture, see Valle forthcoming. For a metaphorical use of σφραγίς similar to that in Rolefinck's text, see *CR* 5, 263.
13 HAB Cod. Guelf. 1169 Helmst., fols 206^v–207: "Philippus in lectione publica. Herodotus inquit mulier deposita veste deponit pudorem In Italia est consuetudo ut viri et mulieres sine ullis tegumentis accedant ad balnea si ego ibi essem consul curarem eos virgis caedi ut quisque suum tegeret." The quotation is from Herodotus, *Histories*, I.8.3: ἅμα δὲ κιθῶνι ἐκδυομένῳ συνεκδύεται καὶ τὴν αἰδῶ γυνή.
14 HAB Cod. Guelf. 1169 Helmst., fol. 158^{r-v}; Diogenes Laertius, *Lives* 7.6.177.
15 HAB Cod. Guelf. 1169 Helmst., fols 20^v, 71^v–73, 125, and *passim*. See also the many entries concerning Charles V: for example, HAB Cod. Guelf. 1169 Helmst., fols 64, 66^{r-v}, 67^v–68, 204^v–205^v, 209.
16 HAB Cod. Guelf. 1169 Helmst., fols 22^v (Nuremberg), 35^v (Worms).
17 The examples are based on Van Rooy and Feys (2024). For DaLeT, see www.dalet.be. Last accessed April 30, 2024.
18 The data are taken from DaLeT Annotation IDs 971–3.

References

Ascham, Roger. 1865. *The Whole Works of Roger Ascham, Now First Collected and Revised, with a Life of the Author*. Edited by Giles Ascham. Vol. 1/2: Letters Continued. London: John Russell Smith.

Barnard, Jody A. 2017. "The 'Erasmian' Pronunciation of Greek: Whose Error Is It?" *Erasmus Studies* 37 (1): 109–32.

Bindseil, Heinrich Ernst, ed. 1863–6. *D. Martini Lutheri Colloquia*. 3 vols. Lemgo–Detmold: Meyer.

Blair, Ann. 1989. "Lectures on Ovid's *Metamorphoses*: The Class Notes of a 16th-Century Paris Schoolboy." *The Princeton University Library Chronicle* 50 (2): 117–44.

Brinkmann, Stefanie, Giovanni Ciotti, Stefano Valente, and Eva Maria Wilden, eds. 2021. *Education Materialised: Reconstructing Teaching and Learning Contexts through Manuscripts*. Berlin–Boston: De Gruyter.

Bywater, Ingram. 1908. *The Erasmian Pronunciation of Greek and Its Precursors: Jerome Aleander, Aldus Manutius, Antonio of Lebrixa*. London–Oxford: Henry Frowde & Oxford University Press.

Calis, Richard. 2019. "Reconstructing the Ottoman Greek World: Early Modern Ethnography in the Household of Martin Crusius." *Renaissance Quarterly* 72 (1): 148–93. https://doi.org/10.1017/rqx.2018.4.

Cohen, Thomas V., and Lesley K. Twomey, eds. 2015. *Spoken Word and Social Practice: Orality in Europe (1400–1700)*. Leiden–Boston: Brill.

Drerup, Engelbert. 1930–2. *Die Schulaussprache des Griechischen von der Renaissance bis zur Gegenwart: Im Rahmen einer allgemeinen Geschichte des griechischen Unterrichts*. 2 vols. Paderborn: F. Schöningh.

Ellis, Anthony. 2020. "Greek History in the Early-Modern Classroom: Lectures on Herodotus by Johannes Rosa and School Notes by Jacques Bongars (Jena, 1568)." In *Receptions of Hellenism in Early Modern Europe: 15th–17th Centuries*, edited by Natasha Constantinidou and Han Lamers, 113–40. Brill's Studies in Intellectual History 303. Leiden–Boston: Brill.

Leonhardt, Jürgen, and Claudia Schindler. 2007. "Neue Quelle zum Alltag im Hörsaal vor 500 Jahren: Ein Tübinger Forschungsprojekt zur Leipziger Universität." *Jahrbuch für Historische Bildungsforschung* 13: 31–56.

McKenzie, D.F. 1990. "Speech–Manuscript–Print." In *New Directions in Textual Studies*, edited by Dave Oliphant and Robin Bradford, 86–109. Austin, TX: Harry Ransom Research Center.

Ogorodnikova, Darya. 2021. "'I heard it from my teacher': Reflections on the Transmission of Knowledge in Islamic Manuscripts from Senegambia and Mali." In *Education Materialised: Reconstructing Teaching and Learning Contexts through Manuscripts*, edited by Stefanie Brinkmann, Giovanni Ciotti, Stefano Valente, and Eva Maria Wilden, 127–51. Berlin–Boston: De Gruyter.

Ong, Walter J. 1958. *Ramus, Method, and the Decay of Dialogue: From the Art of Discourse to the Art of Reason*. Cambridge, MA: Harvard University Press.

Ong, Walter J. 1967. *The Presence of the Word: Some Prolegomena for Cultural and Religious History*. New Haven: Yale University Press.

Sacré, Dirk. 2014. "Pronunciation of Latin." In *Brill's Encyclopaedia of the Neo-Latin World*. Leiden–Boston: Brill. https://referenceworks.brillonline.com/entries/encyclopaedia-of-the-neo-latin-world/pronunciation-of-latin-B9789004271012_0014. Last accessed August 24, 2023.

Sonntag, Corinna. 2019. "Melanchthons 'Schola Domestica': Wissensdistribution eines spezifischen Bildungssystems im Zeichen von Reformation und Späthumanismus." In *Frühneuzeitliche Bildungssysteme im interkonfessionellen Vergleich. Inhalte – Infrastrukturen – Praktiken*, edited by Christine Freytag and Sascha Salatowsky, 145–65. Stuttgart: Franz Steiner.

Thüringer, Walter. 1982. *Die Melancthonhandschriften der Herzog August Bibliothek*. Frankfurt a.M.: Vittorio Klostermann.

Valle, Tomás Antonio. Forthcoming. "Making 'Affection' Matter: A Case Study in Wittenberg Knowledge Production." In *Classical Reformations: Beyond Christian Humanism*, edited by Micha Lazarus and Lucy Nicholas. Turnhout: Brepols.

Van Rooy, Raf. 2020. "Het Grieks gedomesticeerd: De Erasmiaanse uitspraak en de taalideologie van Adolf van Meetkercke (1528–1591)." *Lampas: Tijdschrift voor Nederlandse classici* 53 (4): 447–71.

Van Rooy, Raf, and Xander Feys. 2024. "Activating Greek at the Leuven Trilingue? Rescius' Use of Greek in his 1543 *Odyssey* Course." In *Reading, Writing, Translating Greek in Early Modern Universities and Beyond*, edited by Johanna Akujärvi and Kristiina Savin, 159–201. Lund: Lund University Press.

Van Rooy, Raf, and Toon Van Hal. 2018. "Studying Ancient Greek at the Old University of Leuven: An Outline in a European Context." In *The Leuven Collegium Trilingue 1517–1797: Erasmus, Humanist Educational Practice and the New Language Institute Latin – Greek – Hebrew*, edited by Jan Papy, 129–53. Leuven, Paris, and Bristol, CT: Peeters.

Further reading

Burke, Peter. 1993. *The Art of Conversation*. Ithaca, NY: Cornell University Press. A set of five essays exemplifying the value of approaching social history through orality.

Clanchy, M.T. 2013. *From Memory to Written Record: England, 1066–1307*. 3rd edn. Oxford: Wiley-Blackwell. The classic work on the establishment of textual authority during the Middle Ages.

Fox, Adam. 2000. *Oral and Literate Culture in England, 1500–1700*. Oxford: Oxford University Press. An analysis of the intertwinement and mutual influence among speech, manuscript, and print in early modern England.

Horodowich, Elizabeth. 2012. "Introduction: Speech and Oral Culture in Early Modern Europe and Beyond." *Journal of Early Modern History* 16 (4–5): 301–13. The historiographical introduction to a special edition of *JEMH*, containing five studies focused on orality in different geographical and cultural contexts.

Lord, Albert Bates. 2019. *The Singer of Tales*. 3rd edn. Edited by David F. Elmer. Cambridge, MA: Harvard University Press. An exploration of epic poetry as an oral genre, building on the work of Lord's teacher Milman Parry.

Ong, Walter J. 2002. *Orality and Literacy: The Technologizing of the Word*. 2nd edn. New York: Routledge. A philosophical examination of orality and literacy as fundamentally different ways of approaching the world.

Parry, Milman. 1971. *The Making of Homeric Verse: The Collected Papers of Milman Parry*. Edited by Adam Parry. Oxford: Clarendon Press. The major writings of a pathbreaking scholar of Homeric poetry, interpreting it in light of oral composition techniques.

Roth, Carla. 2022. *The Talk of the Town: Information and Community in Sixteenth-Century Switzerland*. Oxford: Oxford University Press. An exemplary recent study of early modern orality from the perspective of social and cultural history, with a detailed historiographical introduction.

CHAPTER 11

Socio-Cultural History

Maximilian Schuh, Xander Feys, and Raf Van Rooy

1. Introduction

Teaching and learning at premodern universities were embedded in the daily life experiences of masters and students. Student notes give evidence of this close entanglement, and illustrate that daily life and current events took an important place in various academic settings. These notes represent traces of different oral communication situations in the lecture hall or private tutoring. Therefore, these notes not only contain academic and learned information. In addition, they can provide insights into current political affairs, into economic and social settings as well as into the masters' and students' everyday life. This information was either given by the master during the lecture as part of a didactic plan or—for various reasons—introduced into the notes by the students themselves. Against this background, the chapter examines student notes from different cultural, academic, and educational settings. Case studies include student notes from fifteenth-century lectures at arts faculties in Scandinavia (Uppsala) and the Holy Roman Empire (Ingolstadt); notes relating to the private Greek studies of Milanese princess Ippolita Maria Sforza in about 1465; and notes on the Ottoman threat featuring in the exegesis of Vergil at the Leuven Trilingue in 1549. The chapter aims to provide first insights into some of these notes and to show their value not only for the study of academic practices but also for the study of premodern life at large.

2. Case study 1: The arts faculties at Uppsala and Ingolstadt

To understand life at large in student notes from Uppsala and Ingolstadt, we have to consider the social and economic circumstances of studying at universities in Scandinavia and in the Holy Roman Empire. The premodern university was not an institution of tertiary education but a privileged place of teaching and learning in the medieval society. The social structure within the universities, therefore, reflected the hierarchies of the premodern society defined by estate and rank. The majority of the students stayed at the university for only a few semesters, primarily because of high fees for graduations and cost of living. Both money and social connections were necessary to achieve any academic advancement. Therefore, most students enrolled in the faculty of arts, in order to acquire knowledge and skills that would be useful in a non-academic work environment. At the end of the fifteenth century, between 80 and 90 percent of masters and students from a variety of social and economic backgrounds taught and learned at this faculty (Schwinges 1992; Schuh 2014). It was thus the very center of the premodern university in Central and Northern Europe.

Student text collections and student notes allow insights into life at the late medieval university on different levels (Schuh 2018). Student text collections, for example, help to assess to what extent the curricular norm was actually followed in the classes. They enable us to leave the prescriptive perspective of the statutes and to identify the textbooks read in class (see also Chapter 6). A thorough examination of the manuscript material produced at the arts faculty in Vienna revealed, for example, that students' interest was primarily directed toward the trivial subjects of grammar and rhetoric (Glaßner 2010). Therefore, texts discussing grammatical and rhetorical topics were more frequently collected than those treating philosophical subjects (Schuh 2013: 174–94). The curriculum, on the other hand, placed logic, natural, and moral philosophy at the center of the study program in the arts (Lorenz 1985). Since only a small proportion of students sought academic graduation, personal interests and utilitarian considerations seem to have provided a more important impetus than university curricula.

Moreover, the works actually used and annotated in class shed more light on unspecific titled textbooks in the statutes (for example, *liber rhetoricalis*). In a first step a master used self-authored textbooks, which followed humanist ideas. In a second step original Italian textbooks, such as the *Elegantiolae* by Agostino Dati, were used in the classes. Towards the end of the fifteenth century these textbooks then became part of the faculty's official curriculum.[1] It is also possible to trace the topics taught in class in more detail. This is especially true for textbooks whose complete treatment was not possible in the lectures—some of them were very limited in time—due to their volume.[2] The orality of university teaching is reflected in these student notes (see also Chapter 10). Although the concrete proceedings in the lecture hall cannot be completely reconstructed, student notes point to certain strategies in the masters' presentation and the students' learning of the course subjects (Miethke 2004; Leonhardt 2008; Schuh 2015). Against this background, in this first case study we examine student notes from Uppsala and Ingolstadt, showing how everyday life is reflected in these texts created in lectures and other teaching contexts.

2.1. *Uppsala*

A small set of student notes with different status from the university of Uppsala in Sweden shows how the master brought daily life into the lecture hall in the late fifteenth century. For instance, Ericus Olai had studied the arts and theology at Rostock before he began to teach both subjects in Scandinavia (Piltz 1977: 15–16). Notes taken by students in his lectures in Uppsala show that Ericus and other masters were eager to include in the teaching references to daily life beyond the university. The aim was probably to support the students' understanding of the matters taught. From his experience at the university of Rostock in the Holy Roman Empire Ericus included references to vernacular expressions in his Latin teaching. He used, for example, the juridical German term *Brautschatz* ("dowry") in his theological lecture to explain St Bonaventura's teaching regarding the symbolic *dotes* ("dowries") of the bodies and the souls. The master dictated the text during his lecture in Uppsala (Piltz 1977: 29 and 75). The student Olaus Johannis Gutho, who heard this lecture, however, was unable to understand the German term, as he noted down in his manuscript version of the lecture following misspelled expression:

> [...] dos est id, quod datur sponse a patre sponsi vel ab his, qui sunt ex parte sponsi, et vocatur Almanice "brudzchal" (Piltz 1977: 32)

> Dowry is that, what the bride is given by the husband's father or by his family, and it is called "brudzchal" in German.

Referring to examples beyond the experiences of the student audience was not helpful as the listeners were not able to make sense of the explanation relying on a language they did not understand. Some of the students at the Swedish university may have been able to understand some German, but the manuscript evidence points to problems in grasping the sense of German words used in the lecture.

The same is true for an unknown master's references to German towns at the coast of the Baltic Sea. For the discussion of questions on logical conclusions in Aristotle's *Prior Analytics* an anonymous student noted down the following example in his revised copy of the lecture:

> Rokstoksenses pugnare contra Syndenses est malum, ergo **Visbysenses** pugnare contra Lybenses est malum, quia sicut Rokstoksenses et Syndenses sunt vicini, sic et **Vismarienses** et Lybisenses. (Piltz 1977: 32–3)

> People from Rostock fighting against people from Stralsund is bad, therefore people from Visby fighting against people from Lübeck is bad, because as people from Rostock and people from Stralsund are neighbors, so are people from Wismar and Lübeck.

The student note-taker in Uppsala was obviously not familiar with the German towns Rostock, Stralsund, Wismar and Lübeck the lecturer had in mind. Therefore, he changed *Wismarenses* to *Visbysense* in the first half of the sentence, thus referring to Visby, a town known to him on the Swedish island Gotland far away from Lübeck (Piltz 1977: 33). The didactic strategy of referencing local towns and including contemporary political conflicts into the logic teaching was created for a student audience in Rostock. It did not work as smoothly at the university in Sweden. The student was not familiar with the towns mentioned in the lecture and substituted the unknown town Wismar with Visby. This change alone renders the sentence senseless. But by doing this only in the first half of the sentence, the whole example loses its power, as Visby does not appear in the second half. Instead, the correct town Wismar is mentioned. Thus, the syllogistic set-up of the example disappeared. The Uppsala student was probably rather at a loss when reading his notes again and had to make an additional effort to understand the example correctly. As it was the case with other slips of the pen when noting down complex logical rules.

Other student notes from Uppsala, taken in Petrus Olai's *exercicium Zophistrie* and in his lecture on the *Obligationes*, reflect another didactic strategy and refer to examples from a Swedish background discussed in logic classes: "Totus thesaurus Holmensis est in cista mea" ("The whole of Stockholm's treasure is in my coffer"), and "Tu es Rome, ergo non es in Vpsalia" ("You are in Rome, therefore you are not in Uppsala"; Piltz 1977: 33). Additionally, there are two explanations with references to Swedish words in lectures explaining the Bible text (Piltz 1977: 34).

These examples from late medieval Uppsala show what kind of problems could arise when masters, especially ones with academic experiences from abroad, were making use of daily life in their lectures. References to linguistic or geographic phenomena unknown to the student audience did not provide any firm support for understanding the topics taught. Instead, the hardly understandable examples made it far more difficult for the students to grasp the complex matters explained in the lectures. Ericus Olai and the anonymous master probably reused teaching material they had created in Rostock for their lectures in Uppsala. Petrus Olai, on the other hand, included some references to Swedish words and daily life in Sweden to make his teaching more accessible for the student audience in Uppsala.

2.2. Ingolstadt

The second set of examples comes from textbooks used in rhetoric classes at the Bavarian university of Ingolstadt situated in the south-east of the Holy Roman Empire. The *Elegantiolae* written by the Italian humanist Agostino Dati offer an introduction to classical Latin grammar and style (Warner 2012). The work was a very popular textbook in rhetoric classes at universities in the Holy Roman Empire during the second half of the fifteenth century. The book—originally written for use in Latin schools in Italy—explains the subject on a very basic level and offers a wide range of illustrative examples. Twenty manuscript copies of the *Elegantiolae* that were either written or used by Ingolstadt students from the late 1470s to the 1490s can be identified today. These manuscripts allow us to assess the extent of intellectual changes in learning at the university as they show which books were actually copied, used and deemed worth preserving by the students (Schuh 2013: 174–94).

The codex Augsburg, Staats- und Stadtbibliothek, 2° Cod 213 exemplifies the roads that student manuscripts could take. Conrad Hess copied the text of the *Elegantiolae* in the 1470s while studying at the arts faculty in Vienna. A short entry at the beginning of the codex states the scribe's name and the location.[3] In 1481, Hess left Vienna and continued his studies at the university of Ingolstadt. Apparently, the copy of the *Elegantiolae* was no longer of use to him there, and he sold it to another Ingolstadt student named Johannes Stetmaister. The manuscript contains glosses written by two hands, one belonging to Hess, the other to Stetmaister, who repeatedly referred to himself in the glosses (Spilling 1984: 221–2).

Official Ingolstadt arts faculty documents, for example from the documentation of the bachelor exam in 1479, show that Johannes Stetmaister ranked at the very end of the university's hierarchy. He held the last position at the solemn act of the bachelor promotion in autumn 1479. This was not an expression of poor academic achievement but of his limited social and economic possibilities within the personal network of the university. His rank within the university reflected his standing in fifteenth-century society (Schuh 2013: 202–3). Under such circumstances, a used textbook copy bought from another student illustrates how even a poor student could find affordable ways to acquire the relevant texts. After his university studies Stetmaister was able to make some social advancement as he managed to secure a position as a substitute priest (*vicarius*) in Adriach in Austria in about 1500 (Schulte-Strathaus 1926: 29).

The student manuscripts of the *Elegantiolae* allow the scholar insight into late medieval lectures and student life. The layout of the textbook is representative for university manuscripts. In the student copies, the text of the *Elegantiolae* is written in larger script. Additionally, there is room for notes between the lines and at the margins of the pages. Glosses inserted between the lines explain the meaning of single words, give synonyms, and name grammatical phenomena. Probably dictated by the master, they were written down by the students during and revised after the lectures. The glosses in the margins of the manuscript pages, however, show a more intensive intellectual engagement with and a deeper understanding of the *Elegantiolae*. They contain no grammatical or lexical explanations. Instead, these notes offer more examples of the correct use of the grammatical and stylistic rules explained in the main text (Schuh 2013: 194–6). The margins provided space for the masters' and students' own ideas that reflect university and student life.

For instance, the following section of the *Elegantiolae* explains the correct use of the Latin adverbs *multo* ("much") and *longe* ("far") with the comparative of adjectives:

> De comparativo. Comparativis vero vel multo vel longe preponi solet, ut: Justicia multo preclarior est ceteris virtutibus. Et: Aristoteles longe aliis philosophis sapientior.[4]

> "On comparatives: *multo* and *longe* are usually put before comparatives. For example: Justice is much more magnificent than the other virtues. Aristotle is far wiser than the other philosophers."

In his marginal glosses, Johannes Stetmaister noted further examples of this stylistic advice: "Exempla: [...] Rex Ungariae multo fidelior est christianitati aliis regibus. Johannes Stetmaister longe carior est puellis ceteris waccalareis" ("Examples: The king of Hungary is much more faithful to Christianity than the other kings. Johannes Stetmaister is far more popular with the girls than the other bachelors"). While the master may have provided the first added example, it seems rather unlikely that he dictated the second example. Apparently, Johannes completely understood the stylistic guideline and was able to actively formulate a Latin sentence that included a reference to his everyday life. His alleged popularity with girls is a distinct aspect of his personal experience and became part of the textbook. The correct use of the ablative of comparison is an important feature in this gloss. In medieval Latin an analytic construction with the particle *quam* would have been common practice. Another anonymous Ingolstadt student glossed this grammatical alternative in his copy of the *Elegantiolae* between the lines of the textbook: "quam alii philosophi" ("than the other philosophers").[5] This anonymous student—maybe encouraged by his master—added himself some examples reflecting his life at the university in the marginal glosses to the same section of the *Elegantiolae*. He wrote in the left margin of the page:

> Longe vel multo, ut: Johannes Latino eloquio multo prestantior est Petro. Johannes longe doctior est Petro. Vinum multo preclarius est cervisia. Studium Ingolstatense est multo vigorosius Lipsense.[6]

> "'Much' or 'far,' for example: Johannes is much better at Latin eloquence than Peter. Johannes is far more learned than Peter. Wine is much better than Beer. The University of Ingolstadt is far more lively than the University of Leipzig."

Another section of the *Elegantiolae* discusses different ways to praise or condemn individual persons in refined Latin:

> Iam uero explicandum est qua ratione quampiam personam aut laudari aut uituperari oportet, quod ad decorum sermonis pertineat. Nam id trifariam posse fieri comperimus ex monumentis litterarum, ut si uelim ostendere M. Catonem habere magnam uirtutem cum uerbo sum, es, est, ita commodissime fiet: Marcus Cato est magnus uirtute; M. Cato uir est magnae uirtutis; M. Cato vir est magna uirtute. (Warner 2012: 102)

> "But now it must be explained how one should either praise or condemn some person, which may affect the decorum of speech. For we discover from books of literature that it can be done in three different ways, so that if I should wish to show that Marcus Cato has great virtue with the verb *sum, es, est*, it will occur most fittingly as follows: 'Marcus Cato is a man great in virtue'; 'Marcus Cato is a man of great virtue'; 'Marcus Cato is a man with great virtue.'" (Warner 2012: 103)

In his marginal glosses to this stylistic explanation, Johannes Stetmaister included references to his family as well as to other Ingolstadt students, bachelors and masters of the arts faculty in the examples he formulated:

> Mater Johannis Stetmaister mulier est pulcri vultus, pulcro vultu. Thomas Preischuech baccalarius est bonus laude. Johannes Stetmaister amat magistrum Petrum suum ob doctrinam eius poeticam.[7]

> "Johannes Stemaister's mother is a woman of a beautiful face, with a beautiful face. Thomas Preischuech is a bachelor good in praise. Johannes Stetmaister loves his master Peter because of his Poetics teaching."

Further marginal notes also illustrate the rules taught in the *Elegantiolae* regarding the use of *et* and *tum* with simple examples reflecting Stetmaister's personal experiences:

> Johannes Stetmaister est et orator et poeta. Ulricus Stetmaister est bonus tum medicus tum mercator. Georgius Czingel est preclarus tum magister tum doctor.[8]

> "Johannes Stetmaister is an orator and a poet. Ulrich Stetmaister is a good doctor as well as a good merchant. Georg Zingel is a famous master and doctor."

The examples discussed above indicate that teaching the *Elegantiolae* occurred playfully, or at least that the student tried to make the learning experience pleasant. With the mention of town names, other students and masters as well as family members, preferences for alcoholic beverages, and inter-university competition, student notes reveal the daily lives of magisters and students, in this case of an arts faculty in late fifteenth-century Ingolstadt. On the one hand, this reveals the masters' didactic strategy of activating their students by motivating them to compose their own examples. On the other hand, the case of Ingolstadt demonstrates the students' methods of making the subjects their own. In sum, these sources do not simply reveal the students' ability to formulate correct Latin sentences but show that they learned to apply their skills to everyday life. These findings cast doubts on the thesis that oral communication in Latin at the late medieval universities mainly moved along prefabricated text modules (Haye 2005: 77–82).

3. Case study 2: Triangular teaching in Milan in about 1465

Quite different from the university context described in the first case study is the situation of princess Ippolita Maria Sforza (1445–1488), who studied Ancient Greek in private courses at the Milanese court in about 1465.[9] The duke of Milan Francesco I Sforza, Ippolita Maria's father, exploited knowledge of the Greek language and literature as cultural and political capital to make his daughter an excellent wedding candidate, as he wanted to strategically involve her in the ongoing struggle for power on the Italian peninsula. The Sforza princess was promised to Alfonso, then duke of Calabria and son of king of Naples Ferdinand I, and later for a short time king of Naples himself (as Alfonso II), whom she married after ten years of engagement at age twenty in 1465. For this event, she moved from Milan to Naples, together with an entire entourage, including her teachers, the Italian humanist Baldo Martorelli, who served as her and her brother's Latin teacher, and the Greek refugee scholar Constantine Lascaris (1434–1501). Indeed, at about that time Ippolita Sforza seems to have been studying Greek with the migrant Lascaris, then about thirty years old and only recently settled in Milan, after a period of captivity and travelling across the Mediterranean following the fall of Constantinople in 1453.[10] What is more, a manuscript dedicated to Sforza even suggests that the princess formed part of a didactic triangle, where she occupied the position of learner, facing the migrant Greek expert Lascaris, on the one hand, and her local and loyal teacher Martorelli, on the other.

How do we know about this peculiar social set-up? And why was the private course organized like this? The main source is the largely autograph manuscript that Lascaris dedicated to Ippolita Maria Sforza and wrote for her use, today preserved in the Bibliothèque nationale de France, Paris (BnF, grec 2590). A paleographical analysis of this document has led to the hypothesis formulated at the end of the previous paragraph. The manuscript contains a Latin dedicatory letter authored by Lascaris but copied by an anonymous Italian scribe, perhaps because Lascaris' Latin handwriting skills were not yet in keeping with the standards of his new host country. The few Greek phrases in the letter have been added by him afterwards. The rest of the manuscript contains his epitome of Greek grammar, one of the earliest copies known, written in his hand, with occasional corrections of his fellow migrant Greek scholar Demetrios Kastrenos and marginal summaries of another Greek, George Hermonymus of Sparta, probably added at a later stage. All this text is written in Greek. What is, however, most relevant for our purposes are the Latin notes found both in the margins and between the lines of the main text: annotations offering for the greater part translations of Greek examples and grammatical terminology, as well as Greek letter drawing exercises (see Figure 11.1).

While the Greek main text and contributions of the three Greek migrants had been recognized in previous scholarship, the Latin notes and Greek drawing exercises had been completely overlooked. Comparison of Lascaris' and Sforza's Latin hands led to the conclusion that they could not be the authors of the annotations, although certain variants of Sforza's handwritings did come near. A third option turned out to come much closer to the truth: the Latin translations should be attributed to Sforza's trusted teacher and secretary Martorelli (see the evidence in Van Rooy 2022). The Greek pen exercises—written in a different ink—may, in turn, reflect Sforza's efforts to make the language her own (Figure 11.1). Martorelli, in conclusion, wrote down Latin translations of Greek words, supporting his protégé in a context where contacts with a relatively young migrant may have been considered inappropriate and at the same time providing handiwork he was accustomed to do for Sforza as her secretary: writing things down on her behalf. Additionally, Lascaris' knowledge

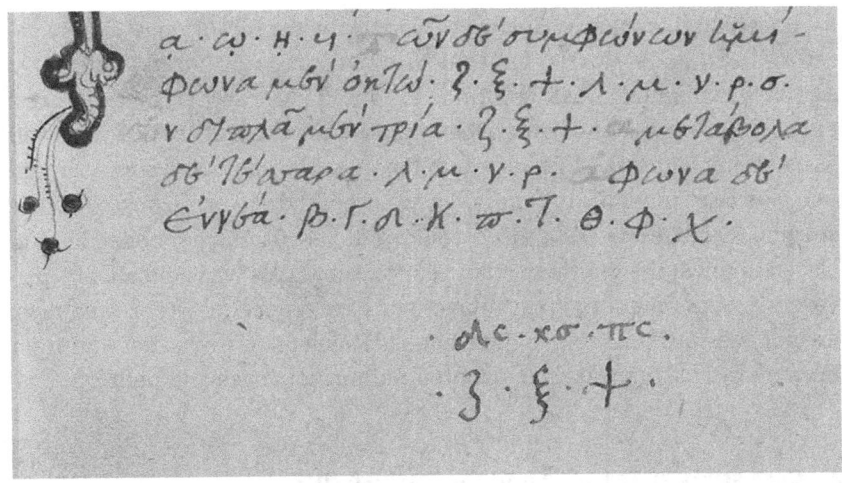

Figure 11.1. Greek letter exercises at the bottom and top of the folios and Latin interlinear translations. BnF, grec 2590, fol. 3r-v.[11]

of Latin may still have been limited, triggering the need to have him assisted by Martorelli, who no doubt must have been more fluent in this language, while he only had a superficial command of Greek. Lascaris and Martorelli were, in other words, a complementary team that taught Sforza, the presence of Martorelli perhaps also being a plus on account of his loyal service and trustworthiness as a local.

Based on this manuscript, then, we may picture a very peculiar social set-up for this Greek course at the Sforza court in Milan in about 1465: Lascaris explained Greek grammar to Ippolita Maria Sforza in the presence of Martorelli, who helped the migrant out with the Latin glosses and assisted the princess in noting them down, while she made some limited pen exercises herself. Student notes, in sum, can help us reconstruct very specific social interactions, offering us a glimpse of what happened behind closed doors at the Milanese court. There, a princess was educated by private teachers on a humanist subject par excellence, the Greek language, even if she does not seem to have booked much progress, as her attention became increasingly absorbed by Neapolitan court life and politics.

4. Case study 3: *Aeneid* 12 and the Turkish threat

Now, let us once more focus on Trilingue student Nicolaus Episcopius the Younger whom we already introduced in a previous contribution (see Chapter 2.3). From September 24 to December 9, 1549, he attended Petrus Nannius' lectures on *Aeneid* 12, diligently recording his notes in a textbook printed by Servaes van Sassen.[12] In essence, Vergil's epic tells the story of the Trojan hero Aeneas, whose adventures en route to and victories on the Italian peninsula ultimately paved the way for the emergence of Rome. In the twelfth and final book, war is the central theme. In spun-out battle scenes, the fate of the Trojan and Latin armies is in the end settled by means of the duel between Aeneas and his adversary Turnus. Since war is of all ages and to make the reading of the Latin classic more relevant for his audience, Nannius did not refrain from referencing contemporary conflicts and struggles during his lectures. In the first half of the sixteenth century, the so-called Ottoman or Turkish Threat was the subject of much debate with some parties arguing in favor of a war, while others held a pacifist view. The pressing nature of the issue becomes evident when one looks at the array of books, essays, pamphlets, and so forth that were published on the topic. Nannius, too, had voiced his opinions on the matter, when, in December 1535, he took part in a quodlibetal disputation organized by the Arts faculty. The topic of discussion was whether war had to be waged against the Turks, the ethnonym used to designate the inhabitants of the Ottoman Empire. Nannius, who at the time was trying to make a name for himself in the humanist milieu, argued to take up arms and had his ornately written speech soon published by Rutgerus Rescius.[13] Due to the academic and somewhat artificial nature of the debate, one could argue that Nannius' call to war does not necessarily reflect his real-life opinions. By 1549, the Ottoman threat had not yet subsided and still prompted reflection in the classroom. Judging by Nicolaus' notes, Nannius mentioned the Turks at least on three separate occasions. In line with his quodlibetal speech, these references put the Turks in a negative light, indicating that the professor leaned more toward a bellicose than a pacifist view. The first mention occurs at *Aen.* 12.206, describing the moment when king Latinus, holding a scepter, solemnly swears to Aeneas that their truce is everlasting:

> DaLeT Annotation ID 2246
> **Vt sceptrum** ·/· Regium nanq[ue] erat iurare i iuramenta per sceptrum. nam sceptru[m] Iouis propriu[m]. Est enim sceptrum cingulum iustitiæ. Reges aut[em] nu[n]c solent iurare p[er] sua[m] corona[m] et suu[m] diodema. Turci uero per suos dentes iurant.
> "just as this scepter": Indeed, it was befitting of a king to swear his oaths by the scepter. For the scepter belongs to Jupiter. Furthermore, the scepter is the girdle of justice. Now, however, kings are used to swear by their crown and their diadem. The Turks, on the other hand, swear by their teeth.
> AL: 12.206: Vt septrum hoc (dextra septrum nam fortè gerebat)

This cultural note conveys information about the practice of oath-swearing. The custom of the ancient and contemporary kings is depicted as a ceremonious happening, where the use of stately objects emphasizes the importance of the act of swearing itself. This dignified happening is then contrasted to the practice of the Turks, as indicated by the adversative adverb *vero* ("on the other hand"). Even though it is not explicitly stated, the impression is given that the Turkish custom, seemingly lacking any form of grandeur, is inferior to that of kings in Europe at the time. We were unable to pinpoint the source where Nannius might have found that the Ottomans swore oaths by their teeth.

A second example of how the Turks are negatively represented in Episcopius' notes is found at *Aen.* 12.511. In this passage, Turnus has just killed two minor characters, Amycus and Diores, hanging their heads from his chariot. This cruel scene led to the following remark:

> DaLeT Annotation ID 3029
>
> **Curruq[ue]** ·/· Immanitatem Turni hic habemus. Hoc solent adhuc Turci contra christianos exercere. et Veneti et Hungri co[n]tra Turcos ut q[ui]cu[m]q[ue] Turci caput referat pro quolibet capite soluatur ei ducatus un[us]. ein tugnde "[then, hanging from] his car [the severed heads of the two, he bears them off dripping with blood]": Here, we have the cruelty of Turnus. To this day, the Turks are accustomed to practice this method [of decapitation] against the Christians. And the Venetians and Hungarians against the Turks so that anybody who brought back the head of a Turk was paid one ducat for every head. ein tugnde ["a virtue"].
>
> AL: 12.511: Hunc mucrone ferit, currúque abscissa duorum

In this note, Nannius puts the cruelty of Turnus on a par with the savagery of the Turks. Inspired perhaps by a folk etymological association (*Turnus–Turcus*), he highlights the fact that the Ottomans still ("adhuc") decapitate their enemies, just like Aeneas' monstrous foe in mythic times. Furthermore, Nicolaus' note states that the act of beheading was eagerly adopted by the Venetians and Hungarians, two nations that had long been at war with the Ottoman Empire.[14] Apparently, money was paid in return for each beheaded Turk. What is more, claiming the head of a Turkish enemy as booty was regarded as a symbol of Christian victory, something that led to the concept of the "Turk head," a recurrent theme in European Heraldry.[15] Interestingly, the student added a short meta-comment in German, his native language, revealing that, like his professor, he advocated a war against the Turks.

The last mention of the Turks appears at *Aen.* 12.857. In this passage, one of the Furies is sent to Earth by Jupiter as a sign for Juturna, Turnus' sister, that the war is lost. Vergil compared the swift and ill-omened descent of the Fury to a poisoned arrow shot by a Parthian. In Nicolaus' note, we read the following:

> DaLeT Annotation ID 3982
>
> **Armatam** ·/· Expositio est elegans. Armatam id est uenenatam, nam quum uis teli ictus per se hominibus mortem inferat, tamen quò magis sit lethalior ueneno ~~aeil~~ aciculam teli solent ungere quod solent iam Turci contra Persas et Hunguros. Venenu[m] aute[m] fit ex succo cæpe, allij etc.
>
> "[an arrow,] armed [with the gall of fell poison]": This is an elegant exposition. "Armatam" ("armed") this is "venenatam" ("poisoned"), for when the power

of a missile, thrown on its own, brings about death in men, how much more lethal would it be with venom. [The Parthians] are used to besmear the small tip of an arrow, something which the Turks are now wont to do against the Persians and the Hungarians.[16] The venom is, furthermore, made from the sap of an onion, garlic, etc.

AL: 12.857: Armatam sæui Parthus quam felle veneni

The Parthians were notorious for their accuracy with bow and arrow, a reputation they had earned, among others, due to Vergil's description. The Turks, in turn, were not known for this. Nevertheless, they were sometimes equalled to the Parthians, hence the parallelism.[17] It is unclear where Nannius might have come across the notion that the Turks also used poisoned arrows. At any rate, the professor also referred to the Ottoman–Hungarian Wars, which culminated in the Battle of Mohács (1526), as well as the wars fought between the Ottoman and Safavid (Persian) Empires.

In the three notes above, the cruelty of the Turks takes center stage. They reveal that Nannius did not shy away from broaching political (and possibly sensitive) subjects and consolidated his negative portrayal of the Ottoman people in a classroom context, building on views he had publicly upheld in the past. In the notes, the Turks are depicted as a barbarian and cruel people who inspired fear.[18] Quite plausibly, Nicolaus agreed with the professor, judging by his own vernacular addition. By way of concluding this case study, it is worth pointing out that there are other, perhaps less charged, coeval references present in Nicolaus' notes, too. In one of them, Nannius discusses the clothing of Roman priests, at the end of which he makes a passing remark about the clothing of contemporary Dutch women.[19] In another note, the professor mentioned an alliance between the Helvetians, the Venetians, the king of France, and the pope, possibly to be understood in the context of the Second Italian War (1499–1501).[20] In still another annotation, we find that Nannius must have advertised a work of his that had been published a little over six months prior to the start of the lectures on *Aeneid* 12.[21]

5. Conclusion

Understanding life at large in student notes requires the consideration of the institutional, economic, and social conditions of teaching and learning in early modernity, before analyzing the respective texts. To find and identify respective student text collections and notes, intensive research is necessary. Corresponding projects initiated for the arts faculties in Paris (Weijers 1994–2012) and Vienna (Glaßner 2010) have resulted in considerable success. Further comprehensive research projects are desirable since in-depth descriptions in manuscript and incunabula catalogs are only partly available. The geographic and thematic limitation to the study of one textbook or subject at a specific university represents a manageable research strategy for handling the quantity of extant manuscripts or prints. Dated colophons in books used for academic teaching are of great use in this context, as is the systematic identification of manuscript scribes and owners and their social markers. Other texts noted in professorial and student text collections, such as letters, sermons, and orations as well as wordlists, timetables, and lecture announcements, provide additional insight into premodern university life. Student notes represent an extremely informative source genre whose potential for research has so far only been rudimentarily exploited due to the manifold challenges connected with their identification and analysis, even though the few clues we have may lead to far-reaching conclusions, as the Sforza case study has endeavored to show. In the case of Episcopius, we have seen that ongoing political conflicts, such as the Turkish threat, were not avoided in the Trilingue classroom. On the contrary, at several instances current events were actively incorporated in the interpretation of Vergil's *Aeneid*.

The approach of this chapter has been to combine micro-history with serial analysis to arrive at a nuanced image of the social contexts of learning in early modern Latin Europe. Indeed, the main take-away of this final chapter should be that by getting to know the Stetmaisters, Ippolita Sforzas, and Episcopiuses of the early modern world you can also get a glimpse of the diverse social contexts in which they operated. Notably, even though we can discern general trends in the history of early modern education, micro-historical approaches like the ones showcased in this chapter show how teachers and students adapted the teaching materials and methods, often drawing on ancient and medieval traditions, to their specific contemporary situations. To enrich the picture, further serial analysis of individual cases is needed, ideally combined with a thorough comparison.

Notes

1. For rhetoric lectures in Ingolstadt, see Schuh (2013: 104–9).
2. For the mathematical textbook *Tractatus de algorismo* in Ingolstadt, see Schöner (1994: 150–2).
3. Augsburg, Staats- und Stadtbibliothek, 2° Cod 213, fol. 1^r: "Conradus Heß ex Novoforo waccalareus studii Wiennensis."
4. Augsburg, Staats- und Stadtbibliothek, 2° Cod 213, fol. 7^v.
5. München, Bayerische Staatsbibliothek, clm 14644, fol. 64^v. On this anonymous student, see Schuh (2013: 183). For the codex, see Helmer and Knödler (2015: 478–84).
6. München, Bayerische Staatsbibliothek, clm 14644, fol. 64^v.
7. Augsburg, Staats- und Stadtbibliothek, 2° Cod 213, fol. 11^r.
8. Augsburg, Staats- und Stadtbibliothek, 2° Cod 213, fol. 13^r.
9. This case study is based on Van Rooy (2023).
10. On Lascaris see, for example, Martínez Manzano (1994).
11. © BNF. Reproduced with permission.
12. For a complete edition of Nicolaus' notes, see Feys s.d.
13. On Nannius' *Declamatio quodlibetica de bello Turcis inferendo*, see Jaspers (2020, 2024).
14. The Ottoman–Hungarian conflict culminated in the Battle of Mohács in 1526, which led to the partition of the country. Venice, too, had been continuously at war with the Ottomans, with the Third Ottoman–Venetian War (1537–40) most fresh in Nannius' and Episcopius' minds by the time of the lectures on *Aeneid* 12.
15. We have found no other accounts of soldiers being paid one ducat for beheading Turks. Nannius makes no mention of this in his *Declamatio*. More on this topic in Brummett (2015: 87–238; esp. 209 and 225, respectively, for examples of Hungarians and Venetians beheading Turkish soldiers).
16. In between "teli" and "solent," Episcopius crossed out a word, most likely the subject of the first "solent," and in doing so he rendered it completely illegible. To make any sense of this annotation, we have to assume that the Parthians are the subject of this "solent," as suggested by the Vergilian context.
17. Morton (2016: 216).
18. Cf. Jaspers (2020: 532–3).
19. DaLeT Annotation ID 1977.
20. DaLeT Annotation ID 3864.
21. DaLeT Annotation ID 4029.

References

Brummett, Palmira. 2015. *Mapping the Ottomans: Sovereignty, Territory, and Identity in the Early Modern Mediterranean*. Cambridge: Cambridge University Press.

Feys, Xander, ed. S.d. "Nannius-Episcopius Annotations on Vergil's *Aeneid* 12 (Latin, 1549)." With contributions by Jan Papy, Andy Peetermans, and Raf Van Rooy. DaLeT: Database of the Leuven Trilingue. <www.dalet.be/copy/5>. Last accessed April 9, 2024.

Feys, Xander. 2024. "Language and Literature Teaching in the Sixteenth Century: Vergil and Homer at the Leuven Collegium Trilingue." Unpublished PhD dissertation, Leuven: KU Leuven.

Glaßner, Christina. 2010. "Wiener Universitätshandschriften in Melk: Bemerkungen zum Lehrbetrieb an der Wiener Artistenfakultät." In *Die Universität Wien im Konzert europäischer Bildungszentren. 14.–16. Jahrhundert*, edited by Kurt Mühlberger and Meta Niederkorn-Bruck, 87–99. München–Wien: Oldenbourg-Böhlau.

Haye, Thomas. 2005. *Lateinische Oralität: Gelehrte Sprache in der mündlichen Kommunikation des hohen und späten Mittelalters*, Berlin–New York: de Gruyter.

Helmer, Friedrich, and Julia Knödler. 2015. *Katalog der lateinischen Handschriften der Bayerischen Staatsbibliothek München: Die Handschriften aus St. Emmeram in Regensburg. Bd. 4: Clm 14401–14540*. Wiesbaden: Harrassowitz.

Jaspers, Martijn. 2020. "Lazy but Cruel: Oriental Stereotypes in Petrus Nannius' *Declamatio de bello Turcis inferendo* (Leuven: Rutger Rescius, 1536)." *Bibliothèque d'Humanisme et Renaissance* 82 (3): 515–33.

Jaspers, Martijn. 2024. *Should We Declare War on the Turks? Nannius' Declamatio de bello Turcis inferendo (Leuven: Rutger Rescius, 1536)*. Leuven: Peeters.

Leonhardt, Jürgen. 2008. "Classics as Textbooks: A Study of the Humanist Lectures on Cicero at the University of Leipzig, ca. 1515?" In *Scholarly Knowledge: Textbooks in Early Modern Europe*, edited by Emidio Campi, Simone De Angelis, Anja-Silvia Goeing, and Anthony T. Grafton, 89–112. Genève: Droz.

Lorenz, Sönke. 1985. "*Libri ordinarie legendi*: Eine Skizze zum Lehrplan der mitteleuropäischen Artistenfakultät um die Wende vom 14. zum 15. Jahrhundert." In *Argumente und Zeugnisse*, edited by Wolfgang Hogrebe, 204–58. Frankfurt am Main: Lang.

Martínez Manzano, Teresa. 1994. *Konstantinos Laskaris: Humanist, Philologe, Lehrer, Kopist*. Hamburg: Universität Hamburg–Institut für griechische und lateinische Philologie.

Miethke, Jürgen. 2004. "Die mittelalterlichen Universitäten und das gesprochene Wort." In *Studieren an mittelalterlichen Universitäten: Chancen und Risiken. Gesammelte Aufsätze von Jürgen Miethke*, 453–91. Leiden–Boston: Brill.

Morton, Nicholas. 2016. *Encountering Islam on the First Crusade*. Cambridge: Cambridge University Press.

Piltz, Anders, ed. 1977. *Studium Upsalense: Specimens of the Oldest Lecture Notes Taken in the Mediaeval University of Uppsala*. Stockholm: Almqvist och Wiksell International.

Polet, Amédée. 1936. *Une gloire de l'humanisme belge: Petrus Nannius 1500–1557*. Louvain: Librairie Universitaire Ch. Uystpruyst.

Schöner, Christoph. 1994. *Mathematik und Astronomie an der Universität Ingolstadt im 15. und 16. Jahrhundert*. Berlin: Duncker und Humblot.

Schuh, Maximilian. 2013. *Aneignungen des Humanismus: Institutionelle und individuelle Praktiken an der Universität Ingolstadt im 15. Jahrhundert*. Leiden–Boston: Brill.

Schuh, Maximilian. 2014. "Making Renaissance Humanism Popular in the Fifteenth Century Empire." In *Renaissance Now! The Value of the Renaissance Past in Contemporary Culture*, edited by Brendan Dooley, 81–101. Oxford et al.: Peter Lang.

Schuh, Maximilian. 2015. "Wein ist viel herrlicher als Bier: Praktiken der Wissensvermittlung und -aneignung im universitären Rhetorikunterricht des Spätmittelalters." In *Akademische Wissenskulturen: Praktiken des Lehrens und Forschens vom Mittelalter bis zur Moderne*, edited by Martin Kintzinger, Sita Steckel, and Julia Crispin, 121–41. Basel: Schwabe.

Schuh, Maximilian. 2018. "Kolleghefte, Vorlesungsmitschriften." In *Universitäre Gelehrtenkultur vom 13.–16. Jahrhundert: Ein interdisziplinäres Quellen- und Methodenhandbuch*, edited by Jan-Hendryk de Boer, Marian Füssel, and Maximilian Schuh, 255–63. Stuttgart: Franz Steiner.

Schulte-Strathaus, Ernst. 1926. *Wiegendrucke: Mit 150 Abbildungen von Typen/Holzschnitten. Miniaturen und Einbänden*. München: J. Halle/Antiquariat.

Schwinges, Rainer Christoph. 1992. "Student Education, Student Life." In *A History of the University in Europe*, vol. 1: *Universities in the Middle Ages*, edited by Hilde de Ridder-Symoens, 195–243. Cambridge: Cambridge University Press.

Spilling, Herrad. 1984. *Die Handschriften der Staats- und Stadtbibliothek Augsburg 2° Cod 101–250*. Wiesbaden: Harrassowitz.

Van Rooy, Raf. 2022. "Baldo Martorelli as Latin Annotator of BNF, grec 2590." *Humanities Commons CORE Repository*. https://doi.org/10.17613/ezf9-mx73.

Van Rooy, Raf. 2023. "Ippolita Maria Sforza, Student and Patron of Greek in Milan." *Renaissance Quarterly* 76 (3): 848–92.

Warner, J. Christopher. 2012. "Quick Eloquence in the Late Renaissance: Agostino Dati's *Elegantiolae*." *Humanistica Lovaniensia: Journal of Neo-Latin Studies* 61: 65–240.

Weijers. Olga. 1994–2012. *Le travail intellectuel à la Faculté des arts de Paris: Textes et maîtres (ca. 1200–1500)*. 9 vols. Turnhout: Brepols.

Multilingual Glossary[1]

English	Page numbers	Gloss	Latin	French	German
approbation	103	official approval of the contents of a book by a censor, typically a cleric	*approbatio*	*approbation*	*Approbation*
autograph (less common: holograph)	40, 212, 246	a work written down in the hand of the author themselves	*autographum autographon*	*autographe*	*Autograph*
bifolium	76–77, 80	a sheet folded once (four sides)	*bifolium*	*bifeuillet*	*Doppelblatt*
binding	31, 53, 74, 77–79, 83, 89, 99, 105, 108–109, 115, 117, 121, 177	the joining together of the quires and securing them within a cover	*ligatura compactio compactura compaginatio*	*reliure*	*Bindung Einband Bucheinband*
bound volume (less common: convolute)	28–2, 29, 112, 115, 117, 184, 186	a single volume that contains multiple works (often by different authors or on different topics) bound together		*recueil factice*	*Sammelband*
censorship	101, 103–104, 113, 121–122	estimation of the contents of a book, (dis)allowing the publication of a book	*censura*	*censure*	*Zensur*

[1] The multilingual glossary has been composed by the editors, inspired by the *Lexique* in Jean-François Gilmont and Alexandre Vanautgaerden's 2008 *La page de titre à la Renaissance* (Turnhout: Brepols), at the suggestion of Ann Blair. Some contributors also suggested terms to add to the glossary.

English	Page numbers	Gloss	Latin	French	German
colophon	28–29, 68, 75, 80, 85, 89, 99, 160, 252	a note at the end of a manuscript or printed book providing information about its production	*colophon*	*colophon*	*Kolophon*
commonplaces	33, 51, 60, 141, 182, 228	notable quotations, ideas, or passages from various texts, typically collected in a notebook	*loci communes*	*lieux communs*	*Gemeinplätze*
compass	31, 36	one of the bookbinder's tools	*circinus*	*compas*	*Zirkel*
dictation	14, 27, 29, 32–42, 49–51, 57–58, 60, 63, 65, 74, 85, 87, 128–129, 134, 144, 191, 201–202, 207, 211, 213, 239, 242, 243	the act of reading out loud the exact words that students needed to note down in view of transmitting and reproducing knowledge	*dictatio*	*dictée*	*Diktat*
endpaper (= pastedown + flyleaf)	77, 79	folded sheet of paper that is partly pasted onto the inside of a book's front or back board (= pastedown) and partly remains unglued between the board and the pages of the actual book (= flyleaf)		*page de garde*	*Vorsatz-(-blatt)/ Nachsatz-(-blatt)*

MULTILINGUAL GLOSSARY

English	Page numbers	Gloss	Latin	French	German
explicit	60	note signaling the end of the book		*explicit*	*Explicit*
	31–34, 37, 64, 179	layout with wide margins and interlinear spacing, intended for note-taking		*feuille classique*	
first edition	103, 180, 187, 201	the first issue of a printed book	*editio princeps*	*édition originale*	*Erstausgabe Urdruck*
first-order notes	29, 37, 39, 74, 159, 161, 224–226, 231	notes taken during the lecture			*Mitschriften*
folio	31, 43–44, 76–78, 80–83, 89, 91, 105–106, 113, 141, 247	one leaf of a codex, consisting of two pages (recto and verso)	*folium*	*feuille(t)*	*Blatt*
(book) format	31, 37, 64, 98, 105–106, 108, 113, 115, 124, 201	size of a book, as determined by paper size and folding (folio, quarto, octavo, sexto decimo...)		*format pliage*	*Buchformat*
gloss	64, 162, 169, 176–177, 180, 242–244, 248	a brief explanation, definition, or commentary to a text	*glossa, glossema, scholium, scholion*	*glose*	*Glosse*

English	Page numbers	Gloss	Latin	French	German
imprint	45, 83, 101, 104, 115, 117	indication of place, publisher, and/or year of the edition, sometimes also mentioning the bookseller and the printing privilege	*impressum*	*adresse bibliographique*	*Druckvermerk*
incipit	60	the opening words of a manuscript or book, sometimes used as a title		*incipit*	*Incipit*
interleaving	31, 50, 64, 69, 77–78, 82–84, 86, 88, 108, 117, 130, 175, 179–180, 182, 186	the practice of putting blank sheets between the regular folios of a book	*interfoliatio*	*interfoliage*	*Interfolierung*
interlinear	29, 32, 37, 42, 64–65, 106, 113, 130, 160, 179, 247	written or printed between the lines of the text	*inter lineas*	*interlinéaire*	*interlinear*
leather	31, 74, 77, 79	the treated animal hides used in the binding of manuscripts and books	*cutis, corium*	*cuir*	*Leder*
lemma	29, 50, 64	1) word or phrase that is repeated in student notes and receives commentary; 2) key word, standard form of a word or phrase as it features in a dictionary	*lemma*	*lemme*	*Lemma Stichwort*

MULTILINGUAL GLOSSARY 261

English	Page numbers	Gloss	Latin	French	German
ligature	16, 55–56	the combination of different letters into one symbol, usually remnants of the handwritten tradition	*abbreviatio*	*ligature*	*Ligatur*
manicule	42, 44, 63, 117, 191, 213	hand symbol drawn in the margin to draw attention	*manicula*	*manicule*	*Zeigehändchen*
margin	13, 29, 32, 33, 42, 44, 50, 57, 64–65, 73, 80, 83, 85, 88, 106, 113, 115, 117, 130, 160, 179, 212, 242–246	white space around the printed text, typically on all four edges of the page	*margo*	*marge*	*Rand*
	105	physical appearance of a book (for example, format, binding)		*mise en livre*	
	105–106	layout of a printed text		*mise en page*	
paleography	17, 49, 54–60, 67, 75, 133–134, 246	the study of historical handwriting, used for dating and authenticating manuscripts	*palaeographia*	*paléographie*	*Paläografie Paläographie*

MULTILINGUAL GLOSSARY

English	Page numbers	Gloss	Latin	French	German
paper	14, 28, 35, 39, 57, 73, 76–79, 83–84, 92, 96, 98–99, 105–106, 108–109, 113, 117, 133, 159, 179, 182, 187	writing and printing support made from textile, often old rags	*charta, papyrus*	*papier*	*Papier*
parallel sets of notes	58, 85, 129, 133	two or more sets of notes taken by different students during the same course			
paratext	32, 40, 73–74, 103, 107–109, 123–124	text accompanying the main text of a manuscript or print, before, after, or in the margin of the main text		*paratexte*	*Paratext*
parchment	31, 76–77, 96, 98, 108, 115, 133, 172	writing support made from animal hides (typically sheep, goats, or calves)	*membrana/ pergamena [charta]*	*parchemin*	*Pergament*
privilege	102–103, 107, 121	legislative procedure to protect against pirate reprints, officialized by printing the privilege text in early modern editions	*privilegium*	*privilège*	*Privileg*

MULTILINGUAL GLOSSARY 263

English	Page numbers	Gloss	Latin	French	German
provenance note/mark	17, 49–53, 58, 67–71, 79, 88, 109–110, 120, 130, 133, 175	annotation revealing the identity of a book's owner(s)	*ex libris*	*provenance*	*Provenienz*
quire/ gathering	76–82, 84, 86–87, 89–91, 105, 108, 115	a collection of leaves made from a folded sheet or sheets; the quire constitutes the building block of a codex and typically consists of four to six folded sheets	*quaternio quaternus*	*cahier*	*Lage*
	27–28, 45, 49–51, 57–58, 60, 63, 74, 134	selective note-taking of speech at regular speed (as opposed to verbatim note-taking under dictation, at slower speed)	*reportatio*		
second-order notes	29, 37, 39, 42–43, 49, 64, 85, 159, 161, 180, 224–226	notes revised after the lecture		*copie propre/ au net*	*Reinschriften*
sewing	77, 79–83, 108–109, 115	joining together of quires of folded paper using needles and thread	*sutura*	*suture*	*Naht*
tachygraphy (shorthand)	27, 39	fast writing	*tachygraphia*	*sténographie tachygraphie*	*Kurzschrift Schnellschrift*

English	Page numbers	Gloss	Latin	French	German
third-order notes	37, 73, 159, 161	notes revised more than once, possibly in view of publication			
title page	28, 30, 52, 64, 68, 73, 99, 102, 107, 111, 115, 192, 204, 211, 216	first or one of the first pages in a printed book, typically on the recto side of a page, offering basic information about the text printed, its author, and its publisher	*pagina tituli*	*page de titre*	*Titelseite*
watermark	74, 79–80, 82–84, 92, 117, 119	a symbol embedded into a sheet of paper to indicate the paper's manufacturer (best visible when holding against the light)	*filigranum*	*filigrane*	*Wasserzeichen*

www.ingramcontent.com/pod-product-compliance
Lightning Source LLC
Chambersburg PA
CBHW071406300426
44114CB00016B/2201